The Jazz-Girl, the Piano, and the Dedicated Tuner

About the Author

Nicky Gentil (née Jenkins) is a British national who has lived in Paris since 1988 where she began her career as a translator shortly after obtaining her degree in French and German from Oxford University. A married mother of two, today – in addition to her writing and translation work – she performs piano jazz in public whenever she can.

The stories in this book are all, without exception, based on her personal experience.

The Jazz-Girl, the Piano, and the Dedicated Tuner

Stories for Piano Enthusiasts and Novices Alike!

Nicky Gentil

Nicky Gentil first published this book in France (Editions Beaurepaire - March 2016)
under the title "La jazz-girl passionnée et son dévoué accordeur".

Matador
9 Priory Business Park,
Wistow Road, Kibworth Beauchamp,
Leicestershire. LE8 0RX
Tel: 0116 279 2299
Email: books@troubador.co.uk
Web: www.troubador.co.uk/matador
Twitter: @matadorbooks

ISBN 978 1788037 631

British Library Cataloguing in Publication Data.
A catalogue record for this book is available from the British Library.

Printed and bound by CPI Group (UK) Ltd, Croydon, CR0 4YY
Typeset in 11pt Aldine401 BT by Troubador Publishing Ltd, Leicester, UK

Matador is an imprint of Troubador Publishing Ltd

When my children were little, they would regularly ask me a question which I found genuinely amusing:

'Mummy, what do you prefer – us or jazz?'

Despite my amusement, I never, ever teased them on this crucial subject. In my view, it was important always to give exactly the same straight reply:

'You, of course.'

'Really? You love us even more than you love jazz?'

'Of course I do. There's absolutely no comparison.'

They would then pause for an instant – the time it took them fully to comprehend the enormous implications of these words – before going on to exclaim, every time, as if they were only just realising it for the first time:

'Wow! That means you must really love us, Mummy! Is it true? Do you really love us more than jazz?'

'I do.'

This amazing "revelation" unfailingly made their eyes shine with absolute happiness – a deliciously contagious form of happiness since it rendered my own complete. I shall never forget these moments of pure bliss, which is why I have decided to dedicate this book to my family in the following manner:

For my husband and my children – whom I love even more than jazz!

A surprising session at the piano...

One day, I found myself sitting at the piano doing something I rarely ever do – I was playing a piece of very sad classical music, more precisely a Chopin waltz with a tragic theme for, having just received some bad news, I was in no mood for jazz improvisation.

It did not take me very long, however, to start regretting this particular choice of piece; any endeavour on my part, to make Chopin's composition sing, was proving to be extremely frustrating, which in turn was doing nothing to help my sad state. In other words, my piano playing lacked finesse and, as had so often been the case in the past, I felt limited by the constraints of classical music – a genre which requires the musician to comply with every single instruction indicated on the score, right down to the very last note.

That day, my piano tuner, who himself happens to be an excellent classical pianist, was following my practice session long-distance via an exchange of text messages. While saddened by my bad news, he was also intrigued – almost amused – to discover that I was playing a type of music which I tend to reject because, being of a naturally joyful disposition, I find it does not suit me.

After a while, thoroughly disappointed by my terrible performance, I decided to abandon the exercise.

And so it was that my piano tuner, in a bid to encourage me, sent me the following message:

"Great works are born out of tragic emotions. Melancholy, despair, anger... these are ALL amazing sources of inspiration. Do not be afraid of this sadness, which is so very alien to you, for it actually carries a positive charge. Go back to Chopin and rather than looking at the notes with your eyes, look at them with all those emotions that are currently running so high within you. This will set you free. Free to play with all your soul. Please try. I'm listening..."

The effect of these words was astonishingly powerful. I returned to the piano and it was as if somebody had suddenly waved a magic wand over my playing.

I decided to recount this anecdote here for the simple reason that it contains the best piece of advice I have ever received for the successful interpretation of classical music on the piano.

Contents

Prologue

There's a week in March, the last official week of winter, when the weather traditionally changes overnight, as if the season of short cold days and long, even colder nights has suddenly decided to take a quantum leap into summer, cutting out the middleman – that is spring – along the way. It lulls everyone into a false sense of security. People believe what they so want to believe – that summer has come and is here to stay; which is not, in fact, the case. On the contrary, the weather can turn very cold again, particularly in April. However, for that one blissful week everyone is willing to be deceived. Entire wardrobes are transformed. Lightweight linen suits replace dark woollen ones. Leather boots are exchanged for strappy sandals. And if the number of people wearing shades is anything to go by, the entire city looks as if it is populated with an unusually large proportion of film stars. Stroll along any street during this time and you will find that the terraces of the numerous cafés and restaurants are full to bursting. Yet, in spite of all of the above, the main indication that this special week is upon us actually comes from the sky. The light at this time of the year is so exquisitely golden that if you have not already understood why Paris is generally considered to be one of the most beautiful cities in the world, you do then.

It all started during one such week…

That Friday afternoon, my piano tuner, who had become a good friend over the years, had invited me to have a drink with him in a café on the Place de la République and, just like everyone else, we too were sitting outside, sporting our shades and basking in the joyful mood brought about by the ubiquitous, sun-induced smiles. And so it was, as I happily sipped my citron pressé, that I decided to put an idea to my tuner – an idea which had been playing on my mind for some time.

'Have you ever thought about writing a book?'

Now to say that his reply took me slightly aback would be putting it mildly.

With a proud grin, he explained:

'Actually, I've already written a few short stories. My most recent one is an erotic fairy tale.'

Hmmm… Not quite the answer I had been expecting!

'You know, François, you really are one very surprising person,' I said, as I burst out laughing. 'Just what sector of the literary market were you targeting with that?'

'I wasn't. I wrote it for a girl I met a few weeks ago. I'll show it to you if you like.'

'Thanks, but I think I'll pass on that one if you don't mind. Tell me about the other stories you've written.'

'Oh, they're all about piano tuning. One's about the time I had to tune a Steinway grand for an extremely rich old lady who took something of a shine to me. She consequently had her butler serve up platters of canapés and kept pouring all these glasses of Champagne as I worked. The thing is, it was only ten in the morning so pretty soon I was completely off my head. Absolutely pissed as a newt! I had no idea what I was doing. I could no longer distinguish a bass note from a high note, let alone tune the damn things. Anyway, she must have liked what I did because when I left she phoned the piano tuning department and asked if I could be her permanent tuner!

Oh, and come to think of it, I've written another really funny one. Actually, this one's my favourite… I was tuning for a family who was obsessed with white. Their entire flat was painted brilliant white, their floor was covered with brilliant white tiles throughout and they'd commissioned a Steinway in – yes, you've guessed it – brilliant white. It was a special type of paint, ordered from Japan. They'd waited six months just to get the paint delivery! So, you see, it was exactly the type of instrument where you wouldn't wish to break anything because every new part has to be specially ordered and, generally, it takes up to six months to produce it. Anyway, they had just been delivered of their brand new, shiny white piano – ugh!' he said, visibly shuddering. 'And I had come to tune and voice it.[1] You should have seen them.

---

1   Voicing a piano is a process which is at one and the same time manual, technical, artistic and enigmatic. Using a three-pronged tool, the tuner makes tiny holes in the felt-covered heads of the hammers. This serves to soften the felt, which in turn changes the timbre of the note when the hammer hits the strings. Voicing requires both physical strength and, paradoxically, a delicate approach in order to pierce the felt in exactly the right place required to produce the desired sound.

They were so proud. Well, that is to say, they were – until disaster struck. There I was, dismantling the piano to do the voicing, when I dropped the wooden bar – which runs the length of the keyboard – on the floor and heard this almighty crack. I didn't dare look down for ages. I was convinced I'd broken one of their tiles, but it was worse than that. All the tiles were intact but the bar from the piano had snapped in two! I was absolutely horrified – although I have to say they were really nice about it. Actually, they seemed to think it was all a bit of a hoot. And that night I began to see the funny side too, so I wrote up the story to give my colleagues a laugh and of course they love teasing me about it even now, despite the fact that it happened months ago.'

'Well, there you go,' I said, 'that's exactly the sort of thing I had in mind. You see, I have an idea I want to talk to you about… You come into contact with so many people through your profession. I mean, just think about the various individuals you meet in their homes, not to mention the really famous artists you get to work for. Let's face it, you encounter people from all walks of life and from all over the globe. And on that basis, surely you have a whole bunch of stories to tell, just as you've done now. So why don't you keep a diary of your experiences? Then, one day, you could write them up and put them in a book. I'm convinced you could write a bestseller. If you like, to get you started, I'll write the introduction for you… Oh, and one last thing. Because it's my idea, I'll settle for fifty per cent of the royalties!'

'Oh, I see. And what are you thinking of saying in your introduction? Something along the lines of: "This book was my idea"?' he suggested, a broad grin once again spreading across his face.

'Yep. That's pretty much it!' I replied, as we now burst out laughing together.

We then went on to fantasise about how this future bestseller was going to make us both filthy rich, until it was time to leave the café and go our separate ways – to another piano waiting to be tuned, in his case; and back to the flat – to greet my children as they arrived home from school –, in mine.

With hindsight, it would appear that the idea to write a book must have followed me home that day…

A few days later, the conversation in the café was going round on a loop inside my head, eventually inciting me to write a spoof introduction to a book that was then but a mere figment of my imagination. The text was full of jokes about my various pianistic experiences and my tuner duly found it hilarious but, precisely because it was full of in-jokes, nobody else could possibly have understood it. So, just like the erotic fairy tale, the reading public for my writing was limited to the one person who had sparked it off, albeit for very different reasons!

However, since I had so enjoyed writing this piece, the following week I found myself sitting down, once again, to write…

This time I wrote a more serious text documenting how I met my tuner and the circumstances in which we became friends. Its essential message was about the power of music to form the most unlikely, and therefore all the more precious, of friendships. Astonishingly, as I wrote I found I did not really have to invent anything. I just put down on paper what had happened and there I found myself with a touching story, a story of a shared passion for pianos and music. I sent it to my tuner that Saturday night and it actually moved him to tears – provoking a response which now appeared to have a sense of urgency about it:

'We *have* to write the book.'

It was as if he already knew that very soon, for the best possible reasons, the sort of gaps in his schedule, which had hitherto enabled him to put his stories down on paper, would be a thing of the past…

In the months that followed, my tuner's career as a concert technician started to take off and then, to the great delight of his family and friends, including me, literally soared. The downside was that he no longer had time for meeting friends in cafés for drinks. As for his story writing, well, that would now quite probably have to wait until his retirement.

I, on the other hand, just seemed to keep on writing, until I had produced a whole book – a collection of short stories – which I wrote in French and which was published here in France in March 2016. When the book came out, family and friends on the other side of the Channel were curious to know more. Consequently, I decided to write this, the English version of that very same book – thus finding myself, for the first time in my life, in the happy position of being able to translate my own work. I say "happy" because for once I knew exactly what the author wanted and meant to say; "happy" also because I could take liberties with the original version, something a translator does not and should not normally do. This is not to say that this book radically diverts from the original in any way. The stories are essentially the same but there are a few additions, such as events which occurred subsequent to the publishing of my French book and which I considered worth sharing, or details which make certain situations clearer to a reader who does not live in France. Conversely, the various explanations required for a French reader to understand the quintessentially British references in the original book have obviously been removed from this version.

Now, the real question in all of this is how in the first place did I, a British national, who back in 1988 shortly after leaving university moved to Paris to work as a translator, find myself in the position where I was able to write a book about jazz improvisation, pianos and the mysterious, fascinating art of tuning? I have to admit that even today it never fails to surprise me but, there again, life is full of surprises and so, it would seem, is music.

Here is how my personal journey brought me to this point:

I discovered piano blues late on in life. As a child, I had studied classical piano for a few years and then – like countless people before and, no doubt, since – given it up. Many years later, I took up the piano again when the very first digital pianos – the Clavinovas – started to emerge and my husband bought me one as a surprise present for my thirtieth birthday. Around this time, in order to reawaken my, by now, dormant knowledge of music, I took some piano lessons with a Japanese teacher who was utterly ferocious regarding technique. This enabled me to recover my level of classical playing – Chopin waltzes, Bach Two-Part Inventions and Mozart sonatas – at an unexpectedly swift pace. In parallel, I started to delve into a book – *The Joy of Boogie and Blues* – completely unaided by my teacher, who remained firmly anchored in the classical repertoire and seemed to view my deviation as a mere form of light entertainment, an indulgence she would have to tolerate. It was patently obvious to me, on the other hand, that, although I knew incredibly little about my new subject, I was rapidly becoming addicted to this specific category of traditional jazz: piano blues together with its rapid, percussive, extremely joyful descendant, boogie-woogie.

Be that as it may, due to various personal commitments, a good few years were to pass before my nascent addiction would truly be allowed to flourish. This finally happened when, one day, serendipity stepped in to propel me on my way by offering me a golden opportunity: a chance discovery of exactly *the* teacher required to help me pursue an in-depth study of this subject that so captivated me…

It was Wednesday afternoon and my son was taking his weekly piano lesson in the sitting room when, suddenly, I heard his teacher interrupt the gentle tones of the classical piece he had been trying in vain to teach his flagging pupil, to give – quite probably with a view to waking this little eight-year-old up – a thundering performance of a fast and furious boogie-woogie. At the end of the lesson, I questioned the teacher about this and discovered, to my great surprise, that although he was giving classical lessons to my son, his speciality was in fact jazz!

The following week, I took a trial lesson in order to play some of the pieces I had learnt a few years earlier and obtain advice as to where I should go from there. According to the teacher, I was on the right track in that the swing rhythm, which actually defines jazz, was clearly present in my playing. Apparently, some people play this rhythm naturally, some eventually manage to learn it and some never get it at all. So, since I had the good fortune to fall into the first category, I was already past a major hurdle without even having had to try.

Then something happened that changed my life forever…

The teacher pointed out a series of codes – Fmaj7, C7, Bb6, etc. – written above the treble clef of the pieces and asked me if I knew what they were for. Now, I had always thought that these referred to chords for guitarists. However, he set me straight on this point by explaining the following principle which lies at the heart of all jazz improvisation: on the sheet music of a jazz standard, the chords forming the harmony of the piece are indicated – via these codes – above the treble clef. Each chord consists of four notes. When you improvise on the piano, you can play these notes wherever you wish to, in whatever order you choose and, better still, this applies to your left or your right hand, or both at the same time[2].

When I say this revelation changed my life forever, it really is no exaggeration. From that moment on, I was never to look at the keyboard of a piano in the same way again – for the simple reason that I could no longer see it as a long line of black and white keys.

---

2   This is the type of simple explanation that a jazz teacher will give to a beginner. However, as a jazz student progresses, he or she learns that the chords actually provide somewhat more complex, seemingly endless, possibilities for improvising than just four mere notes.

Now I saw it divided into groups of notes, which would enable me to improvise on any piece of music and thus create an infinite number of new melodies because I had just been given the freedom to organise and reorganise these notes as I saw fit. This possibility, this potential access to a profound source of a multitude of melodies, seemed like a dream. And quite suddenly, the keyboard of my piano appeared to light up in front of my eyes, exactly like the magical moment when the button is pressed to illuminate the Christmas tree. In short, the man who was about to become my jazz teacher had just given me a key. I owe him so much. With that key, I opened a very big door and stepped – musically speaking – into a completely undiscovered, enchanting new world.

A few months later, I started to take weekly jazz lessons in the simple hope that I would manage to learn the basics of improvisation; in spite of the life-changing revelation about the chords, the subject, at this stage, still remained rather a large mystery to me and, frankly, learning the basics already struck me as such a daunting task that to succeed in doing that alone would more than have sufficed as far as I was concerned. This, of course, was to seriously underestimate the power of music.

In reality, my jazz lessons turned out to be but the mere beginning of a very long and profoundly enriching journey. (Looking back, I compare these lessons to seeds which grew into a kind of tree whose branches never cease to amaze me because music, to this day, continues to take me on a truly astonishing, magical and, for the most part, completely unexpected, trip).

Thus it was that, once I had entered this new musical domain, I set about discovering all the Parisian jazz clubs. I started to attend boogie-woogie festivals, which gave me the opportunity to meet some extremely talented musicians. I wrote a jazz improvisation method for beginners who, just like me, already knew how to play classical piano and required help making the transition. I began giving lessons. And, to my utter surprise, I also began to play in public – regularly in a local brasserie, from time to time at private lunches and once in the sophisticated setting of a sumptuous Parisian reception room.

To top it all, some years after starting my jazz lessons, I had the immense good fortune to be able to purchase the piano of my dreams – a beautiful Steinway baby grand. This led to my discovery of another completely different branch of the music world – that of the intriguing, fascinating, mysterious work of a piano tuner.

Today, I freely admit, not without a certain degree of shame, that when I purchased my piano, I genuinely believed it would suffice to have it tuned just once a year – as if it were to be maintained in the manner of a car or a boiler requiring its annual service! Thankfully, I happened to meet an extremely talented piano tuner, a man who to this day remains completely and utterly dedicated to his profession and who was willing to take the time and trouble to teach me all about the internal workings of the piano and more generally about the nature of sound. As a result, I am now in a much better position to understand the complexity of piano tuning, an activity which strikes me as being extremely complete for the human brain because it is at one and the same time manual, technical, intellectual and – when performed at its highest level – artistic and creative. Seen, then, from a purely cerebral point of view, the act of tuning a piano is not dissimilar to that of playing an instrument.

Observing my piano tuner at work has also enabled me more specifically to understand that a good tuner is capable of creating a tailor-made sound in order to satisfy the precise requests of a pianist: bright and brilliant for Hélène Grimaud because she is about to play Rachmaninov, or soft and mellow for Lang Lang because he has been booked to play Mozart, for example. Thus, the reason a piano sings with a particular voice is threefold: its sound is fashioned and shaped not only by the hands of the person who manufactures the instrument and those of the pianist who plays it but also, sometimes especially, by the hands of the tuner who prepares it. In other words, two tuners of equal ability can tune the same piano at four hundred and forty hertz[3] but each will give it a different sound depending on his or her specific way of working and on the characteristics defined and requested by the pianist.

As is the case with the majority of new pianos, my own instrument actually took quite a while to stabilise – which meant that at first it would go out of tune rather quickly – and it was during this period that I really began to understand just how important the role of the tuner is. General opinion asserts that a talented pianist can bring a good sound out of any piano and this

---

3   Four hundred and forty hertz refers to the frequency of the A situated above middle C on the keyboard, and serves as a general tuning standard.

is indeed true to a certain extent. Be that as it may, even the most talented pianist in the world will *never* be capable of making a piano, which is out of tune or poorly tuned, sound otherwise. Only the tuner can do that.

Now, as I stated previously, during the years when my tuner worked regularly on my piano – prior to his meteoric rise into concert hall work – he became a good friend.

That people from completely different backgrounds (in the case in point, my tuner is very much a product of the artistic world – the complete opposite of me) can transcend barriers to forge strong friendships, born of their shared passion, is, as far as I am concerned, clear proof of the power of music[4]. And, interestingly, this seemingly mysterious, potent capacity of music – to bring together people from all walks of life – seems to be a direct reflection of the manner in which musical harmony itself operates, in the sense that musical harmony systematically pulls off the impressive feat of combining many different melodies in such a way as to enable them to co-exist, quite happily, within one and the same work. A simple illustration of this can be found in orchestral music where each instrument plays a different piece. The part written for the violins is not the same as that written for the flutes, to take just one example. Yet, when all the instruments play, the orchestra sings with one single voice due to the harmony at

---

4   In today's world, a particularly powerful illustration of music's capacity to bring together people from all walks of life can be seen in the West-Eastern Divan Orchestra – founded by the Argentine-Israeli conductor and pianist Daniel Barenboim, together with the late Palestinian-American academic Edward Said, to promote understanding and tolerance in the Middle East.

Every summer, around eighty young musicians – from Israel, the surrounding Arab states (Syria, Lebanon, Egypt and Jordan) and the Palestinian territories – come to Seville to rehearse during the month of July before embarking on a world tour in August.

In Elena Cheah's book – *An Orchestra Beyond Borders* – members of this orchestra describe their personal experiences. Surprisingly, these descriptions all have a common thread running through them: the musicians, in spite of their initial firm intentions *not* to talk to their orchestral neighbours, invariably find themselves striking up solid friendships with these very neighbours – people whom they would normally consider to be their political and/or religious enemies. And, quite often, once they do start talking to one another, these young musicians are astonished to realise that they tend to use exactly the same arguments to defend their respective opposing points of view!

the basis of the work, which quite masterfully binds the individual parts together to form a beautiful melodious whole.

Pursuing this aside on musical harmony for an instant, I would add that its role in jazz is particularly impressive because it is the very harmony of any given piece, which allows jazz musicians to improvise – in other words, to compose and play spontaneously together – or, as the jazz musicians themselves say, to jam.

A couple of years ago, I was lucky enough to be able to do just that with the immensely talented Pierre-Yves Plat[5] when he was performing, one Friday night, in a restaurant in Versailles. That evening, during the break, Pierre-Yves asked if anyone would like to play a duet with him in the second half. Now, in the normal course of things I would never have dared to attempt to play the piano alongside such a great artist. However, due to my husband's encouraging words – and possibly also due to the rather fine bottle of red wine we had just downed! – I decided to have a go. And by merely saying to Pierre-Yves that I was going to play "Swanee River" in C major, I actually gave him more information than he needed because, in order to improvise on this piece, strictly speaking, he did not even require the title of the song. Just the key – C major – would have sufficed, given that this information alone provided him with the required chords. And it is precisely this – the chord structure or harmony – which meant that Pierre-Yves, a young, immensely talented, professional pianist and I, a somewhat less young but nevertheless passionate and enthusiastic pianist, were able to perform together on that Friday night, having never previously met, let alone rehearsed, and absolutely bring the house down receiving, much to our delight, unanimous rapturous applause.

To return to the subject of my piano tuner, in the beginning music actually succeeded in creating a quite unusual – indeed, as far as we were concerned, unique – form of friendship between us in that, initially, our friendship was mainly based on letter writing. This came about because, shortly after we met, an injury to my right hand – a devastating blow since at the time I feared it could forever deprive me of my piano playing – incited us to start writing to each other about our shared passion for music and just how much that passion meant to us. And it is thanks to these epistolary exchanges that we gradually

---

5   Pierre-Yves Plat is a French pianist who specialises in jazz arrangements of well-known classical pieces.

made the transition from the status of tuner–client to that of good friends[6].

Furthermore, over time it was these very exchanges that began to reveal in both of us a taste for story writing. Thus it was that I first wrote a few stories for the dual pleasure of pursuing a private, but nevertheless incredibly satisfying, creative activity, while at the same time providing my piano tuner friend with reading matter which he seemed to find hugely entertaining.

Interestingly, the more I wrote about my musical experiences, the more it became apparent that I did not actually have to look very far for the subject matter; music – just like life itself – regularly injects funny, touching, moving, sometimes even magical moments into my existence, moments which in my view are far better than anything I could possibly invent.

Before long, three close female friends of mine were asking if they too could take a look at my work and, surprisingly, all three of them came back asking for more. I say surprisingly because none of them plays an instrument and at the time, none of them knew much about jazz improvisation, still less about piano tuning.

Receiving such a positive enthusiastic response from three novices was naturally extremely encouraging for me and spurred me on with my writing in the hope that, one day, I would produce an entire book which could convey to a wider public the immense joy which my passion for pianos and jazz improvisation constantly brings to me.

The linguistic exercise was also an enticing incentive to continue writing. I happen to love playing around with words and expressions, which no doubt explains why I studied foreign languages and became a translator. And on this subject, I would just like to point out that it is not at all unusual for people who are passionate about music to be equally passionate about language because these apparently different subjects are actually two branches of a single, deep-rooted – more often than not subconscious – interest in communication in its various forms.

Personally, I derive particular pleasure from the complementary

---

6   In my view, it is a wonderful paradox of modern technology that relatively new inventions – such as the computer and the mobile phone – provide an ideal opportunity for people who like writing to return to a rather old-fashioned form of communication, that of letter writing, since letters can now so easily be sent by email or text message. I address the subject of this paradox in greater detail later in the book.

nature of music and language. I use the term complementary because music is surely the ultimate means of universal communication, in that a French musician, for example, can perform in a concert hall in Tokyo and will not require the services of a translator to communicate his message through his art. And if, in this respect, music can be perceived as a form of language, language is conversely a form of music due to the musical rhythms found in both the spoken and the written word.

In the light of all of the above, then, once I started studying jazz improvisation, writing about it was actually a natural, logical next step for me.

So there you have it. A long, detailed and hopefully informative explanation as to the origins of this book – a collection of stories, based on my personal journey with music, which pay tribute along the way to the little known and sometimes undervalued piano tuning profession.

Finally, a word about the characters you are about to meet. I deliberately chose to write these stories in the third person and have also changed the names of the majority of the people appearing in them. Thus, for the purposes of this book, my tuner is known as François Pradel, while my character is called Nina Somerville – a name I invented as a tribute both to Nina Simone and to the Oxford college at which I had the immense privilege to study. That said, Nina is more generally referred to as the Jazz-Girl – a nickname whose origin will become apparent as you read.

My reason for adopting the third person form is that, by doing so, I was able to take a step back and thus feel sufficiently free to put my personal experiences down on paper. This is linked to the reason for changing people's names: paradoxically, fictitious names give an author greater freedom to tell the truth. And while the stories which follow may vary widely – due to their diverse range of funny, moving, complex, simple, occasionally hilarious if not completely surreal, scenes – the one thread binding them together is that, aside from the odd additional detail or exaggeration for effect, they are all, as I stated earlier, pretty much based on my own experience. So, in this particular case, for once, the opposite of the standard assertion is true: the names are indeed fictitious but any relation to fictitious persons or events is purely coincidental!

Having said that, a third main player in this book – Apollo[7], the God of music, who pops up now and then in his capacity as father of all musicians – is obviously a blatant invention or, to put it another way, pure poetic licence on my part.

My decision to include Apollo came about because I feel that my passion for jazz improvisation just seemed to drop into my life from nowhere, at a time when I was not particularly searching for anything, at least not consciously. And since this passion has brought me so much in terms of personal fulfilment, alluding to Apollo is my (admittedly highly romanticized) way of expressing my gratitude towards the powers that govern our universe, for sending me this precious gift. Moreover, it so happens that Apollo adds a fairy-tale dimension to my stories which, I hope, aptly conveys the magical aspect of everything I have experienced, and continue to experience, for the simple reason that, one day, music apparently just came looking for me.

So now, without further ado, it is with the greatest pleasure that I hereby invite you to step into another world and discover the following tales of a Jazz-Girl with a passion, a piano with a soul, and a most dedicated tuner…

---

7   Apollo, as the Greek mythology experts will tell you, is not just the God of music. He is also, among many other things, the God of light, art, poetry and knowledge.

In Search of a Piano Tuner

Her first encounter with the man who would later become, in his own words, her "most dedicated piano tuner" marked an important milestone on her journey with music. Finding him had been difficult. And when she met him, she could not possibly have known that, one day, this man would help her overcome a devastating accident for the passionate jazz pianist she had by then become – an injury to her hand – that, subsequently, he would personally prepare the piano of her very first professional performance, let alone that over the years he would become a good friend. However, of one thing she could be sure: here was a man with a true passion for pianos.

Now, in order to require the services of a piano tuner, one does indeed need to have a piano, which is why this story begins with the acquisition of a very beautiful instrument.

One day, the Jazz-Girl purchased a piano, an exquisite baby grand.

Twenty years previously, a chance discovery had given her the opportunity to play on a Steinway for the first time in her life. Blessed with a sensitive ear, she had truly savoured the pure sound of this beautiful instrument, which seemed to sing to her like no other piano. It was an experience that was to leave an indelible trace on her auditory memory, inciting her to make a crucial decision: if ever she were to buy a piano, it would be a Steinway or nothing. This was her little private joke, her personal fantasy, which she reasonably presumed would remain so for the entirety of her days spent on this planet.

Twenty years later, when first she began taking jazz improvisation lessons, the Jazz-Girl was perfectly content to play on her digital piano – a Clavinova – with the headphones firmly plugged in. Since she lived in a flat in Paris, it was a good way of keeping the peace with the neighbours and, in any event, given her somewhat basic level of piano playing at the time, her Clavinova was more than good enough for her.

1

Then a miracle occurred…

A set of totally unexpected, extraordinary circumstances provided her with the means to buy the very piano of which she hitherto could only have dreamed. This was just one of the many magical moments that music would bring to her over the years, moments imbued with such a fairy-tale-like quality that, from that day forward, she would privately attribute them to the God of music, Apollo – for what possible explanation could there be other than that for such amazing events to occur, a force greater than ours must be at work? And, secretly, she liked to harbour the romantic belief that Apollo toiled to orchestrate such incredible events for his musician children, thus encouraging them all to grow and progress, be they great or, as in her case, small.

In a bid to strike while the iron was hot, she immediately started enquiring about all types of Steinway pianos and, once she had carefully measured the designated space in her sitting room, opted for a Model S – the smallest baby grand. The baby-baby, if you will. Then, in order to test it out, she arranged an appointment for the following Saturday morning.

That day, as she set off with her husband and their two children in search of the piano of her dreams, the sky, as if to announce the magical nature of the experience to come, appeared to be putting on a very beautiful show. An abundance of large, fluffy snowflakes was painting the entire city of Paris in a pristine shade of white.

As the four of them entered the shop, the Jazz-Girl introduced herself.

'Bonjour, Madame Somerville,' replied the salesman. 'The Model S is just over here. Yesterday, when we heard you were coming to test it, we had it tuned specially for you.'

They'd had it tuned *specially* for her! She thought she must be in a dream.

When she saw the piano, it was love at first sight. The instrument was absolutely beautiful – so truly magnificent that she scarcely dared to touch it. She simply wished to admire it. To venerate it!

After a few minutes of standing there motionless, she nevertheless managed to sit down and play some bars of soft, bluesy music. The resulting sound made it hard for her to believe that these melodies were actually emerging from beneath her fingertips.

Just to be sure, she went all round the shop and tested a number of other pianos, but the Steinway with its purity – a clarity of sound which so many years previously had made such an impression on her – kept enticing her back.

Enquiring as to the maintenance of the piano, the Jazz-Girl learnt that a new instrument always required special treatment. Initially, she would need to have it tuned regularly and often, and during the first session, the tuner would also do the voicing[1]. Furthermore, it would be advisable to have a tuner with specific Steinway training.

The Jazz-Girl had already heard about tuners who practised the profession to this level – a breed apart due to their auditory acuity[2]. And to think that if she were to buy this piano, a "mythical" tuner would take care of it. It was better and better…

Continuing with her enquiries, she finally arrived at the end of her long list of questions and, once everything seemed perfectly clear to her, was at last able to sign the documents relating to the purchase of this magnificent instrument. Only then did she realise that she had been a good three hours in the shop! The time had literally flown by.

In order to thank their son and daughter for their patience, the Jazz-Girl and her husband decided to take them to a restaurant for lunch, where they celebrated this historic purchase with fizzy drinks for the children and a glass of Champagne for the parents.

The Jazz-Girl felt blissfully happy; some moments in life are truly magical and this was indeed one of those moments. She had just spent *the* most amazing morning in the piano shop and now here she was, sitting with the three people she loved most, sipping a glass of Champagne, while at the same time watching the snowflakes gently drift down onto the streets of Paris.

Life was really good that day – and even more so when, a few days later, the piano was delivered to her home and installed in the designated space, a space that seemed absolutely perfect for this new addition to the family, right in the middle of the sitting room!

Once again, before daring to touch it she spent a long time simply contemplating her instrument and, pausing to reflect on its appellation – baby grand – suddenly understood, for the very first time, the juxtaposition of these apparently contradictory words. She

---

1   See the footnote on page xii for a definition of voicing.
2   With their exceptional ears, many piano tuners find it hard to attend concerts because, even from a distance at the back of a concert hall, they are capable of detecting the slightest imperfection in the sound of any instrument. In the music business, the precision of their hearing is considered to be legendary.

had just acquired the smallest grand piano available – the baby – and yet it was indeed "grand" in every sense of the word.

During the days that followed, the Jazz-Girl took the time to become acquainted with her beautiful new piano, delighting in the many nuances of its profoundly rich sound.

A few days later, when her teacher arrived for her weekly lesson, they were like two excited children at Christmas. Just like his pupil, the teacher spent a long time admiring the beauty of the instrument before sitting down to test it. Then he began, somewhat hesitantly, by playing a Chopin waltz, following it up with a few jazzy improvisations. He was undeniably a very accomplished pianist, capable of switching with the greatest of ease between classical music and jazz and, that day, he remained seated at the piano for a good twenty minutes, saying at the end of each piece:

'Just one more and then I'll stop.'

Clearly he was finding it hard to give up his place, which did not bother the Jazz-Girl in the slightest. Admittedly it was her lesson but she was absolutely thrilled to be able to listen to the beautiful sound of her piano, all the while observing the immense pleasure that this very sound was bringing to her teacher.

When finally she did begin her lesson, her teacher, as if to intensify the auditory pleasure of the musical moment, kept his eyes firmly closed to listen to her play. Moreover, although usually extremely rigorous and demanding, that day he accepted absolutely anything. After all, what did it matter if her improvisation were good or bad? Everything seemed to sound beautiful to him, including the numerous wrong notes!

Ultimately, it was not really a day for a piano lesson. It was a day for getting to know a magnificent instrument, held – by both teacher and pupil alike – in awe and admiration.

♪

A few months later, as predicted, the piano required tuning. The Jazz-Girl thus called the piano tuning department for an appointment and the pleasant voice that answered explained that she should allow around three hours – one for the tuning and two for the voicing…

It was Friday morning and she was ready. The Jazz-Girl had created optimum conditions for receiving Monsieur X, the piano tuner, who was about to arrive. In other words, she had just made one final check to ensure that all machines – the dishwasher, the washing machine and the tumble dryer – were resolutely switched off. Consequently, silence now reigned in her flat and, bearing in mind everything she had been told about piano tuners and their exceptional hearing, she was expecting to spend an amazing morning watching Monsieur X at work.

At ten o'clock sharp, Monsieur X duly arrived.

Greeting him in the standard French way, she held out her hand to shake his and said:

'Bonjour, Monsieur.'

To her utter astonishment, he responded by completely ignoring her – instead, heading straight for the sitting room where he dropped his bag of tools on the floor and, looking truly shocked, exclaimed:

'Oh no. No, no, no! This won't do. This room is weird… seriously weird. It's far too light and echo-y.'

He then proceeded to walk all round the room pursuing his line of criticism with:

'No, this really just won't do at all. The piano is completely out of place here. I mean, there's hardly any furniture! You're really going to have to think about furnishing this room. And you should add some plants and a few rugs. But even so, the piano is just *so* out of place…'

Two years previously, the Jazz-Girl and her husband had gone to great lengths to purchase this particular property – the flat of their dreams! Located on the top floor of a large block of modern flats, the view of the Eiffel Tower and the distinctive Paris rooftops was absolutely spectacular, while the property itself was spacious, light and airy, and most definitely furnished in a minimalist style – a deliberate choice on their part for they had always chosen to favour quality over quantity. As for the piano, utterly resplendent, standing as it was right in the middle of their large circular sitting room which opened out onto a magnificent terrace, it appeared, on the contrary, to have landed in just the right spot!

Monsieur X's negative reaction spoke volumes about the man he was – a man who appeared to have absolutely no qualms whatsoever about behaving in a truly unacceptable manner. Naturally, he was not obliged to like her home but the point was that he was not there to give his opinion on the matter. His role was supposed to be strictly limited to working on her piano. And as a client, the Jazz-Girl had just not expected her very first encounter with a piano tuner to commence in this way – a way which appeared to be at complete odds with her impression, based on everything she had hitherto heard, that tuners were a mythical breed; highly-gifted members of an exclusive club dedicated to sound in all its forms.

In an attempt to take a step back from this unpleasant start, she decided to try to keep an open mind. Perhaps this man put beautiful grand pianos on such a pedestal that his sole concern was to do everything within his power to keep these instruments "happy" by ensuring they were installed in what he considered to be the perfect setting.

Unfortunately, what followed only served to confirm the incredibly bad initial impression that Monsieur X had just made on her. Without even so much as bothering to ask for her permission, the tuner began to walk all around the flat and concluded that the piano would be much better off in the study.

At this point, the Jazz-Girl struggled to contain her laughter. This man, who so readily proffered his opinion, irrespective of whether or not it had been requested, appeared to be somewhat immune to practicalities. The fact of the matter was that it would have been nigh on impossible to move the piano into the study for the simple reason that this room was already furnished with a large floor-to-ceiling bookcase, a sofa bed for guests and – unsurprisingly, given its appellation – a desk for studying!

Monsieur X condescended to return to the sitting room and the Jazz-Girl, who was by now forcing herself to remain polite in the face of his somewhat odious behaviour, asked:

'Do you think we could take a look at the piano now? I would like to show you one of the keys in the high notes. It doesn't spring back up properly when I play it. It seems to get a bit stuck.'

His reply was, to say the very least, unexpected:

'You know, I really don't need to bother about the high notes. You're hardly ever going to use them. If you do, it will be just occasionally for an arpeggio at the end of a piece but that's all.'

The Jazz-Girl felt absolutely incensed by this man's complete lack of professionalism! He was, after all, there to tune the entire piano.

However, somehow she managed to remain calm enough to inform him of her requirements:

'I happen to play jazz, which means I use the high notes all the time. *That* is actually how I detected this particular problem. So you see, you have to tune the high notes because I really need them.'

'Okay, I'll tune the high notes for you,' was his begrudging reply – as if to say he were doing her some kind of special favour, beyond the call of duty.

As she continued to show him the piano, the Jazz-Girl pointed out the other teething problems she was encountering – notably a buzzing sound, which occurred when she played certain notes. This problem was going to be quite hard to resolve because it happened on a random basis and generally disappeared after two or three days.

Then, once she had informed him of all the various issues to be dealt with, she decided it was time to leave him in peace to deal with the task at hand.

Barely one and a half hours later, Monsieur X called her proudly to announce that he had finished the tuning and the voicing, and that it had all taken a lot less time than expected.

At this point, the Jazz-Girl was at a complete loss. The pleasant voice at the piano tuning department had told her he was to spend three hours working on her piano. And yet, here was Monsieur X claiming that everything had been sorted out and that the only problem remaining was that of the random buzzing sounds. For this, he advised her that if the problem were to return, she should book an appointment with two tuners, so that one could play the piano while the other would try to identify the cause.

Given that she was perfectly capable of playing the piano herself in order to help a tuner identify a technical problem, the Jazz-Girl found this suggestion a tad excessive. However, far be it from her to dare to contradict Monsieur X. He had already behaved in a gratuitously unpleasant manner and, since she had quite simply had enough for one morning, she was unwilling to provide him with any reason to continue doing so.

Thus it was that the Jazz-Girl accompanied Monsieur X to the lift and, relieved to see the back of him, returned to the sitting room to test out her piano.

To say she was disappointed would be an understatement. Her beautiful instrument was absolutely unrecognisable! The sound was far too bright, metallic almost, and a large proportion of notes were buzzing. Worse still, in the hour that followed, the piano rapidly went out of tune. Horrified by the results of Monsieur X's work, the

Jazz-Girl was on the point of calling the piano tuning department to complain when, suddenly, she thought better of it. All this was, after all, very new to her and she decided it might be better to wait and see how her piano fared over the next few days. That way, she would also be able to obtain a second opinion from her teacher.

A few days later, when her jazz teacher arrived, the Jazz-Girl, in a bid to have his objective reaction, informed him that the piano had been tuned and voiced but refrained from revealing any details. She then invited him to test it – which he only had to do for a few brief minutes before making exactly the same diagnosis as she had.

The next day, she called the piano tuning department and explained the problem:

'Bonjour, Madame. Madame Somerville speaking. I'm calling because Monsieur X came to tune and voice my piano a week ago but I'm not very happy with what he's done. The piano went out of tune almost immediately after he left and I now have several notes that buzz. Would it be possible to send somebody else to take a look?'

While she could see the logic of it, the Jazz-Girl was actually really disappointed by the pleasant voice's reply:

'I'm very sorry to hear that, Madame Somerville, but it's better if I send Monsieur X to correct the problem because he is the one who did the tuning and the voicing. He can come next Friday at the same time if you wish.'

Endeavouring to hide her disappointment, the Jazz-Girl replied:

'Okay. But in that case, you need to send me two tuners. Monsieur X told me that in order to identify the source of the buzzing noise, another tuner needs to play while he looks for it.'

'Very well; in that case I'll send Monsieur Y too.'

𝄞

The following Friday, in response to the Jazz-Girl's explanation of the problem, Monsieur Y, who was the first to arrive, said:

'Okay, while I'm waiting for Monsieur X, I'm going to tune your piano but what you need to know is that I'm not going to be able to give it a radically different sound.'

Unable to contain her astonishment, the Jazz-Girl exclaimed:

'But I'm not asking you to change the sound of my piano! I'm simply asking you to *retrieve* the sound of the beautiful instrument I purchased. Currently, I just don't recognise it.'

In spite of this surprising comment, Monsieur Y appeared to be a much nicer person than Monsieur X and, more importantly, was somewhat more thorough in the way he approached his work. He took his time over the bass notes and was starting on the middle octaves when Monsieur X arrived.

Just as she had done the previous week, the Jazz-Girl politely held out her hand to shake his and said:

'Bonjour, Monsieur,' adding: 'your colleague is already here.'

However, just as he had done the previous week, Monsieur X walked straight past her, without bothering to say "bonjour" back, and continued into the sitting room, whereupon he exclaimed in an angry voice:

'*What* on earth is going on? Amateur pianists have no place calling out two highly qualified tuners to take care of a tiny baby grand! Is this some kind of a joke? Because if it is, it's not funny.'

This time Monsieur X had gone too far. The Jazz-Girl had, after all, acted on his advice and she did not hesitate to point this out:

'Believe you me, I myself do not find this in the slightest bit amusing. By booking two tuners to sort out the problem of the buzzing notes, I was merely following your instructions.'

'The buzz undoubtedly comes from vibrations in the room,' was his immediate reply.

Unflinchingly, she said:

'*That* is just not possible because the problem occurs on a random basis and while the room never changes, the instrument does, which means the buzzing sound can only come from the piano. However, since we're on the subject, as far as I'm concerned, last week you spent far too much time criticising this room. And what you must understand is that we have absolutely no intention of changing it. Furthermore, we are most definitely *not* going to move the piano into another room. Be that as it may, a "highly qualified" tuner such as yourself must surely be perfectly capable of tuning an instrument properly, whatever the conditions of the room. But here's the thing, my piano went out of tune after just one hour and, to my mind, that is not right.'

At this point, Monsieur Y smiled discreetly at the Jazz-Girl as if to show her that he too was not at all happy with the unpleasant behaviour of his colleague.

9

Monsieur X, on the other hand, remained undeterred.

'You know, it's hardly surprising that your piano went out of tune so quickly. After all, it's brand new.'

The Jazz-Girl was on the point of replying that one hour was not actually that long, even for a new piano, when the tuner decided to follow up his words with a comment which was so audacious that it left her completely dumbfounded and Monsieur Y looking incredibly ill at ease.

Turning to his colleague, Monsieur X enquired:

'What do you think of the room?'

Monsieur Y kept his eyes firmly fixed on the piano as he timidly replied:

'I happen to think that this room is rather beautiful.'

Clearly irritated by this answer, Monsieur X angrily pursued the matter of the piano with:

'Okay, you might as well show us the buzzing problem now we're here.'

The Jazz-Girl sat down at the piano and started to play the notes that needed correcting but Monsieur Y was quite unable to hear the problem – with good reason, as it so happened. The simple fact of the matter was that Monsieur X was now going round the room exaggeratedly tapping on the picture frames, the lamps, the coffee table, in fact on anything he could possibly lay his hands on, because clearly he wanted to demonstrate that the buzzing sound was so obviously coming from the apparently echo-y surroundings.

Out of sheer frustration, the Jazz-Girl eventually gave up trying and handed Monsieur Y the list she had prepared earlier of all the notes that buzzed, while at the same time inviting him to take her place so he could test the piano himself.

Monsieur Y played the first two notes on the list and then stopped. He had immediately understood what was happening and did not need to go any further. Suddenly, he removed the action[3] from the piano and began to do the voicing right in front of his colleague. Thus it was that, for the next hour, he toiled relentlessly to do the very job which Monsieur X should have done the previous week, and once he had finished he asked the Jazz-Girl to test the piano.

This she did by playing a short piece of blues, which enabled her to

---

3   The mechanics of a piano's interior – located behind the keys and underneath the strings on a grand piano.

confirm to Monsieur Y that he had indeed cured the buzzing problem while at the same time making a point of expressing her profound gratitude towards him.

It was then that Monsieur X, clearly offended because his own work had been called into question, turned to his colleague and said:

'Okay, let's get out of here now.'

In response, Monsieur Y, who was evidently thoroughly ashamed of his colleague's behaviour, protested:

'But I haven't yet had a chance to tune the high notes!'

Monsieur X vaguely pretended to test the high notes and decreed, once more, that they did not actually need to be tuned!

'They're fine. Come on. We're out of here.'

Poor Monsieur Y was so embarrassed. As for the Jazz-Girl, she no longer had the energy to pursue the matter. Weary of the entire morning's experience, she just gave up and accompanied the two tuners to the lift.

Then she returned to the piano to discover that, unsurprisingly, only two-thirds of her instrument now sang in tune!

Three months later...

It was the day before the children were due to go back to school after the long summer break and, once more, the Jazz-Girl had an appointment with Monsieur X; the punishing Parisian heat during the months of July and August had seriously affected her piano.

On this particular occasion, Monsieur X seemed different. The presence of the children in the flat somehow rendered him less harsh. It turned out that he had two children of his own and was even taking the next day off work to take them back to school and see them into their new classes.

That day, the Jazz-Girl's then eight-year-old daughter, curious to see a tuner at work, asked Monsieur X if he would mind if she stayed in the room to watch. Monsieur X responded to this request by taking the time and trouble to explain to her how he was going to approach the job of tuning the piano, displaying unexpected levels of kindness and patience as he showed her some of the tools he would be using.

As for the Jazz-Girl, she was most pleasantly surprised to observe this radical change in Monsieur X's behaviour. He seemed so much more human, to the extent that she wondered if his ill-tempered demeanour of the previous occasions had ultimately just been due to fatigue. At any rate, she was pleased to discover that Monsieur X could be really quite affable when he wanted to. This gave her a glimmer of hope that she might actually be able to get on with him. And this was something she genuinely desired because she had a real problem dealing with conflict. While some people naturally go looking for it, she was the type of person who actively avoided it whenever she could.

With all this in mind, the Jazz-Girl began to feel rather optimistic about her future encounters with Monsieur X but, unfortunately, her optimism was to be short-lived. Once again, the piano rapidly went out of tune and, once again, the Jazz-Girl found herself calling the piano tuning department to explain the problem to the pleasant voice:

'I'm really sorry but my piano is already out of tune even though Monsieur X tuned it just two weeks ago. I'm actually beginning to think there must be something wrong with my instrument. I realise that the piano being brand new is a factor but still, it just keeps going out of tune far too quickly. In fact, it's never really *in* tune, so I'm beginning to wonder if my piano has some kind of technical defect. Do you think you could send me another tuner to take a look and give me a second opinion?'

The pleasant voice's reply was, yet again, disappointing:

'I understand that you're frustrated, Madame Somerville, but it really is better if Monsieur X takes a look because *he* is the person who did the tuning. That said, I shall indeed be informing our technical director of your complaint.'

While this approach was completely justified, in reality it turned out to be counter-productive – merely serving to make Monsieur X extremely angry.

That Monday morning, just as on previous occasions, Monsieur X walked straight past the Jazz-Girl – without even bothering to utter so much as a "bonjour" – and into the sitting room.

In response, to show him that she really did not appreciate his impolite manner, the Jazz-Girl remained silent – choosing instead to sit down at the piano so she could demonstrate the problem to him. Barely was she seated, however, when Monsieur X looked at her straight in the eye and angrily proclaimed:

'Your piano most definitely does *not* keep going out of tune.'

Not for the first time, the Jazz-Girl was thoroughly shocked by his complete lack of professionalism, and even more so by his complete lack of interest in the piano. How could he possibly know whether the piano was in – or out of – tune? He hadn't even tested it! Her frustration with this tuner was such that she simply did not have the energy to retaliate. Consequently, she ignored his comment and surprised herself by calmly requesting:

'Could I just ask you to play the F of the middle octave?'

This question, while one hundred per cent sincere, actually had the effect of throwing Monsieur X totally off balance because, although he had quite clearly heard it, apparently he needed to make sure he had understood correctly, as he said:

'I beg your pardon?'

She thus repeated the question in a voice which was increasingly calm and even quite pleasant:

'Could I just ask you to play the F of the middle octave? I would like to show you something. If you can tell me that this note is in tune, then you are more than welcome to leave.'

With that, she stood up and invited him to take her place.

Unable to conceal his ever-increasing anger, Monsieur X sat down, vaguely went through the motions of playing the note by lightly pressing on the key, and said in a really irritated voice:

'So what?'

The Jazz-Girl was by now feeling increasingly serene. After all, she had nothing to lose as she approached the piano and played the note herself, pressing the key down for as long as possible so that the tuner would listen properly.

Deep down, she knew it was impossible for Monsieur X, in his capacity as a professional tuner, *not* to hear the problem but, in spite of this, he nevertheless insisted that she give him an explanation when she said:

'Can you hear what I hear?'

'What? Just *what* can you hear?'

'When I press on this key, first of all I hear an F and then, behind that note, there's a sort of wavy, impure sound, which seems to run the entire length of the strings. I'm really sorry because I don't know the technical vocabulary to describe it any better than that.'

For one brief instant, the Jazz-Girl felt that she could detect something resembling a glimmer of respect in Monsieur X's eyes.

Then it was his turn to throw *her* totally off balance with *his* question:

'Do you by any chance play the violin?'

At this point, she could only think that she had completely lost the plot! Just what exactly was he getting at? In spite of her utter confusion, however, she answered:

'No. I only play the piano and not very well for the time being. Why the question about the violin?'

'Because generally it takes a violinist to hear what you can hear. You have a truly excellent ear and the noise you're hearing is what we call the "meowing". You see this note? Well, it has three strings and the tension of one of the strings is not equal to the tension of the other two, which means that the note has lost its "unison" and that is why it's producing this so-called meowing sound.'

'Well, whenever I play the piano,' said the Jazz-Girl, 'I can hear the meowing on lots of notes and it is precisely for that reason, and for that reason only, that I asked you to come back.'

In response, Monsieur X began to play a piece so he could make a true diagnosis of the state of the piano. It was high time! His chosen piece was a well-known hit by Serge Gainsbourg – a type of music at complete odds with his image. Clearly this man was full of surprises! Then he took his time to tune the piano in a way which was meticulous and thorough – worthy of both her instrument and his profession. And the results were undeniable. The piano stayed in tune for a good few months, until winter came along…

When next the Jazz-Girl booked an appointment, she sincerely hoped that she was going to start afresh with Monsieur X. She had earned his respect on the previous occasion and genuinely believed that this would act in her favour.

Unfortunately, the fact of the matter was that while she had indeed won the battle, she had most definitely *not* won the war. That day, when he arrived, Monsieur X was more unpleasant than ever. Thus it was that he marched into her flat, did his traditional walk straight past her, and headed directly for the sitting room whereupon, seeing her piano, he sighed:

'Oh yes, I'd forgotten. You have a Steinway. I know I shouldn't say this but I actually prefer Bechsteins!'

Privately, she thought: *Well, in that case, why bother to say it?*

Once again, Monsieur X tuned the piano, with his usual superficial approach, at breakneck speed. And, once again, unsurprisingly, a few days later the piano was out of tune.

It was the last straw. The Jazz-Girl's mind was finally made up; she had no choice but to find another tuner. There was absolutely no way she could continue to employ Monsieur X. His work was just too ineffectual. And try as she might, she just could not get on with him. They had a real relationship problem for which she held him mainly responsible. After all, she really had made an effort, as she always did with everyone, but with this man she was at the end of her tether. And if she were to receive a tuner regularly into her home, it would have to be someone with whom she could feel at ease.

Furthermore, she urgently needed to resolve this problem once and for all. Having just written a jazz method for beginners, she was now about to present her book to some music publishers. And in order to illustrate her method, she wished to record the pieces and exercises, which she had specially composed, on her piano.

This all placed the Jazz-Girl in a somewhat delicate situation. How should she proceed with the piano tuning department? While fully aware that she had numerous legitimate reasons to put in a formal complaint about Monsieur X, she nevertheless had absolutely no desire to do so. In addition to the fact that she most certainly did not want to be viewed as a troublemaker, she was just utterly weary of the whole Monsieur X scenario and simply wished to draw a line under this most unfortunate episode of her otherwise magical journey with music.

Clearly, then, what she really needed to do now was find a diplomatic way to approach the piano tuning department…

♪

It was the winter half-term break and the Jazz-Girl, together with her husband and their two children, went to Venice for *the* most amazing holiday. They had always loved Venice in this season and, as with their previous trips there, this exquisitely picturesque corner of the globe did not fail to enthral them.

Then, upon her return to Paris, the Jazz-Girl, now in fine fettle due to her recent days of *far niente*, came up with a brilliant idea for resolving her problem. That year, the half-term break was very early – just six weeks after the Christmas break – with the result that an awful lot of Parisians had decided to go away in the second week. Thus, she reasoned, if she were to call for an appointment now, there was a good chance that Monsieur X would be away on holiday with his family and that the pleasant voice would suggest a replacement.

Firmly crossing her fingers, the Jazz-Girl picked up her telephone and called the piano tuning department:

'I'm sorry to have to tell you this, but my piano is *yet again* out of tune. It's only been two weeks! I know full well that a new piano can be a bit unstable, especially during the first year. That said, I have been having mine regularly tuned for over a year now and it is still not approaching anything resembling stability.'

'I'm sorry to hear that you're not satisfied,' replied the pleasant voice.

'The fact of the matter is that I really need to sort this out as quickly as possible because I'm going to be making a recording this week and for a recording, the piano has to be absolutely perfect.'

It was at this point that the pleasant voice asked the traditional question:

'May I have your tuner's name please?'

'Yes, of course. It's Monsieur X.'

'I'm really sorry but Monsieur X is on holiday this week. Would you like me to send somebody else?'

Upon hearing these words, the Jazz-Girl suddenly felt a tremendous urge to jump up and down for joy!

Thankfully she just managed to curb it in time to give the cool and collected reply required:

'Yes please. I would like that very much.'

'Would three o'clock today be possible?'

'Yes. Definitely. Three is perfect for me.'

'Very well, in that case I'm going to send you Monsieur Pradel. Monsieur François Pradel. And I can guarantee that *he* will do a really good job.'

As the Jazz-Girl rang off, she breathed a huge sigh of relief – getting through this first stage had been relatively easy.

Be that as it may, she remained intrigued as to what would happen next and, although she was curious to meet this Monsieur François Pradel, she suddenly realised that she actually felt slightly sorry for him. He had a huge amount of work to do on her piano and, unbeknownst to him, he now carried upon his poor shoulders the heavy burden of restoring in her eyes the reputation of the entire piano tuner population!

Naturally, she could not have known that Apollo was apparently at work again...

Patently aware of the fact that his little Jazz-Girl desperately wished to retrieve the beautiful sound of her instrument, Apollo had indeed decided to intervene, personally handpicking François Pradel to be her new tuner – a man one hundred per cent dedicated to his profession who, when seated before a piano, would metamorphose into a true artist.

Furthermore, that day, the God of music, while always happy to oblige where his children were concerned, was particularly excited, for he firmly believed that, here, he was orchestrating a truly magical meeting of musical minds. And so convinced was he that these two musical spirits would get on well together that he was incredibly eager to observe the fruits of his labours.

With this in mind, he settled down in an armchair, rubbed his hands together in glee and simply said to himself: '*Showtime!*'

At a quarter to three, the Jazz-Girl's telephone rang.

'Madame Somerville?'

'Yes?'

'Bonjour, Madame, François Pradel speaking; I'm booked to tune your piano today.'

'Ah, bonjour, Monsieur; yes, that's right, our appointment's at three o'clock, isn't it?'

'Well, that's what was booked, but the thing is I'm a bit early. Actually, I'm just approaching your building, so I was wondering if it would be okay to come up now.'

'Absolutely, of course, please do. I'll see you in a few minutes, then.'

'See you in a few minutes. Au revoir, Madame.'

This initial contact left the Jazz-Girl feeling utterly delighted; it had only taken this short telephone call for François Pradel to make an incredibly good impression on her. He had actually said "bonjour". Unbelievable! Moreover, by taking the trouble to warn her that he would be a few minutes early, he was clearly very polite. And, to top it all, he had a really lovely voice. With her sensitive ear, the Jazz-Girl always noticed people's voices.

A few minutes later, the man who entered her flat most definitely did not disappoint her. On the contrary, this young thirty-something tuner, with his pleasant smile, was a perfect match for his agreeable voice.

The Jazz-Girl duly shook his hand and then – old habits die hard – stood there, expecting François Pradel to continue walking. François Pradel, however, was most definitely *not* Monsieur X, so he too stood there looking at her quizzically, until he eventually, tentatively, said:

'Would you like to show me where the piano is? After all, that's what I'm here for.'

Kicking herself for having made such a ridiculous start, she abruptly came to her senses and said:

'Yes. Yes, of course. Follow me; it's over here in the sitting room.'

François Pradel was now grinning at her in utter bemusement, doing little to conceal the fact that he clearly viewed his new client as being one sandwich short of a picnic! And, frankly, she could see his point. Knowing the location of the piano was, after all, a minimum requirement for him to do his job! But she bit her lip to refrain from giving him any explanation, since she had absolutely no wish to tell him that it was Monsieur X's impolite behaviour of the past that had caused her to pause in the hall. This would undoubtedly have put him in an awkward position regarding his colleague and her priority was to make a fresh start with this new tuner.

It turned out that she need not have been unduly concerned for things began to look promising from the moment François Pradel laid eyes on the piano.

'Wow! You have a Model S! I really love this piano. It's an amazing example of technical prowess. Such a little piano, yet such beautiful bass notes.'

The piano actually looked rather enormous to her but she knew what he meant and his reaction made her relax sufficiently to cut to the chase:

'It is indeed a very beautiful piano and I'm really lucky to have it. I am well aware that it is somewhat excessive given my current basic level of playing but you only live once and, last year, an unexpected windfall enabled me to make a wild dream come true to become the proud owner of this Steinway piano.'

Upon hearing this, François Pradel smiled at her and said:

'What a wonderful story! I do so love it when dreams come true.'

'So do I,' replied the Jazz-Girl as she smiled back at him, before continuing with: 'I chose this particular make of piano because I am extremely sensitive to the pure Steinway sound. That said, I regretfully have to admit that I am somewhat disappointed because my piano is just never in tune – which means that my dream is now turning into an absolute nightmare. It's a most unexpected, unpleasant surprise. When you invest so much money in such a beautiful instrument, you do not expect to be disappointed and you should not, under any circumstances, be disappointed.'

The piano tuner now looked crestfallen and immediately began to reassure her:

'You know, this is one of the problems which occurs with new pianos. They do tend to take a while to stabilise. Some pianos are also more fragile than others but in such cases we research the problem in order to find a specific way to stabilise them and then we adapt our tuning techniques accordingly. By the way, who *is* your tuner?'

'Monsieur X.'

'I just don't understand. He's actually a really good tuner.'

The Jazz-Girl only just managed to refrain from replying: *not as far as I'm concerned.* Obviously, the situation was extremely delicate and it was her firm intention to concentrate solely on her requirements regarding the piano.

In reality, however, she was unable to prevent herself from spilling a few of the beans as she said:

'You know, I'm not really in a position to say whether Monsieur X is a good or bad tuner because I have not really known any others. All I know is that my piano never stays in tune and I also know that I am thoroughly disappointed in Monsieur X and his general attitude. You see, the thing is, Monsieur X seems to be more interested in criticising my home than in tuning my piano. He is always saying that the problems are our fault because the room is just too light and too minimalist. Now, while I accept that our home may not be to everybody's taste, to be brutally frank I'm not actually that interested in whether a piano tuner likes or dislikes the way my flat is furnished and decorated. My sole concern is that the piano be properly tuned.'

François Pradel could clearly see that she was indeed extremely disappointed with her piano, with Monsieur X and most likely with the prestigious shop where she had purchased her instrument.

Consequently, as he began to set out his tools, he sat down at the piano and once again spoke to her in a gentle, reassuring voice:

'I completely agree with you. When you purchase this kind of piano, it's just not right that you should be disappointed. Quite clearly, we're going to have to do a lot better than this. From now on, I promise you, we're going to work twice as hard until we do actually get it right.'

Upon hearing the words "we're going to work twice as hard", the Jazz-Girl felt immensely relieved. Here was a man who was willing to support her. Clearly, he took her seriously. Even more importantly, he took the problem of the piano very seriously indeed. And, suddenly, she realised just how pleasantly surprised she was to meet this new tuner.

What followed rendered her, quite simply, surprised... full stop!

Barely had François Pradel sat down when he leapt up from the piano stool – his eyes shining with undiluted excitement. He was now wearing that distinctive look of a child who has just noticed all the presents under the Christmas tree, to the extent that the Jazz-Girl thought he might actually start jumping for joy. She was utterly intrigued. What on earth was going on? What had he just seen to put him in this state? He was no longer the calm, composed man who was there to resolve the problems on her piano. Here was an animated little boy who, having apparently just made *the* most amazing discovery, requested:

'Before I set to work, would it be okay if I asked you a little question?'

Unable to hide her amusement at such an abrupt change in this man's behaviour, the Jazz-Girl began to laugh. Then, flashing him a teasing smile, she could not resist giving him the type of answer she generally reserved for her children:

'As far as I'm concerned, you can even ask me a very big question if you like. I just lurrrrve questions!'

Realising that his behaviour had taken his client aback, the tuner took her teasing in good part and started to laugh with her, before questioning her about the sound system under the flat screen, which dominated the television area of the sitting room.

The thing is, the piano actually divided this room in two. Consequently, upon entering, the tuner had only been able to see one half of it. However, when seated at the piano, he had found himself directly facing the other half of the room – the television area. Now, this part of the sitting room was really the domain of the Jazz-Girl's husband, filled as it was with gadgets, equipment and remote controls galore – or "toys for boys", as she liked to call them. And François Pradel's attention had immediately been drawn to the magnificent sound system.

This spontaneous, enthusiastic reaction spoke absolute volumes about him, and the Jazz-Girl was increasingly enchanted by what she was witnessing. Clearly, this man took a keen interest, just as she did, in sound and the quality of sound, whatever form it came in.

Better still, upon seeing François Pradel's eyes shine so excitedly, the Jazz-Girl was able to detect something which was incredibly familiar to her – a glimmer of childlike wonderment, a glimmer which could only come, without a shadow of a doubt, from a man or a woman imbued with a passion. And in that instant, this man's passion for sound, for music and for pianos seemed to shine visibly all around him in a lovely halo of charismatic light. It was at that precise moment that the Jazz-Girl became convinced that she had just met a man who carried within him a musical flame which burned with the same intensity as that which she carried within her.

The tuner eventually got over his excitement, sat down again and, in order to identify the precise areas of the piano requiring attention, began to play a piece of classical music. A mere few bars were all it took for it to become apparent that he was a truly excellent pianist – his light, delicate touch revealing an inner finesse and sensitivity which all augured particularly well for the work he was about to carry out on the piano.

As for the Jazz-Girl, she was delighted to sit back and enjoy this superb performance on her instrument. The music was absolutely glorious. And it was a piece she knew well. In fact, she clearly remembered learning to play this piece herself during the years when she had studied classical piano. However, she could not for the life of her remember the title. All she knew was that this piece was by Chopin, undeniably by Chopin. A novice, even a child, would most likely have been able to recognise the composer of this music. And now, completely and utterly transported by the tuner's performance, she suddenly felt a strong urge to learn to play this piece again, but somehow the title stubbornly refused to come back to her. She thus decided to ask the tuner about it when he finished playing but so thoroughly absorbed was she by the music that she ended up putting her question rather badly:

'That was beautiful. Indeed, it was quite exquisite. Thank you very much... By the way, what was it?'

Fortunately, the tuner had remained seated because otherwise he would undoubtedly have fainted at this point. Suddenly he looked rather shocked – in fact, utterly horrified would probably be a better way of putting it. Clearly, he was wondering how it was actually possible for someone to be so very culturally vacuous!

With the colour draining from his face, rendering him completely ashen, he looked the Jazz-Girl straight in the eye and lowering his voice, so as to encourage her to lean in and listen attentively, he whispered: 'It was Cho-pin,' emphatically separating the syllables as if to help her remember the name.

For a few brief seconds, the Jazz-Girl felt incredibly small, not quite knowing how to react for the best. Should she observe a minute's silence out of deference for the genius whose name had just been uttered? Or would she be better off crawling into a corner, where she could roll into a little ball and lie in the foetal position, so that the tuner could no longer see her?

Then, quite suddenly, she snapped back into reality, bursting out laughing as she said:

'I know full well that the piece you just played is by Chopin. I used to play it all the time when I studied classical piano. It's merely the title that escapes me.'

A look of blessed relief appeared on François Pradel's face and, the colour now gently returning to his cheeks, he duly informed her of the title.

And so it was that, in order to avoid creating any more cultural shock waves, the Jazz-Girl stood up and said:

'I think it's probably time I left you in peace to work. If you need anything at all, just give me a shout. I shall be working next door in the study.'

In spite of the Chopin incident, the Jazz-Girl left the sitting room with a huge smile on her face. In the space of ten brief minutes, she had had more pleasant exchanges with this man than in all the many long hours she had spent with Monsieur X.

Settling down in the study, she set to work, fascinated by the background music, a mysterious mix of exotic sounds, produced by the tuner as he carried out his work.

Each tuner has his own specific way of proceeding and François

Pradel's preferred method was to begin with the middle octaves, where his thorough, meticulous approach revealed him to be a true perfectionist. He really took his time, lingering over those notes which required particular attention, correcting them, testing them, going back over them again and again until they were just right. Then he began to tune the high notes. He was actually tuning the high notes! At last, she had a tuner who was prepared to do this! And finally, he dealt with the bass notes. And so it was that, for two long hours, he worked relentlessly, not letting up for one single second.

Then he began to play some more classical music – this time it was a piece by Bach. Once more, the Jazz-Girl recognised the piece. And, once more, she could not for the life of her remember the title. However, on this occasion, she decided that her curiosity would just have to go unsatisfied; she was desperately hoping that François Pradel would accept to become her permanent tuner and therefore concluded that it would be wise to avoid further offending this artistically sensitive man.

Believing this classical performance to be a sign that the tuner had now finished his work on the piano, the Jazz-Girl grabbed her chequebook and returned to the sitting room to pay the bill where, in a bid to enjoy the Bach performance to the end, she sat down comfortably in an armchair.

As it happened, being seated was probably for the best for, unbeknownst to her, it was soon to be *her* turn to receive the most enormous musical shock.

In the seconds following the end of the performance, the tuner quite simply underwent a change of personality...

It was then that this sensitive man, whose hitherto delicate touch on the piano had made such an impression on her, suddenly turned into a kind of monster who started to attack the instrument like a wild animal – the only difference being that a wild animal would undoubtedly have played with more finesse!

The tuner's ten fingers were now hitting the keys with such force that it looked as if they had turned into hammers. She had never seen anything quite like it, which was surprising because she was used to seeing boogie-woogie specialists go completely crazy on the piano – playing chords with their feet, hitting the strings with their fists, not to mention climbing onto the top of the instrument at the end of the show. However, *this* was a whole new ball game. What on earth was going on? She was actually beginning to wonder if she had a schizophrenic in her midst. And, ultimately, she was wondering if she might just be better off accepting that all piano tuners were seriously weird. Or was it merely a case of having had the gross misfortune to happen upon the two most unpredictable piano tuners of the entire planet? She no longer knew what to think.

At the end of what seemed like an eternity, the tuner eventually ceased to thump the piano like a savage beast and turned to look at the Jazz-Girl. Clearly, he was genuinely amused by what he saw: her usually diaphanous complexion had become transparent!

Flashing her *the* most wicked of grins, he quite simply said:

'I'm trying to make your piano tremble.'

Unfortunately, the piano was not the only thing trembling in the room; the Jazz-Girl was currently trembling from head to foot for her instrument, her treasure, her baby – and sorely wishing she could take it into her arms to console it.

Now, at a complete loss as to what to think about this tuner, she decided to remain seated in the armchair so she could jealously watch over her piano in the manner of a young mother who, out of a fierce primeval desire to protect her newborn baby, seems to metamorphose into a she-wolf!

The decision to stay in the room proved to be a good move. During the hour that followed, the Jazz-Girl began to understand precisely what was going on. And she was also reassured to observe that this tuner was not, in fact, completely mad!

Due to François Pradel's fierce attack on the piano, some of the unisons had been very slightly affected and he was now making the tiniest adjustments imaginable. Here, the finesse of his work was really quite remarkable. It was as if his tuning lever were actually a paintbrush, and he, an artist who was completing a beautiful oil painting with light, delicate brushstrokes.

After three solid hours of toiling relentlessly, the tuner was at last satisfied. As for the Jazz-Girl, she was literally stunned. The time this man had spent on her piano only served to confirm to her that Monsieur X had not done his job properly. François Pradel had had to work really hard to turn the piano back into the very beautiful instrument she had chosen in the shop.

In the normal course of things, she would now have tested the piano but on this occasion she refrained from doing so. She was genuinely impressed, even slightly overwhelmed, by this tuner's pianistic skills which meant that she was not yet ready to reveal her own somewhat basic level of playing to him. And in any event, testing the piano seemed quite unnecessary. Her instrument was different, transformed and that was clear for all to hear.

The tuner tidied his tools away and then asked the Jazz-Girl to show him where he could wash his hands. She thus invited him to follow her to the kitchen where she was ashamed to observe that the sink was full of dirty pans but it was unfortunately too late to do anything about it now.

The tuner, for his part, did not seem unduly perturbed by the state of the kitchen. As he took his time to wash his hands, he looked all around and then proclaimed:

'Your flat may be minimalist but, in my view, it really is very beautiful.'

He could not have paid her a better compliment. After all, it was she who had designed the kitchen! Thus it was that she now found herself thanking him for his kind words while desperately trying to control her smile which seemed intent on spreading itself from one ear to the other, for the simple reason that she felt genuinely happy to have met this new tuner. He had not put a single foot wrong. And yet, the best was still to come…

As they returned to the sitting room to deal with the invoice, the Jazz-Girl took the opportunity to express her profound gratitude to him for the work he had just carried out. And it was at this point that he seemed to realise how very relieved she was to meet somebody who was prepared to do such a thorough job on her piano.

In response, he spoke to her once again in a most gentle, reassuring voice:

'You know, it's really important to entrust your instrument to the right person – somebody in whom you have complete faith. Would you like my telephone number? Then if there is anything about the piano, anything at all, which you're worried about, you can ring me and we'll discuss it together.'

His kindness rendered her speechless. The contrast with Monsieur X's minimum service behaviour was so very stark! Clearly, François Pradel was one hundred per cent dedicated to his profession, his art.

Noticing that she was obviously moved by his suggestion, the tuner decided to answer on her behalf:

'Look, here's my number. Call me if you have any queries at all.'

With that, the Jazz-Girl accompanied him to the lift and then he was gone, leaving something resembling a trail of musical charisma in his wake…

𝄞

In the days that followed, the Jazz-Girl derived enormous pleasure from playing her piano. Its voice was, as before, pure and true. The base notes were beautifully deep, the medium range astoundingly mellow, while the high notes chimed like delicate little bells. This was the sound for which she had so longed.

A few days later, her jazz teacher, just back from his own holiday, came to give her her weekly lesson. That day, as she played, he listened particularly attentively, until he could no longer conceal his surprise:

'This is amazing. Unbelievable. I have rarely seen you let yourself go on your instrument in this way. There's a huge difference in the way you play. And your touch is greatly improved.'

Then, teasing her in a friendly manner – as was his wont to do – he enquired:

'Come on. Out with it. What's going on? Just *what* has happened to you?'

In response, the Jazz-Girl explained how hard François Pradel had toiled to return the original, magnificent sound to her piano, a sound so pure that it was actually helping her progress as she endeavoured to be equal to it. She then invited him to play the piano himself, intrigued to know what he thought since he had the good fortune to be blessed with perfect pitch.

Her teacher sat down to play and shortly afterwards confirmed what she believed; the piano was once again the beautiful instrument she had chosen, its clarity of sound undeniable.

It was on the basis of these comments that the Jazz-Girl decided it was time to give François Pradel some positive feedback. She thus called him, thanked him profusely and concluded by asking him if he would think about becoming her permanent tuner.

Unfortunately, his response was totally unexpected. As luck would have it, he turned out to be extremely reticent about the whole idea:

'You know, I'm not sure I can take on your piano. I already look after so many. And you must understand that Monsieur X is actually a very good tuner.'

This reaction left the Jazz-Girl feeling profoundly disappointed. Why the reticence? Was he afraid of repercussions between him and his colleague?

As for Apollo, he was completely beside himself. 'No, no, *no*! This just will not do,' he found himself saying. This was not at all the outcome he had set his heart on. He had, after all, gone to great lengths to orchestrate this magical meeting. He could see these two musical spirits working really well together and was hoping, if everything went as planned, that one day they might even become friends. So it was not for the tuner, however talented he may be, to decide otherwise.

Aware that speed was of the essence, Apollo immediately proceeded to rush to the Jazz-Girl's aid by sending her the exact words required to convince the tuner that he must, at all costs, take on her piano.

Thus it was that the Jazz-Girl actually surprised herself by responding in a much more direct manner than usual:

'Please allow me to make one thing very clear. I have every intention of finding a new tuner. I can no longer continue to work with Monsieur X. After all, what possible reason could I have to do so? I really don't like his sound, the piano never stays in tune and, to add insult to injury, he is thoroughly unpleasant with me. I am naturally telling you all this on a strictly confidential basis since I have absolutely no wish to cause any trouble within the piano tuning department. My sole concern lies with finding a decent tuner and here is how I propose to go about it. Whenever I call for an appointment, the first thing they ask for is the name of the person who looks after my piano. The next time, I would really like to be able to give your name. No details, just your name. If this poses any problem at all, then I can see that it would obviously be better to let me know sooner rather than later.'

Her direct words paid off. This time the tuner, reassured to know that any repercussions would be highly unlikely, responded favourably to her request.

As she put the telephone down, the Jazz-Girl could not help but breathe a huge sigh of relief.

As for Apollo, well, naturally, he punched the air and cried: 'Yessssss!!!'

The Jazz-Girl was on the point of calling the piano tuning department for a new appointment when she hesitated, pausing to reflect for an instant on the stark contrast between Monsieur X and Monsieur Pradel – two tuners diametrically opposed in their approach to their work. And it was then that she suddenly became aware of the extremely valuable lesson which Monsieur X had inadvertently taught her: thanks to him, she had finally understood the true importance of a tuner's work because she now realised that, whatever the quality of the piano, if an instrument is out of tune or poorly tuned, then it just cannot sound beautiful. In other words, even the most talented virtuoso in the world, seated in front of the best piano known to man, will struggle to make his or her music sing gracefully if the instrument itself has not been properly prepared. And this is precisely where the person preparing it has a crucial role to play. A highly skilled, talented tuner will add a personal touch, thus breathing life into a piano to help it find its true voice. An indifferent tuner will do just the opposite. Seen, then, from this point of view, a piano is quite simply as good – or as bad – as the person who tunes it.

The Jazz-Girl now actually started to feel quite sorry for Monsieur X. What could possibly have happened during his life to make him so disillusioned with his profession? Why on earth was he so sad and bitter, despite the fact that he too carried within him this very ability to bring beautiful pianos to life in order to ensure they sang gracefully? Had his passion for pianos been harmed by the disdainful attitude of unpleasant divas? Or had he just never had the passion? Was he consequently worn out by years of working in a profession which did not interest him in the slightest? She had absolutely no idea. Monsieur X's behaviour would forever remain a mystery to her and, in any event, she no longer had any more time to waste on his case because she currently had to deal with a much more pressing matter. Just as she had promised François Pradel, it was imperative she avoid going into any detail about her decision to change tuner and, in order for that to happen, the pleasant voice *had* to ask her the habitual question.

And so it was that, without further ado, the Jazz-Girl picked up her telephone, dialled the number and requested an appointment for her piano.

'Could you just remind me of the name of your tuner please?' asked the pleasant voice.

Suddenly, an immense feeling of happiness began to descend on the Jazz-Girl as, in the knowledge that she was about to enter a new phase of her personal journey with music, she proudly responded by saying:

'Yes, of course. My tuner's name is François Pradel.'

And that is how a long and beautiful working relationship between a Jazz-Girl with a passion and a most dedicated piano tuner was born.

Apollo was smiling joyfully. *This* was merely the beginning…

The Piano Tuner Boogie-Woogie

The creative process is incredibly unpredictable. At times, an artist will toil over his, or her, work without obtaining the slightest results. On other occasions, new ideas seem to arrive from nowhere, like gifts landing effortlessly in the hands of the very same artist who had previously been struggling. These gems of creativity more than compensate for all the feelings of frustration arising from the fruitless periods.

Emmanuel Carrère[4] mentions this type of experience in one of his books – *The Adversary*. At one point, he had to stop writing it because another book – *Class Trip* – just started "writing itself"; a book which he describes as the best thing he had ever written at the time. When questioned about this, he was keen to point out that he had been mulling over the idea for this book for several months, years maybe, feeling his way around a vague subject and storyline. He draws the following conclusion: "A long and somewhat arduous period of subconscious gestation, then sudden fruition."

That the subconscious mind carries on working at a very deep level long after the artist thinks that he, or she, has forgotten the subject which was frustrating him, or her, so much, does indeed appear to be the only possible explanation for these instances of creative bliss.

Interestingly, this magical process, giving rise as it does to apparently effortless, spontaneous, artistic creations, seems to be

4   Emmanuel Carrère is a best-selling French author and I happen to be a huge fan of his literary style. When I was writing this story, I contacted him via his publisher to ask him if he would allow me to quote him on this subject and also to check that my facts were right. He promptly replied with a kind, detailed letter containing lots of useful additional information. I particularly appreciated receiving his help because at the time of our exchange he was an extremely busy man. He had just brought out a new book and was on an intensive promotional tour. My sincere thanks go to this great writer for his invaluable contribution to this story.

particularly present in musical composition. Illustrations of this abound, both among classical and contemporary composers. A perfect example can be found in the song "Let It Be". In interviews, Paul McCartney will often recall how one night he dreamt of his mother, who had died many years previously when he was just fourteen years old. The next morning, he awoke to find that this new song had just suddenly dropped into his mind and the rest, as they say, is history.

At times like these, the musician does not really feel that he, or she, is actually composing the work but more that he, or she, is a mere vehicle for receiving it. And paradoxically – just as Emmanuel Carrère points out when talking about his experience writing *Class Trip* – those compositions which seem to come from nowhere, without any apparent effort on the part of the musician, are generally the best.

The most amazing thing about this mysterious, magical process is that it happens to be very democratic. Such spontaneous creative works are not only sent to the great, highly gifted artists of our planet but also to mere beginners, as the Jazz-Girl discovered, to her utter astonishment, when first she started to study piano jazz...

Once she had learnt to read the chords – an essential very basic first step required for jazz improvisation – her teacher Zach considered that she was ready to study blues harmony. He thus began by teaching her three pentatonic scales[5] and then gave her an exercise to work on for the following lesson: she was to use these scales to compose some bluesy phrases.

This, however, posed a problem: an imminent trip to London for a family party meant that the Jazz-Girl was about to find herself with little access to a piano for the best part of a week. Consequently, prior to her departure, she learnt her blues scales by heart, in the hope that they might just inspire her during her stay in England.

Alas, her approach turned out to be in vain. Try as she might to sing her blues scales every day, ideas for bluesy phrases were simply not forthcoming.

At least, that's what she thought, until the day she was on her way home when, suddenly, an idea – not for one simple musical phrase but for an entire melody – dropped into her mind. Back home in Paris, she played it on the piano – a piece of twelve-bar blues that actually sounded quite... well... bluesy! Zach confirmed this during the following lesson; according to him, her melody had a "great blues

---

5   Five-note scales used in blues.

sound". This was her very first composition and since the melody came to her while she was travelling through the Channel Tunnel, she decided to call it "Eurostar Blues".

Miraculously, the more the Jazz-Girl studied jazz, the more she seemed to have access to these magical moments of creative bliss…

One day, while contemplating the sunrise, the idea of playing one of her favourite riffs[6] backwards[7] suddenly came to her. In order not to wake up her family, she sat silently at her digital piano, plugged in the headphones and began to play; a new piece of blues, based on this inverted riff, appeared spontaneously on the keyboard. She named it "Sunrise Dream".

Once again, her teacher congratulated her profusely on her work, yet she did not really feel she deserved his congratulations because the piece had seemingly revealed itself without any particular effort on her part. As the great and famous artists regularly point out, she too was under the impression that her best work just dropped easily and spontaneously into her hands and, in order to receive it, all she had to do was remain present in the musical moment.

A few weeks later, a totally unexpected source of inspiration gave the Jazz-Girl *the* most surprising, spontaneous, creative experience she had ever had…

From the moment François Pradel had become her official piano tuner, he had established a strategy, with a view to stabilising the piano, which was based on the simple principle of "a little and often"; in other words, the piano was to be tuned as soon as it displayed the slightest signs of requiring it. Given the superb quality of this instrument, which deserved to be regularly maintained, coupled with the fact that the Jazz-Girl clearly had a very demanding ear, in his view, they would be able to declare victory the day they reached a stage where the piano would require tuning just twice a year.

Due to her piano tuner's remarkable work, the Jazz-Girl was already at a stage where she was only required to have her piano tuned every three or four months – more often than average but nevertheless a good pace for a brand-new piano of this type. That

---

6   A riff is a musical phrase played repeatedly and used to create tension in jazz improvisation.
7   A useful tip for anyone struggling to find new ideas for a composition and something I only discovered subsequent to this experience: many composers – when seeking inspiration – do actually play phrases of music backwards.

said, the frequency of the tunings never failed to amuse her jazz teacher…

It was Tuesday afternoon and Zach had just arrived to give her her weekly lesson. As she greeted him, she proudly announced:

'We're going to have a great time today. I've literally just had the piano tuned. It's absolutely perfect!'

'You know,' retorted Zach, 'in my view, you'd be better off having a bed installed for your tuner just here, right next to the piano. Let's face it, you're always calling him in!'

Laughing and entering into the spirit, she responded with:

'Why not? He's such a nice guy, he's always welcome!' Then she paused for thought, before adding: 'You know, by calling him in so often, I'm only following the advice he gave me, but I do freely admit that I truly love the whole process of having the piano tuned. It's actually a really peaceful experience. First of all, I make sure the flat is as quiet as possible and then, while the tuner is here, I sit in the study next door, allegedly working, but in fact I spend most of my time listening to the "music" of his precise and meticulous work. I really love the sounds it makes.'

With that, she repeatedly played two intervals – a fourth and a fifth – and, turning to look at her teacher, she enquired:

'Isn't that a bit how it sounds when a tuner works on a piano?'

Zach nodded his head to indicate that it was indeed quite a good imitation of a tuner at work, which encouraged her to develop her idea – this time by playing a major third, followed by a fourth and a fifth. Now on a roll, she went one step further to play a minor third, a major third, a fourth, adding a chromatic note – F sharp – for good measure, and ending once again on a fifth. Then, having suddenly stumbled upon this bluesy phrase, a potential new riff which really appealed to her, she turned to her teacher and, displaying a hugely mischievous grin on her face, as if to say she had just made *the* most amazing discovery, exclaimed:

'Well, there you have it! *That* is precisely why I love listening to my tuner at work. You see, when he tunes the piano, he's actually playing blues riffs. This is what I'm always trying to tell you. It all comes down to blues in the end.'

Zach burst out laughing. His pupil had just scored a point in a game they played regularly, and he knew it!

It so happened that the Jazz-Girl and her teacher had diametrically opposed tastes in music and every week they would each try and defend their respective corner. Zach preferred sad music because he found it particularly moving. The Jazz-Girl, on the other hand, only liked happy, feel-good music. This had always been the case, dating right back to her childhood days. As a little girl, when first she had started taking piano lessons at the age of nine, she had been quick to invent a system which enabled her to "brighten up" the works of Chopin, Beethoven and Bach, in that assured kind of belief, which so often goes hand in hand with all the confidence of youth, that these great composers should quite simply not have written such melancholic pieces! Her system consisted of transposing any piece originally written in a minor key into a joyful major key. Then, just before her piano lesson, she would quickly relearn the piece exactly as it had been written in order to avoid a scolding from her teacher!

Now, while her desire to modify her pieces to suit her tastes, coupled with her obvious ability to create her own arrangements, were clear signs that one day she would abandon classical piano in favour of jazz improvisation, her preference for happy music had never once wavered. Not for a single second. She freely admitted that she liked feel-good melodies and loved teasing her teacher mercilessly about his somewhat darker tastes in music, dropping regular hints that his favourite pieces were comparable to dirges.

Zach, for his part, would generally retaliate by referring to the different eras of their radically divergent tastes. Whereas he loved the dissonant, innovative sounds of contemporary jazz, the Jazz-Girl preferred traditional jazz – more precisely, blues (of course!) and its rapid, joyful, percussive descendant, boogie-woogie. Consequently, he never ceased to use this as ammunition for teasing her back: from a musical standpoint, she was quite incapable of leaving the 1930s!

And so it was that the weekly lessons would revolve around this joyful game of musical ping pong, which left no stone unturned, including that of classical music, for while they were more than happy to concede that they did actually both like Chopin, as far as the Jazz-Girl was concerned, only one composer really mattered: Mozart. Zach, unsurprisingly, preferred slightly less accessible music, expressing a strong preference for Debussy and Ravel. In his view, the more one had to scratch away at the surface of a piece to understand it, the better.

Be that as it may, in spite of their widely opposing tastes, their teacher–pupil duo worked wonderfully well for the simple reason that they were both in complete agreement on one essential point: together they shared the same fascination with jazz improvisation and the profound source of melodies it offered. Moreover, their contrasting tastes in music actually added something to their teacher–pupil relationship because from time to time one of them would succeed in influencing the other in an amazingly positive way.

This was the case the day Zach taught his pupil that magnificent jewel of jazz improvisation known as the tri-tone substitution.

Almost immediately, the Jazz-Girl was utterly captivated by the beautiful, mathematical perfection of this improvisation technique, to the extent that dinners with her equally enthralled husband started to revolve around this subject on a regular basis. However, in spite of her total fascination with the theory of the tri-tone substitution, she struggled to use it in her improvisations for the simple reason that the sound was way too dissonant for her somewhat traditional ear.

Recognising the difficulty, Zach, endowed as he was with solid pedagogical skills and levels of patience bordering on the superhuman, would gently encourage the Jazz-Girl to surmount the problem, each week painstakingly separating this exceedingly complex technique into several simple and easy stages, until one day she finally managed to integrate it into one of her improvisations. Zach responded to her work with a combination of astonishment and delight. She was at last beginning to create extremely modern, jazzy, innovative sounds. Better still, she actually got a taste for these new sounds and started to use the tri-tone substitution in ways Zach would never have "dared" to, such as in traditional boogie and blues pieces!

Conversely, over time, the Jazz-Girl managed to "contaminate" her teacher with her enthusiasm for boogie-woogie. Never having been the type of musician to do things by halves, Zach spent a whole summer studying the entire boogie-woogie repertoire, completing his studies by taking lessons with a well-known jazzman. Subsequently, with touching role reversal, Zach would regularly begin the lessons he gave to the Jazz-Girl by updating her on his progress, playing his new pieces for her and even going so far as to ask her for advice!

It was precisely due to their great teacher–pupil relationship that the Jazz-Girl made huge progress with Zach and, that day, once she had finished playing around with the riff imitating a tuner at work, they then got down to the serious business of studying a new jazz standard…

The intellectual stimulation of her weekly lesson always gave the Jazz-Girl an amazing feeling of wellbeing, a feeling so intoxicating that – just like any drug – it would leave her wanting for more which is why as soon as Zach left her, precisely one hour later to go to his next pupil, she decided to sit right down at the piano again.

Intrigued by her new "discovery" – the piano tuner riff – she suddenly started playing it repeatedly with her right hand. Then her left hand, not to be outdone, began playing too, adding a typical boogie-woogie accompaniment: eight quavers to the bar played on a swing rhythm. And, bingo! Suddenly, she found herself playing a sixteen-bar boogie-woogie based on the riff. It was a truly magical experience! The piece was composing itself. She barely had to do anything. Just as on previous occasions, all that was required of her was to remain present in the musical moment.

For the next lesson, she wrote out the piece in order to be able to show the sheet music to her teacher.

Upon seeing it, Zach deemed it to be her best composition to date, so much more sophisticated than the pieces she usually wrote. This encouraged her to develop it into an arrangement that would follow the order in which François Pradel tuned her piano. In other words, the arrangement would start in the middle octave and move gradually up into the high notes, before going on to the passages in the bass notes. Then, in order to imitate the way her tuner checked the piano at the end of each tuning, she would conclude the piece with a passage crossing the entire keyboard from left to right.

During the week that followed, the Jazz-Girl proceeded to work on her arrangement. Or so she thought... In fact, the piece just seemed to arrange itself. Every time she sat down at the piano, the ideas would simply flow. Once again, the creative process was in charge and, consequently, things seemed to be happening without requiring the slightest effort on the part of the Jazz-Girl, despite her allegedly being the composer of this piece, to the extent that she felt she really did not deserve the many compliments she subsequently received. When she played the piece for Zach, he congratulated her on the depth and rich quality of her music. He loved the variety of the left-hand accompaniments and some of the riffs in the right hand were so sophisticated that he had to listen to them at least twice before being able to understand their structure. As for François Pradel, the next time he came to tune the piano, the Jazz-Girl proudly played the entire piece for him. And so touched was he to learn that his profession had served as the inspiration for a new composition that he took a copy of it away with him.

A few years later, François told the Jazz-Girl an anecdote about this piece that made her even more proud. One of his clients was a very famous French composer, specialising in music for films. One day, this particular client had asked him if he could record him at work for he had just had a brilliant idea – he intended to compose a piece based on the sounds created by a tuner on the piano!

François had replied:

'Regarding the recording, no problem, but as far as the composition is concerned, you should know that another client of mine has already beaten you to it!'

That said, the Jazz-Girl's greatest source of pride lay elsewhere, in her access to these amazing, quite incredible, moments of spontaneous creativity – which would come to her seemingly from nowhere, just as they did to the great authors and composers such as Emmanuel Carrère or Paul McCartney! Admittedly, she would never be able to write in the sublimely poetic style of her favourite contemporary French author. Nor would her music ever hold a candle to Paul McCartney's compositions – unless Apollo were to perform some kind of miracle and she sincerely believed that the God of music had already done more than enough for her in that department! However, despite the vastly differing levels of talent between these famous artists and herself, it did indeed seem that she too had the immense privilege of experiencing the truly magical, mysterious aspects of the creative process, a process which, from time to time, would offer her *the* most astonishing musical gems and which, one day, had produced, just as it had done on previous occasions for these two great artists, one of her best works; a composition which had been really well received by her jazz teacher and which had so touched her piano tuner that he had actually requested a copy of it.

And while the original inspiration for this composition had been utterly surprising and unexpected, the title, which the Jazz-Girl should bestow upon it, seemed completely obvious to her.

Thus it was that The Piano Tuner Boogie-Woogie[8] was born.

---

8   If you would like to obtain a free copy of this piece, please do not hesitate to contact me: lajazzgirlpassionnee@gmail.com.

The Music Stand

Whenever her piano tuner was due to arrive, the Jazz-Girl would go through the same precise ritual. First of all, she would ensure silence reigned by walking round her flat to check that all the electrical appliances – the washing machine, the tumble dryer and the dishwasher – were resolutely switched off; no machine was allowed to go "beep" in the presence of François Pradel. She would then clean the inside of her piano, paying particular attention to the dampers[9], delicately dusting them lengthways, just as her tuner had taught her. And finally, she would play a few pieces in order to verify – one last time – the exact state of her instrument.

That day, she had just completed her ritual when she received a text message. François was struggling to tune a somewhat recalcitrant piano and was going to be at least half an hour late. She thus returned to her piano and took it upon herself to remove the music stand – an imposing piece of wood, running the entire width of the instrument. Since this was usually the first thing her tuner did on arrival, she thought it might just speed things up a bit. Then, somewhat absentmindedly, she sat down and started to play the piano again.

It was in that very instant that she had *the* most amazing revelation…

The sound was completely transformed. And there was a very specific reason for this. Without the wooden barrier, which the music stand essentially formed, the notes of her music were now able to travel in a straight line from the inside of the piano all the way to her ear. Consequently, her instrument was singing with impressive clarity. A beautiful sound which was purer than ever!

---

9   The small felted pieces of wood which drop down (in the case of a grand piano) onto the strings to stop the vibrations.

That said, the amazing clarity of sound was truly unforgiving and before long she had detected a weird vibration on a note in the middle octave.

When François finally arrived, the Jazz-Girl attempted to convey the problem to him by repeatedly playing the vibrating note. Unfortunately, in response he *repeatedly* claimed that he really could not hear anything wrong with it, all the while displaying a weary expression on his face – that look which was becoming increasingly familiar to her and which seemed to say: "Your ear is way too demanding. You seem to hear things which other pianists just don't hear." Maybe, but in this particular case her ear was even worse than that – detecting noises that were quite clearly failing to reach even her tuner's highly sensitive ear!

Applying her last resort tactic, she invited François to take her place at the piano and play the note himself, which he only had to do once before turning to her to declare:

'You're absolutely right. In fact, it's blatantly obvious. There's a major vibration on this note. I think it's coming from the bar of wood in front of the keyboard. It doesn't seem to be properly attached. If you put your hand here you can actually feel the vibrations.'

It was now her turn to be completely in the dark. Try as she might, her hand placed firmly on the bar, she simply could not identify the culprits but, in any case, the main thing was to cure the problem. This François did by swiftly removing the bar of wood, putting it back in place and then hitting it really hard – three times! – with his right hand. Miraculously, the note once again sounded truly pure. That such brutal treatment could produce such a graceful sound was a complete mystery to the Jazz-Girl but the ends clearly justified the somewhat unorthodox means because this solution had apparently been extremely effective.

One hour later, his work finished, the tuner proceeded to go through his own precise ritual of tidying his tools away, washing his hands, preparing the invoice and, in the normal course of things, replacing the music stand on the piano. However, just as he was about to do this, the Jazz-Girl stopped him with a request:

'Actually, would you mind leaving the music stand off, please? I'd like to play with the piano completely open today. I've only just discovered the clarity of sound you get when you remove the stand, and I love it. It's absolutely amazing! It's as if I've just found a new toy.

Admittedly, it's a highly sophisticated toy but, nevertheless, to me it's a toy and I can tell you, I'm about to have a really great time.'

François remained silent; no words were necessary as he stood there smiling at her in the manner of an indulgent parent. While her demanding ear most certainly did not facilitate his work as a tuner, he always seemed to take great delight in the childlike sense of wonder she would display when seated at her beautiful piano. And that day, the little girl in her was clearly visible as he left her happily playing with her newfound "toy".

Better still, this "little girl" was not about to be disappointed. The more she played, the more she discovered *just* how amazing the piano was when completely open; the visual aspect was turning out to be as magical as the auditory transformation, for she simply could not take her eyes off the dampers as they went up and down – giving her the impression that they were putting on a show specially for her, a show in which the performers no longer seemed to be dampers but tiny little puppets!

The visual aspect also had a surprise in store for her since it brought a major improvement to her piano playing… The Jazz-Girl had always struggled to maintain a regular tempo. Frequently, she would allow herself to become carried away by the music, accelerating the pace as she improvised. Moreover, the problem persisted since she was utterly incapable of using a metronome to correct it. The dampers, on the other hand, appeared to be providing her with a very useful working tool because by merely observing the speed at which they went up and down, she was able to maintain an extremely regular left-hand rhythm, a crucial requirement for a polished boogie and blues performance.

Increasingly fascinated by what was happening, that day the Jazz-Girl found herself unable to leave the piano for a single second. Indeed, she remained glued to the spot for several hours, completely forgetting to have lunch, and ceasing to play only when it became absolutely necessary, to go and pick up her daughter from school.

And when finally she, somewhat unwillingly, detached herself from her ever-beckoning piano, the delicious feeling of musical intoxication arising from this long bluesy session incited her to take a very important decision: from now on she would always play the piano without the music stand – which naturally posed a problem. Where was she to put the sheet music? As a student of jazz improvisation, arguably full music scores were not necessary. However, she knew she would feel more at ease if she were able to play with her grids[10] in front of her, particularly during her hour-long music lesson…

$$\oint$$

It was Tuesday afternoon and Zach had just arrived. That day, the sight of the piano came as something of a shock to him:

'*What* on earth is that?'

Admittedly, the sheet music solution was somewhat makeshift, to say the very least! The Jazz-Girl had not come up with anything better than three unsightly blobs of Blu-tack, which were now attaching the piece of paper to the edge of her piano.

'Nina, you just *cannot* do that to a Steinway,' said Zach, as he burst out laughing. 'If you don't remove the Blu-tack immediately, I'm going to take some photos and send them to the Steinway factory in Hamburg!'

In the manner of a repentant schoolgirl, she conceded that it was not exactly ideal and, once the lesson was over, proceeded to search the Internet in order to find a more acceptable solution. Surprisingly, according to the information available, it appeared that Steinway & Sons had thought of producing every accessory imaginable – T-shirts, mugs, shammy leathers decorated with the company's beautiful logo – everything, except any type of object remotely connected to the instrument itself!

Expanding her search, she eventually ordered a metal music stand originally intended for guitarists but which seemed, in her view, absolutely perfect for her piano. At least that is what she thought… When she received it, she discovered that it certainly fulfilled most of her requirements. Lightweight and small, it did not prevent her from seeing the dampers and, even more importantly, it did not absorb the sound. There was however a slight hitch. It was actually so light that it refused to stay in place. Consequently, when she positioned it on the metal structure inside the piano, a small blob of Blu-tack was still required to prevent it from sliding around. And one day, in spite of this precaution, disaster very nearly struck. That day, she was

---

10 The term "grid" refers to the series of chords that form the basis of an improvisation.

playing a particularly lively boogie-woogie when the music stand suddenly slipped backwards, knocking over her rather large book of jazz standards which she only just caught in time before it fell on the dampers – one of the most, if not *the* most, fragile parts of the piano's interior. Clearly it was time to find a more sensible solution and it was at this point that her tuner came on board.

François was very interested in her idea and wanted to help her. He knew that Steinway & Sons sold a different type of music stand made out of Plexiglas, which due to its transparency would have satisfied the visual requirement. However, it was exactly the same shape and size as the original wooden stand and would therefore be likely to create the same sound barrier.

The Jazz-Girl showed him the one she had found on the Internet and explained the problem:

'This stand would be perfect if only we could find a way to stop it from sliding around.'

'What you need is a frame to stand it in,' he replied. 'I have a friend who is a carpenter. I could ask him to make a wooden frame for you. With the right dimensions and a layer of felt on its base, I guarantee that the frame will stay in place.'

With that, he took some precise measurements and left with the metal music stand to see what he could do.

𝄞

A few weeks later, the Jazz-Girl received an unexpected call:

'Hello. François Pradel speaking. I'm calling because the carpenter has just given me a quote for the frame but, in my view, it's much too expensive so I'm currently in a shop looking at ready-made frames to see if there is anything appropriate. I've found some with the right measurements but I'd like your opinion about the colour.'

Touched and even slightly overwhelmed by this gesture, a clear testimony, once again, to François' complete dedication to his profession, the Jazz-Girl began by thanking him profusely for his invaluable help, invaluable because it was enabling her to move one step closer to her pianistic dream.

Then addressing the more specific issue of the frame, after some discussion they decided that he would purchase a frame in natural wood, which the carpenter could then paint in black gloss to match the piano and back with felt as originally planned.

The next week the music stand was ready and François was truly satisfied with the result. So much so in fact that, in the belief other clients might also be interested in this type of stand, he was keen for her to try it out and was consequently coming round specially to deliver it. Unfortunately, at the last minute he was called out to deal with a concert hall emergency and ended up cancelling.

Two weeks later, the Jazz-Girl was delighted to see her tuner's name pop up again on her telephone. She was at last going to receive the stand. However, there was one slight problem: she had just acquired a new mobile phone and had absolutely no idea how to answer calls on it. She tried everything, including, in a fit of frustration, her tuner's "technical" approach of hitting the thing hard, three times in a row, which, alas, turned out to be much less effective on her phone than on the piano!

After several fruitless attempts to speak to her, François finally had recourse to a more traditional method and called her on her landline to inform her of a rather unexpected turn of events. A few days previously, he had whisked the girlfriend of the moment away on a romantic weekend. Before setting off on the Friday night, with a somewhat more pressing affair (so to speak) on his mind, he had, in his haste, thrown his and his girlfriend's luggage in the boot of his sports car with a carefree toss. The ensuing resounding crack had suddenly reminded him that he had left the music stand with its new frame in there. It had also informed him, into the bargain, that the frame had failed to survive the impact and promptly split in two!

The Jazz-Girl was now trying hard not to laugh. She was indeed sorry to learn about what had happened. After all, François had devoted a lot of time to this. Nevertheless, she could not help but see the funny side. The stand had been on some adventures, and all that, merely to arrive back at square one! Furthermore, she would now have to wait some time before receiving a new one. The carpenter friend was obliged to return to his home country for family reasons.

A few months later…

That morning, the Jazz-Girl had just completed a really productive session at the piano when she received a text message. Having gone some months with no news, she was pleased to see it came from her piano tuner and even more so to discover its contents: a series of photos showing the stand placed on a superb frame, painted in black gloss and backed with felt. It looked just right.

A week later, when François came to tune the piano, he duly delivered the new stand to her. Delighted with the result, the Jazz-Girl sent him a message, barely half an hour after his departure, to thank him, declaring it absolutely perfect.

And that is where this story draws to a close.

Well, almost.

This story might have finished here had it not been for a second exchange of text messages some weeks later...

Now unable to play the piano any other way, the Jazz-Girl was using her stand every single day and the more she used it, the more she realised just how utterly thrilled she was with the result. This suddenly made her want to thank her piano tuner one more time. Consequently, she grabbed her telephone and wrote a long text message to tell him just how successful her new stand was proving to be. It satisfied all the auditory and visual requirements. From an aesthetic point of view, it worked really well because it matched the piano – so well, in fact, that it looked like a tailor-made accessory. And it was extremely practical. François had indeed thought of absolutely everything. He had designed it in such a way that the whole stand could be folded and tidied away in a drawer when not in use.

A few minutes later, she received a reply from a totally unexpected place: Cameroon!

"Dear Nina,

Thank you for your message. It's lovely to hear from you and I'm really touched and pleased that you like the stand so much.

You'll never guess where I am so let me tell you – I'm currently in Cameroon with a tuner friend of mine. We're repairing some pianos for a charitable organisation called Arbre à Musique and we're having an absolutely fantastic time. See you soon.

François"

Intrigued, the Jazz-Girl was eager to know more about Arbre à Musique and the next time she saw François, learnt the following...

It all began with a simple but nevertheless surprising observation made by a young Cameroonian student named Raymond Pendé, who was at the time in France, more precisely in Lyons, to pursue his music studies.

44

One day, Raymond remarked on the fact that his flatmate – an amateur musician – had more musical instruments in his bedroom than could be found in the majority of music classes he taught in his home country. This comment galvanized his friends who, in 2005, co-founded the organisation Arbre à Musique, with a view to creating the first music school in Raymond Pendé's hometown, which happened to be the capital city of Cameroon – Yaoundé.

Some years later, the organisation managed to recover fifteen second-hand pianos to donate to the school, which had duly been given the same name (Arbre à Musique), and approached a top piano tuner in Lyons to ask if he would be prepared to travel to Cameroon to repair and tune them. The organisation offered to finance the two-week trip and the tuner duly accepted, while at the same time feeling somewhat daunted by the Herculean task that lay ahead of him. The pianos were old and in very poor condition. In an ideal world, he would have been given several weeks, or even months, to complete the job properly.

Consequently, the Lyons-based tuner decided to contact his good friend and colleague, François Pradel, to see if he would be prepared to accompany him. Unfortunately, Arbre à Musique did not have the means to finance two trips but François was so interested in the project that he accepted the request, while undertaking to pay for the trip himself.

Once they touched down in Yaoundé, these two young, long-awaited tuners were, to their utter astonishment, received like true heroes. The "piano saviours" had at last arrived!

As qualified concert technicians, they were used to performing highly skilled work on some of the best pianos in the world. Here, however, they found themselves fielding comparatively basic problems – such as making sure the pianos had three working pedals and that all eighty-eight keys were "present and correct"[11]. Nevertheless, they found their work thoroughly rewarding because every time a piano was released for use, the pupils in the school – all very young Cameroonian children – would express their gratitude by jumping for

---

11 Photographs of this trip can be found on the website of the piano tuner from Lyons, Damien Conor: techniciendupiano.com. Just click on the heading marked "Cameroun". Furthermore, if you are unfamiliar with the piano tuning profession and wish to become visually acquainted with it, click on "Album photos" where you will be able to see just how intricate and complex this work is.

joy and running enthusiastically to take their lessons, which usually involved two, sometimes three, pupils working together on one piano all at the same time!

And so it was, in this joyful cacophony, that these two piano tuners toiled to achieve the nigh on impossible – repair and tune all the pianos in record time!

In spite of the enormity of the task, François really enjoyed this experience. He initially went to Cameroon with a view to giving but as is so often the case with any act that starts out as being purely altruistic, in giving, he received. This trip brought him so much joy that the moment his plane landed back in Paris he immediately started to plan a return trip for the following year.

When first she heard the touching story of this incredible Cameroonian adventure, the Jazz-Girl could not help but reflect on the amazingly diverse nature of the population for whom François worked: children from poor countries, amateur musicians, highly gifted concert pianists and, unfortunately, extremely demanding divas! A pianist belonging to this last category immediately sprung to her mind – a man whose attitude was diametrically opposed to that of the Cameroonian children: while they were so grateful for so little, the demands of this particular pianist bordered on the obscene.

The American artist in question had been given nothing but the very best for his performance in Paris that night. A magnificent concert hall with near perfect acoustics, one of the best pianos known to man – a Steinway concert grand – and, to top it all, an extremely talented concert technician, the rising star of the profession.

On the day of the concert, François had spent hours preparing the piano. He had begun by completely dismantling it, taking time to sand down the felt heads on the hammers of a particularly delicate octave, before going on to apply, with meticulous precision, the sum total of his knowledge to every last piece of the instrument. And it has to be said that his knowledge was indeed extensive for he had just completed two weeks' intensive training at Steinway & Sons Hamburg, a special, higher form of training offered only to the aces among aces of the profession.

The American pianist, once he had tested the piano, his agent hovering protectively over him, had thankfully given the instrument his coveted seal of approval.

As for the team working in the concert hall, everyone had at that point breathed a huge sigh of relief – no one more so than François Pradel!

And yet, in spite of all the efforts made to provide the American pianist with the perfect conditions for a successful concert, this star had still managed to find a reason to behave like a spoilt child. During the first part of the concert he had left the stage to go and sulk in his dressing room because a member of the audience had had the audacity to cough! During the second part, he had left the stage, never to return, for the same reason, leaving the audience booing loudly and demanding a refund.

It was precisely then, as she considered the stark contrast between the intense joy of the Cameroonian children and the disappointing behaviour of the American pianist, that the Jazz-Girl began to understand for the first time *just* how very versatile François Pradel needed to be in order to practise his profession. Not only did he have to be capable of working for an incredibly varied population – from the beginner to the virtuoso, from children in need to the most temperamental of stars, from the classical pianist to the jazz pianist – but he was also regularly required to perform an extremely diverse range of tasks, from the most basic (repairing old second-hand pianos at breakneck speed) to the more precise highly sophisticated operations (preparing concert grands for world-famous artists), not to mention, from time to time, being called upon to satisfy the odd unusual request (helping to produce a bespoke music stand for a Jazz-Girl with an ultra-sensitive ear).

Clearly, François' ability to be so very versatile spoke volumes about his talent. However, it revealed even more about the very essence of his work because in spite of the diversity of his client base and the wide range of tasks he was asked to perform, it appeared that a unique, magnificent, sublimely poetic thread bound everything together into a beautiful, consistent whole. The point is that François was, all the while, actually devoting his entire professional life to one single, incredibly noble mission – that of providing the pianists he encountered with the means to make their music sing. And in doing so, he was giving pianists from all over the globe and from all walks of life a chance to fulfil their intensely personal musical dreams.

In the case of the Jazz-Girl, some years later François confessed to her that he always found it particularly touching to witness her unbridled joy whenever she played her piano – so much so that the very first time he had seen her seated in front of her baby grand, he had found himself literally transfixed by the sight of what appeared to him to be "a little girl in a fairy tale". This was one of the many reasons why he took enormous pleasure in working for her because it rendered her so very different from those clients whose conversation would never go beyond "Here's the piano" when he arrived and "Here – this is your cheque" as he was about to leave. Equally, she took a keen interest in his work and always enthused about the results, which in turn made him feel the deepest respect for her passion for music; he was proud to play his part and wanted to do whatever he could to enable her to enjoy that passion to the full.

In conclusion, building the music stand had clearly played an important part in fostering the solid working relationship that was now beginning to grow between these two musical spirits.

However, what the Jazz-Girl and her tuner did not yet realise was that, together, they had just embarked on a long journey; a quest to obtain the most perfect sound possible from the Jazz-Girl's piano. And this quest would not only bring them several deliciously triumphant moments of success but also, unfortunately, a major disappointment.

One year later, the Jazz-Girl's piano ran into a humidity-related problem and, with that, entered into an extremely temperamental phase. Consequently, in spite of his immense talent and all his efforts, François Pradel just could not get the piano to stay in tune; the unisons would stubbornly refuse to hold for any reasonable length of time, collapsing every few days like a house of cards, leaving the Jazz-Girl profoundly disappointed and her tuner deeply saddened, for he feared this would seriously affect her passion.

This major disappointment would incite them to work together, more closely than ever, employing all the means at their disposal with a view to treating and curing the sick piano. This would in turn give rise to a totally unexpected, sometimes hilarious, often absurd and, for the most part, truly surreal experience. In short, one of their best musical adventures, which forms, dear readers, the subject of a completely different story…

Post-scriptum

I wrote this story at the behest of my piano tuner, without whose insistence it would probably never have made it into the book, for I was sceptical.

That the music stand perfectly satisfied my requirements was in no doubt. In fact, it went on to transform my life as a pianist! On the other hand, I was not convinced that I could turn this subject into an especially interesting story; in my view, it all boiled down to just one sentence: "The Jazz-Girl was looking for a particular type of music stand, and her piano tuner... well... helped her to obtain it!" However, since my tuner had gone to so much trouble to produce this invaluable working tool, I eventually came round to the idea that the least I could do would be to try to write the story and just see what came out.

Initially, my fears were indeed confirmed in that, as I was writing, when I got to the part where the music stand had at last been delivered to me and I had declared it utterly perfect, I confess I was at a complete loss as to how to draw things to a close. However hard I tried, I simply could not find an interesting conclusion to this story. Consequently, I just left it and gave up.

Then something quite extraordinary happened...

The next morning, a hitherto forgotten detail, the second text message I sent to my tuner to thank him for the stand, suddenly dropped back into my mind and, lo and behold, my story found itself travelling to Yaoundé in Cameroon!

Somehow, the rest just seemed to write itself.

As sometimes happens with my music, here too the magical, enigmatic aspect of the creative process had clearly kicked in because, from then on, no longer was I a master of my work but more at the service of it – acting as a mere vehicle for delivering sentences which were now appearing on the page with the greatest of ease, apparently from nowhere!

It was an immensely powerful experience. And when I read the second half of this story, I realised that the style of my writing had changed! As a result, I had to go back and re-write the six stories, which I had already written (for, here, I should perhaps point out that I did not write these stories in the order in which they appear in the book), in order to render the overall style consistent. (All this naturally refers to when I was writing the original French version of this work.)

In the light of the extraordinary way in which this particular story turned out, it was as if (I concluded) the Cameroon music school – Arbre à Musique – had apparently "decided" that it just HAD to be in my book, and that was not all. Clearly, it had also succeeded in dictating the style of the writing, making my entire work all the better for it and providing me with what was to become a key passage: the one which addresses the true essence of the piano tuning profession.

This gradually led me to the realisation that I actually owed a debt of gratitude to Arbre à Musique. And that is when it became obvious to me that if ever this book were to be published, I should use the royalties to support this music school.

A few weeks before the French version of this book came out in March 2016, I thus contacted Raymond Pendé just to make sure his school still existed because four years had elapsed since my piano tuner's trip there.

This turned out to be but the mere beginning of yet another exciting journey. A new musical collaboration…

When I spoke to Raymond Pendé – once he had recovered from his initial surprise at my popping into his life completely out of the blue! – he told me that at times it is a struggle to run his music school but that he continues to teach children to sing and/or to play an instrument "in order to prevent them from being tempted to pick up a weapon".

These words naturally had a huge impact on me and motivate me to help him to this day.

A few months later, in a touching exchange, Raymond told me that the publication of my book had given him renewed energy for his school and, as a result, the following October he returned to France to visit all his friends in Lyons and to try to drum up some more support. On his way back via Paris, he came to meet us in our home with a childhood friend of his – who is today a singer with the Paris Opera – and, together with my husband, the four of us spent a wonderful evening over dinner, followed by a few ad-libbed musical performances!

It was during this particular trip to France that Raymond managed to meet up with another Lyons-based piano tuner, Boris Mange, who was prepared to offer his services to Arbre à Musique over a ten-day stay. With the initial sales of the original French version of this book, I was able to finance this trip and, in March 2017, Boris Mange and his partner Laetitia travelled to Yaoundé to tend to the large number of pianos – to date, around thirty! – in the music school.

All that to say, it is my dearest wish that this work, in both its French *and English forms, will have a long and happy life so that I may continue to support Arbre à Musique for some time by financing regular piano tuner trips to Yaoundé. This will hopefully ensure that the pianos in this school find – and keep – their true voices, to sing as gracefully as they possibly can.*

And to think that this story very nearly didn't make it onto the pages of my book!

The Piano Shop Showroom and a Most Surprising Surprise!

That day, the Jazz-Girl had been assigned the absolutely delicious task of testing two pianos for a friend who wanted to buy a Steinway but could not decide between the Model S (the same size as hers) and the M (the next size up). The said friend had given her the address of a shop located in the seventeenth arrondissement of Paris, which had both types in stock.

She arrived at the shop just as it was opening and was greeted by a young salesman – a professional piano tuner whose job it was to maintain all the pianos in the large showroom.

Her first priority was to make the purpose of her visit perfectly clear:

'Hello. I confess I haven't actually come to buy a piano. I'm already the proud owner of a Steinway Model S and a digital piano, so I really do have all I need. The reason I'm here is to test two Steinways – the S and the M – for a friend who is looking to invest in a top-quality baby grand but who still can't make up his mind about which size to buy.'

Immediately eliminating any pressure to buy or to sell, this explanation put them both at their ease and so it was that, without further ado, the young piano tuner accompanied the Jazz-Girl to a small room right at the end of the shop where the two pianos were standing facing each other.

'Here they are. I would just like to point out that I tuned the S yesterday but the M is seriously in need of tuning. I'm planning on doing it this afternoon.'

Since the shop was completely empty, before sitting down to play, the Jazz-Girl decided to take the opportunity to ask a few questions. One of them was to do with upright pianos and the length of their bass note strings.

In order to illustrate his answer, the tuner enthusiastically dismantled an upright Steinway with impressive speed before turning to her to say:

'You know, it's a real pleasure to meet someone who is genuinely interested in the manufacture and the mechanics of a piano. Usually, people just want a piano, full stop. They couldn't care less about the workings of the piano itself, what goes on inside, how you tune it and maintain it. And surprisingly, the worst offenders are the concert pianists. All they want to do is play and, frankly, they don't give a toss about what happens behind the keys – or anything else, for that matter.'

Suddenly, she understood what was happening. Here was a man who, just like her and François Pradel, was truly passionate about pianos and clearly he was encouraging her to discuss the subject with him.

They thus began to walk around the shop and the young tuner proceeded to show her a Czech piano which he was in the process of restoring.

'This piano is currently at about fifty per cent of its capacity. I still have an awful lot of work to do on it but it's already really good. Would you like to play something on it? I would be interested to see what you think.'

He subsequently invited her to test an array of pianos with a view to comparing several Asian and European models and, in doing so, he confessed to an unashamed preference for German pianos, since he himself was half-German due to his maternal roots.

It turned out that this young tuner had already made several trips to Germany specifically to visit the factories of the some of *the* best piano manufacturers. And during these trips he had been able to observe the precise, minute, delicate work required to produce the type of piano which, due to a combination of highly refined skills and materials, results in being a true work of art.

As they continued to wander around the shop, the young tuner told the Jazz-Girl a wonderful story...

A few weeks previously, he had refused to sell a Steinway concert grand to a client – a very rich man – who had come to purchase this piano for his country home. Why? Because although this man did not actually know how to play the piano, he nevertheless wished to acquire a beautiful instrument with the sole purpose of decorating his sitting room!

For the young tuner, this type of purchase would have constituted a huge waste. He had therefore explained to his client that it takes at least a year to manufacture a Steinway because the work is almost entirely done by hand. And prior to manufacture, a long period of time is required to choose, prepare and dry the wood, not to mention the time it takes, once the piano has been made, to run a number of rigorous tests without which an instrument cannot leave the factory.

In other words, as far as this tuner was concerned, given the substantial amount of creative and artistic work involved, it would quite simply have been unacceptable to allow the piano in question to end up in a barely inhabited country home. The instrument would consequently have been subjected to major fluctuations in temperature and humidity, most likely causing serious damage to it in the long term. Given these conditions, then, this piano would not have been able to thrive. At best, it would have only just "survived" as a somewhat ostentatious, decorative object.

The Jazz-Girl found this story extremely moving, essentially because of what it told her about this young tuner. It revealed his poetic, sensitive soul, his complete dedication to his profession and, above all, his love of beautiful pianos. Indeed, so intense was his passion for this, the king of all instruments, that it had incited him to take a huge risk with his job. At the time, France was in the throes of a major financial crisis and it had required some courage on his part to refuse a sale of this kind. As a result, the shop had not only lost potentially large takings that day but also, it would seem, a rich client – forever.

In a bid to satisfy his client, the young tuner had actually offered to handpick a piano for his country home. He would have been prepared to seek out a second-hand piano and restore it just for him. Such an instrument would more than have fulfilled the aesthetic requirement desired but, as it turned out, this particular client was never to return to the shop. Thankfully, the young tuner had an intelligent boss. The manager of the shop had congratulated him profusely on his audacious refusal!

His storytelling now over, the tuner, citing a mountain of administrative work awaiting him in the upstairs office, then left the Jazz-Girl alone to test the two pianos.

She began by testing the Model S. It was magnificent. A dream! Not quite as good as her piano, obviously, because hers was quite simply the best in the world – at least according to her! However, even she could not deny that this piano was absolutely superb and perfectly in tune.

She then sat down at the M but she barely played anything. Just as the tuner had indicated, this particular piano was seriously in need of tuning and she therefore felt utterly incapable of assessing it. This served as a reminder of a very important lesson. Ultimately, a piano is as good – or as bad – as its tuning.

And so it was that she returned to the S and, since the shop was still completely empty, decided to take her time. After all, she was really enjoying being in this room. The acoustics were excellent, not to mention the amazing view for this small room overlooked the extensive showroom with its ocean of gleaming pianos. What an exquisite picture!

Before long, she was immersed in her own little world – Planet Jazz – as she proceeded to improvise on all her favourite pieces, completely letting herself go on this sublime gem of an instrument, in front of which it was her privilege to be sitting.

Then, after about half an hour or so, she suddenly realised that she was no longer alone; the young tuner had just returned and was now standing right opposite her.

Looking her straight in the eye, somewhat emphatically he uttered the following words:

'Thank you for playing jazz on a Steinway.'

Caught as she was completely off guard, the Jazz-Girl was not quite sure how to take this comment. Indeed, she had a serious doubt as to its sincerity. Patently aware of the intellectual snobbery sometimes associated with this type of piano – that particular kind of snobbery which asserts that playing jazz on a Steinway is just not the done thing – she could only assume that the tuner was being ironic.

On the other hand, she did not feel in the least bit offended. The young tuner had spent a lot of time with her, patiently answering each and every one of her questions. The last thing she wanted to do was upset this musically sensitive man in any way. Consequently, she decided to appeal to her British roots and respond with that time-honoured lifesaver in so many tricky situations: self-deprecation.

'I'm truly sorry for playing jazz on a Steinway. I totally understand. For you, it's sacrilege. But, believe you me, given my appalling level of classical piano it's so much better for your ears if I play jazz!'

In response, the young tuner flashed her a wide smile and, making as if to leave the room, took three steps back.

Then he re-entered, this time saying:

'Okay. Let me start again. *Thank you* for playing jazz on a Steinway. I promise you, I'm not being ironic. What I'm saying is one hundred per cent sincere. You have absolutely no idea of the number of pianists who would never dare to play jazz on a Steinway. They think that it's not the done thing but they just don't seem to get the amazing capacity of these pianos. You can play anything on them and it's a real shame not to exploit their full potential.'

The Jazz-Girl endeavoured to respond but he was now on a roll.

'The point is, you don't realise how amazing it is to hear jazz being played here. It makes such a change. In fact, it's a real relief. You see, every day we hear exactly the same pieces of classical music – every, single, day. And do you know what? The worst offenders are the concert pianists. (Clearly, he had something against this particular breed!) They come into the shop and play the exact same Chopin pieces, which we hear all the time. On top of which, they are just soooo pleased with themselves. They look at us and they all say the same thing: "I bet it's not often you hear that – a little concert to brighten up your day!" Brighten up our day? Sometimes we're so desperate it makes us want to cry. You have to understand that it's the pianists like you who brighten up our day. I really love jazz. I'm obliged to play classical music for my demonstrations but if I were allowed to, I would play jazz.'

Utterly amazed by what she was hearing, the Jazz-Girl was on the point of thanking the young tuner for his kind words but he had still not quite finished.

'In fact, my boss has just asked me to convey his special thanks to you. He came out of his office and asked me if there was anyone in the shop and I told him: "Yes. There's a *woman* downstairs who's playing *jazz* on a *Steinway*." And this is what he said: "Oh, joy! What a relief to have someone play jazz in this shop for once! Please go and thank her immediately on my behalf." That's actually why I came back downstairs, to thank you on behalf of my boss. And I want to say thank you, too. You've just given us one great concert!'

As he "delivered" the line – "There's a *woman* downstairs who's playing *jazz* on a *Steinway*", emphasising the key words in order to convey the apparently momentous nature of this occurrence – this young tuner gave the Jazz-Girl the impression that he could not have been more amazed if a Martian had descended upon Planet Earth to come inside the shop and improvise on a top-quality grand piano.

Now, the Jazz-Girl did, it has to be said, freely accept that it must indeed come as something of a surprise for people to see a woman like her playing this type of music. As a mother of two children, well into her forties, with a somewhat classical sartorial style, let's face it, her image was somewhat at odds with that of the usual jazz pianist – a field generally dominated by men with a cool, funky look. The tuner's astonishment was therefore justified and did not prevent her in any way from savouring this young man's comments. On the contrary, his personal thanks, together with those coming from the manager, made her feel really happy. And as she left the shop, a big smile started to appear on her face for one reason, and one reason alone: since she had started taking jazz lessons, music had never ceased to bring her many wonderful surprises but, on that particular day, the situation had been different…

That day, two men had gone to work as usual.

That day, these two men had been expecting to hear the same pieces of classical music, as usual – not suspecting for one single minute that…

That day, Apollo had apparently decided to intervene *precisely* in order to prevent things from being… as usual. Thus…

That day, an *un*-usual type of pianist had walked in: a woman who had played jazz on a Steinway. A woman who, by merely pursuing her own daily routine, had succeeded in brightening up the daily routine of the two men listening.

Consequently, just for once, it was the Jazz-Girl herself who had actually managed to create a surprise, something she had not been expecting to do. Which is precisely why she deemed her enchanting experience in the piano shop showroom that morning to have in fact been a most surprising… surprise!

Post-scriptum

Five years after this magical encounter in the piano shop, I had become a confirmed jazz pianist, performing in public whenever I could. I was also the proud author of this collection of stories, which had just come out in France. One day, I decided that it might be fun to try to track down the young tuner in order to thank him for that delightful morning, in the best way I possibly could, by giving him a signed copy of my book.

Here's what happened…

I entered the shop and, on this occasion, was greeted by the manager:

'Good morning, how can I help you?'

'Hello. I've come in search of a piano tuner I met here in this very shop a few years ago.'

'Do you have a name?'

'No. I'm afraid I don't.'

With a slightly bemused look on his face, he replied:

'Well, you see, here's the thing. My entire sales team is made up of tuners. We have three shops and they rotate between them. So I'm sorry, but I really can't help you.'

Never one to give up easily, I decided to adopt another approach:

'I may not know his name but I do know one thing about him.'

'Ah… and what would that be?' asked the manager, his bemusement on the verge of transforming into irritation.

'The tuner's mother is German.'

Relief replaced his incipient irritation as he said:

'Now you're talking. That would be Etienne and he is currently working in one of our shops on the other side of Paris. May I ask why you want to see him?'

At this point, I was privately thinking to myself: how could I have forgotten such a significant name? It was, after all, the same as my husband's and I suddenly remembered that the tuner had indeed told me his name at the time. On the other hand, I was delighted to discover that this Etienne still worked for the same shop, or chain of shops as it turned out, and started to explain to the manager the reason why I was there:

'Well, you see, I happen to be a jazz pianist and…'

He did not allow me to go any further. Suddenly, he had a really happy, excited look on his face. In fact, absolutely ecstatic would probably be a better way of putting it.

'You play jazz? You're a woman and you play jazz?? That's just soooo rare. Could you come this way, please?'

I followed him to the room at the end of the shop where, five years previously, I had tested the two Steinways. A client was playing a grand piano with a view to buying it. However – to my surprise and, I confess, great amusement – the "Wow, we have a female jazz pianist in our midst" *factor seemed so much more important to the manager than a potentially lucrative sale, as he approached his client with the words:*

'Could I just ask you to stop playing for a few minutes?' adding, as if this so obviously rendered his request totally legitimate: ' You see, a female jazz pianist has just come into the shop.'

The idea of ejecting this poor client from her seat was by now turning my amusement into mortifying embarrassment but, apparently unfazed by the request, she got up good-naturedly, enabling the manager to lead me to a concert Steinway, where he said:

'Would you mind playing something for me?'

A concert Steinway! Would I mind? I told him it would be an honour and a few minutes later, while I was playing, he sat down at the neighbouring piano and joined me in an impromptu jam session.

When we'd finished, he exclaimed as if he still couldn't quite believe it:

'Wow! You really can play jazz. It's a sort of traditional, bluesy, New Orleans style, isn't it? I love it! But where does Etienne come in?'

I told him that I wanted to give a signed copy of my book to Etienne, and explained the reason why, and he suggested I come back the following Tuesday when Etienne would be there on desk duty. He also agreed to keep the book a surprise.

Four days later, I duly returned to the shop and this time the manager had the look of an excited child who had been asked to keep a secret but was literally bursting to tell it.

He duly greeted me with:

'Hello. I can't wait to see Etienne's face when he discovers the reason you're here. He's working in the office in the basement. Follow me.'

Down the stairs we went to a small but exceedingly modern, hi-tech office. The manager walked in first and proudly announced:

'Etienne, this lady has come specially to see you.'

Etienne looked up and said, as if only a few days, and not five years, had elapsed since our first meeting:

'Oh, hello, I remember you. You're a jazz pianist. What can I do for you?'

What a charmer, *I thought to myself.* He can't possibly remember me after so long. *Presuming that the manager must, after all, have let the cat out of the bag, I replied:*

'You're kidding! The last time I was in this shop was over five years ago.'

Then, turning to the manager, I said: 'Surely, you must have told him why I was coming.'

The manager raised his hands in protest of his innocence, which Etienne proceeded to confirm:

'I can promise you that I really don't know why you've come to see me but I do remember you coming here to test some pianos. You're English and when I told you I was half-German, you said you'd lived in Germany for a year as part of your studies. However, the thing I remember most about you is that you played jazz, for a whole morning, here in this very shop. You've no idea how rare it is to have a jazz player, let alone a female jazz player, come and test our pianos.'

The young Etienne was undoubtedly charming but, clearly, he was also genuine. He really did remember me.

The manager left me to present my book to Etienne who, upon learning that he was the subject of one of the stories, looked utterly thrilled. I stayed for around twenty minutes as we talked about our shared love of pianos, in-between him fielding the numerous incoming calls. One came from a very irate lady. Her Steinway concert grand had been delivered to the wrong shop for repair and despite Etienne's insistence that he knew it had not landed in this particular shop, she still wanted him to go upstairs to the showroom just to check. He whispered to me: 'She's mad. How could I possibly miss a Steinway concert grand?' It was a fair point well made and we both laughed with that exquisite feeling of complicity which arises from the invisible bond created between two people who barely know each other but who just happen to share the same passion.

It was soon time to be on my way and as I got up to leave, Etienne, who looked as if this surprise had made him truly happy, thanked me profusely, saying that he would probably spend most of the afternoon neglecting his office duty in order sneakily to read my book, under his desk, in the manner of a naughty schoolboy.

For my part, tracking down this young tuner had just afforded me yet another of those enchanting moments which music so regularly brings about. Little did I know, that afternoon I was to have an experience similar to that of my very first encounter with Etienne and, as it happened, to that of my subsequent encounter with the shop manager...

I was running late, so I leapt into a taxi and said to the driver:

'Could you take me to the Café de la Paix on the Place de l'Opéra, please?'

'Off to have tea with our lady friends, are we?' was his reply.

Hmmm… So, no stereotypical assumptions there, then, *I thought to myself, before saying:*

'No. Actually, I'm going there to present my book, which has just come out. Not to the entire café, you understand, but to a guitarist friend of mine.'

'Ah, so you're an author, are you?'

'Well, not exactly. Originally, I'm a translator, but a few years ago I took up piano playing again and then I wrote a book about it, which I actually managed to get published.'

'Goodness. That sounds exciting. What sort of things do you play?'

'I'm a jazz pianist. But I'm not into anything dissonant and innovative. It's very traditional jazz…'

A slam on the brakes screeched the car to an emergency stop as the taxi driver turned round to look at me and say:

'Wow! That's just so unusual. You're a woman and you play jazz?'

Thinking to myself, Well, there's nothing like a bit of mad Parisian driving to spice up this recurring question, *I grinned at him and replied:*

'As long as I'm still alive, I do.'

The surrounding cars were now tooting their horns, so he drove on and, smiling at me in the rear-view mirror, asked:

'You have a slight accent. How long have you lived in Paris?'

'You're right. I'm not French. As you can hear, I'm English, but I've lived here for nearly thirty years.'

Referring to my previous answer, he said:

'So, still not used to Parisian drivers, then?'

'No,' *I said resignedly.* 'And I don't think I shall ever become accustomed to them. It's the formative years and all that…'

'So, tell me about your book.'

I spent a few minutes explaining what the book was about and after a while the taxi driver said:

'You know, I really wish you every success with your literary venture. And I do believe you will succeed. When you talk about your experiences and your book, you have that joy, that happy enthusiasm, which all people who have a passion in life simply exude. And it's so contagious. Just talking to you has made me feel really happy, so much so that I would like to buy your book. In fact, I would like to buy two copies – one for me, and another for a friend of mine who plays the piano. Could you give me the title please, so I can order it?'

With a slam on the brakes, he screeched the car to a halt once again – this time in order to reach for a pen and paper. We were slap bang in the middle of the Place de la Concorde! The Place de la Concorde!! Help!!! I thought it probably best not to waste any time by saying that I actually had a pen and paper as well as some business cards on me. Instead, I just gave him the title in the hope that we could be on our way without further ado and that the increasing cacophony of tooting horns would consequently cease.

A few minutes later, the taxi driver duly dropped me off at the Café de la Paix, once again wishing me every success with my book.

Upon entering the café, I observed – in the taxi driver's defence – that the room was indeed full of elegant Parisiennes daintily sipping their tea. This made it all the more amusing when in walked my guitarist friend Benjamin, larger than life as ever, clad in ripped jeans, a leather jacket and a cowboy hat, his guitar coolly draped over his shoulder. The surrounding elegant female jaws literally dropped!

Kissing me on both cheeks, Benjamin greeted me with:

'Wow! You look great! Radiantly happy! Is it the publication of the book that's giving you this glow?'

'Well, there's that. And, you know, I'm just happy to be alive, really.'

Naturally, Benjamin could not possibly know that I was referring to the treacherous journey I had just survived in order to arrive at the café, so he sat down and said:

'Well, whatever the reason, you look fab! Why don't you hold up your book and I'll take some photos so I can post them on Facebook?'

As he clicked away, the elegant Parisiennes looked on, barely concealing their curiosity, giving me the impression for a few fleeting, but nevertheless delicious, moments that I was some kind of literary superstar who had just won the Prix Goncourt!

A few weeks later, after this great day – seeing Etienne the tuner again, the touching (albeit eventful!) encounter with the taxi driver, and the afternoon spent in the Café de la Paix with Benjamin – I noticed that a certain Nath had given my book a serious thumbs-up by awarding it the maximum amount of gold stars, five out of five, and posting a lovely comment on my publisher's website. It translates as follows:

"I have just finished reading this book and I loved it. The author *has a true passion for pianos and jazz improvisation, a passion which radiates from every page, and she really knows how to convey that passion to the reader."*

As an author, particularly a first-time author such as myself, it is always wonderful to receive such positive feedback. The undiluted pleasure I gained from writing every single word of these stories actually intensifies each time my book is thus received. And with regard to this particular comment, I would just like to take the opportunity to extend my most sincere thanks to Nath because, while I have absolutely no idea who Nath is, I like to think it was the taxi driver.

The Accident

The Jazz-Girl's desire to be worthy of her piano's beautiful sound resulted in her making huge strides, growing and maturing as a pianist beyond anything she could *ever* have believed possible. Her level of progress was in fact such that she had recently reached a stage where she was actually able to perform in public! Naturally cautious about this new stage, she had been taking it in small steps by playing at the odd family party. Now, however, she was preparing to perform at a much bigger event: some friends of hers had asked her to play in front of a hundred people at the annual lunch of a charitable organisation which they had founded some years previously.

Honoured to have been asked and utterly delighted to be able to accept this request, the Jazz-Girl consequently had but just one goal in sight: to rise to the challenge successfully, with aplomb. And in her determination to achieve this, she was spending her days working increasingly hard on the preparation of a full and complete repertoire.

Then disaster struck.

It was Easter Sunday and the Jazz-Girl and her family were in Normandy for the long weekend. That day, they were planning to go sailing for just a few hours, so that they could return to their cottage by late afternoon in time to prepare their traditional Pascal dinner: roast leg of lamb, local cheeses, chocolate lava cake, all washed down with a fine bottle of claret. The Jazz-Girl was so looking forward to this feast that she could already picture a cosy family scene in front of a roaring log fire.

During the course of the morning, while they were waiting for the harbour gates to open, the wind picked up considerably. The Jazz-Girl and her children thus had second thoughts about going out to sea, opting instead to spend the day on land, leaving the Jazz-Girl's husband, or "Etienne le Capitaine" as they liked to call him, to brave the elements alone.

In spite of the wind and the cold, it was a beautifully sunny day and, in a bid to enjoy it to the full, the Jazz-Girl and her children went for a long walk along the beach – their final destination being one of their favourite brasseries, favourite because it served good simple food and offered an absolutely stunning view over the bay of Deauville.

The brasserie turned out to be full inside but the waiters were offering places outside, on the heated terrace, and bright blue blankets for anyone who was willing to give it a go. As a result, the terrace also rapidly became full to bursting and the atmosphere particularly joyful due to the highly amusing visual spectacle: with all the clients snugly wrapped up in their bright blue blankets, it was as if this restaurant were now playing host to some kind of Pascal Smurf Symposium!

The waiters did their best to meet the demands of the packed brasserie but the service was naturally slow and when it was finally time to leave, the Jazz-Girl stood up and was surprised to discover that she was suddenly feeling quite dizzy, a feeling which she could only attribute to the effects of having spent several hours outside in the wind, the sun and the cold. With this in mind, she now wanted to return to the cottage as quickly as possible.

Be that as it may, the walk home seemed increasingly long.

In reality, they only had a few hundred yards left to go but she was so tired that with every step she took, the house just seemed to be one step further away. She was trying really hard to reassure herself. After all, they were not far at all. They had just left the beach to take the little road leading to their cottage. They would soon be home and she would have plenty of time to rest before dinner.

On this road, a large building site had recently been set up from which ran a thick cable all the way to an electric socket situated on the opposite pavement. Heavy duty industrial staples were serving to keep this cable firmly fixed to the ground. Then, all of a sudden, the Jazz-Girl noticed a spot where the cable was not in fact properly attached. It was only missing one staple. However, just as she was thinking that this was nevertheless really dangerous, her foot got tangled in it, causing her to fall to the ground, landing first on her knees and then on her right hand. In doing so, she heard a sharp "crack" following which, she exclaimed: 'Oh no, my piano playing!'

Then everything went black.

'Mummy, Mummy, are you all right?'

Her children's voices, as they kept repeating this question, seemed so far away but little by little they came closer, increasing in volume as she regained consciousness. When the light finally returned, seeing the terrible look of panic on her children's faces, the Jazz-Girl endeavoured to reassure them: all she needed was a few minutes to get up.

Once she did actually manage to stand up, she very nearly blacked out again, with the result that her children had to prop her up for the rest of the way home. And during the couple of hundred yards left to go, they constantly cried: 'Mummy, Mummy, stay with us! *Mummy!*' Subsequently, they would tell her that they had kept shouting because for the rest of the walk they were convinced she would faint once more.

Relieved to be home at last, the Jazz-Girl, who, due to the shock, was now trembling from head to foot, immediately went to lie down. As for her children, so horrified were they to see their mother in this state that they started to do whatever they could look to after her; Charlie rushed to make her a hot-water bottle, while Juliet wrapped her up in a blanket.

In spite of their caring gestures, she just could not get comfortable. The searing pain in her hand was preventing her from resting and during the hour that followed, her hand turned black and blue, and doubled in size! No need to have studied medicine to be able to understand what was happening here; this injury was clearly presenting all the signs of a fracture.

With her panic levels soaring, the Jazz-Girl found herself literally counting the minutes until her husband came home, even though she knew full well that he still had several hours to go, and while she was waiting she decided to do a little test. She had to do it. She just could not stop herself from doing it.

And so it was that she stood up and dragged herself to her digital piano, where her inability to play a simple blues riff with her right hand clearly demonstrated that her little finger no longer seemed to be connected to her brain. As far as she was concerned, this was devastating confirmation of the hard fact that she was indeed looking at a fracture. Consequently, she would most likely be deprived of her piano playing for some time and would undoubtedly be unable to play at the lunch which was due to take place in just two months. In other words, it was the absolute worst-case scenario and she knew that time was of the essence if she were to obtain treatment which would avoid her suffering any long-term damage. Now feeling decidedly weak, she returned to her bed to lie down again.

When her husband finally came home, the Jazz-Girl breathed a huge sigh of relief. They would at last be able to return to Paris so she could be treated in a hospital close to home.

This, however, was to overlook certain deep-seated family values which her husband had unfortunately inherited from his parents…

The Jazz-Girl's parents-in-law proudly made it a point of honour to live their life in the manner to which they had been accustomed during their childhood – that is to say, in "joyful frugality"! This amusing expression owed its origins not only to their strict Catholic upbringing but also – indeed, especially – to the stoic and philosophical approach adopted during the Second World War by their respective families as a very necessary survival strategy to enable the members of these families to cope with the dreadful atrocities to which they were subjected, while still retaining the ability to smile.

The various manifestations of her in-laws' present-day self-imposed philosophy of joyful frugality, admittedly admirable in its origins, would never cease to amuse the Jazz-Girl. Although now retired, her parents-in-law were still, after all these years, in the habit of serving meagre dishes at family gatherings, such as leek soup – or possibly a vegetable gratin when they really wanted to let their hair down! – and this in spite of the hard-earned, well-deserved material comforts afforded to them by a life divided between a large flat in an upmarket leafy Parisian suburb and a country home in Brittany.

Unsurprisingly, given that we are all more or less the product of our parental education, their son was also perfectly capable of reacting according to the sacrosanct values instilled in him by his family's notoriously frugal, austere approach to life. And, in his eyes, one of these values reigned supreme: any manifestation of personal suffering was a form of self-indulgence. In other words, he was a direct product of the school of "put up and shut up". And possibly one of its most successful pupils!

Thus it was that he returned home, utterly euphoric from the effects of several hours spent thrashing it out with the elements at sea, and upon seeing his wife lying on the bed – trembling with shock and caressing her hand in an attempt to render the pain slightly less unbearable – exclaimed:

'Nah! It's just not possible! Don't overdo it. You clearly haven't broken anything. Frankly, I can't even see where it's swollen.'

Without so much as uttering a word, the Jazz-Girl placed one hand next to the other in the hope that this would make him aware of the blatant contrast: one perfectly normal hand alongside a multi-coloured hand with a swelling the size of a tennis ball!

'Okay. I get it. I can see it's very slightly swollen,' he conceded. 'But why don't you get up? Take a shower. You'll see, you'll feel so much better afterwards. And then instead of doing dinner here, we can we all go and eat at the pizzeria.'

Never one to disobey a captain's orders, the Jazz-Girl stood up... then promptly fainted.

That did it. They clearly had no option but to return to Paris.

In reality, the journey only lasted two hours. The Jazz-Girl, however, was under the impression that it took a good two centuries to reach the desired destination, with the result that when her husband finally dropped her off at casualty, never before had she felt so thrilled to find herself in a hospital. Be that as it may, her panic levels had now reached their zenith and all of a sudden she felt a terrible urge to stand in the middle of the reception hall and shout at the top of her voice:

I play the piano! My hand is injured! You have to treat me immediately! Before everybody else!'

Thankfully, her British self-control kicked in just in time for her to walk calmly to the reception desk and register her arrival in a more dignified manner than that to which she felt inclined!

One hour later, a young male nurse came to get her and accompanied her to a small room in order to make the standard checks – temperature, blood pressure, and so on.

Unaware that she was left-handed and therefore still capable of writing in spite of her injury, he then proceeded to fill in a form on her behalf. By now, she was feeling so exhausted that she decided to leave him to it as he said:

'Can I have your surname, please?'

'Somerville.'

'And your first name?'

'Nina.'

'Ah! Nina. What a lovely name! It really suits you. And your profession?'

'I'm a jazz pianist.'

Upon hearing these words, the nurse could barely contain his surprise, which was *not* in fact that surprising. Since her encounter with the young tuner in the piano shop, the Jazz-Girl had become accustomed to provoking this kind of reaction. "Wow! You're a woman and you play jazz!" No, this time the real surprise was in fact reserved for the Jazz-Girl herself who was quite astonished to hear these words emerging from her lips. Just who did she think she was? Immediately, she set about rectifying the situation:

'Actually, I'm a translator. But a few years ago, I took up jazz improvisation on the piano and now, I'm preparing to give my first concert…'

Oh, no. She'd just gone and done it again! Once more, she endeavoured to set the record straight:

'What I really mean is that I'm preparing to play some jazz at the annual lunch of a charitable organisation. And I so desperately want to help this organisation, not to mention my burning desire to perform in public. As a result, I have spent months working on my repertoire. On top of which, you need to understand that my piano playing is like a drug to me. I just can't live without it. So you see, we have to get my hand treated as soon as possible. There's absolutely no time to lose.'

The nurse now had a genuine look of compassion about him as he said in an understanding voice:

'Why don't we put "jazz pianist" as your profession? That way, the doctors will see that your injury urgently requires attention.'

With that, he completed the form and invited the Jazz-Girl to return to the waiting room.

Some time later, the same male nurse entered the waiting room, sat down next to her and announced, rather unreassuringly:

'Madame Somerville, I'm afraid there's something really serious we need to talk about.'

Not for the first time that day, the Jazz-Girl felt her panic levels soaring. She had not even so much as had her hand X-rayed, yet already the nurse apparently had "something really serious" to tell her.

For his part, the nurse observed her look of panic, paused for an instant and then looked at her in a way which appeared to emphasise the fact that he had some *really* grim news for her, until such time as he could keep it up no longer, whereupon he flashed her the widest of smiles and enquired:

'So, you're a jazz pianist, are you? Wow! I want you to tell me all about it! Everything! Your favourite pianists, your favourite jazz clubs, the lot! The whole shebang!'

Spontaneously, the Jazz-Girl burst out laughing before going on to tell this young man, who was kind and considerate enough to keep her company during her difficult wait, all about her love of jazz.

Then, before she knew it, it was time to go down to the X-ray department.

The radiologist told the Jazz-Girl how to position her hand and then proceeded to work in silence as she took seemingly endless photos.

After a few minutes, the suspense was absolutely killing the Jazz-Girl – who freely admitted that she had never been particularly well endowed in the patience department! – so much so that she ended up asking:

'Can you see anything? Is anything broken?'

'Between you and me, it does indeed look like you've broken something but it's not really for me to say. The doctor will tell you what's going on,' was the radiologist's reply.

Devastated to learn that her fear was becoming a reality, the Jazz-Girl returned to the waiting room.

A few minutes later, a junior doctor came to get her, saying:

'Madame Somerville, I'm here to tell you that you *have* actually broken something.'

'Really? What exactly have I broken?'

'A bone.'

Luckily for this junior doctor, her hand was hurting far too much for her to slap him across the face. Otherwise she would have had no qualms whatsoever about responding in such a manner. Just how many years of studying medicine had it taken for him to come up with such a ridiculous answer? *Obviously*, they were talking about a bone. So, when she had asked the question, she had merely wanted to know precisely *which* bone.

Incapable of discussing anything at all with a person whose approach was so unintelligent, the Jazz-Girl did not utter another word for the rest of the consultation, which barely lasted two minutes, during which the doctor explained:

'Okay, I'm now going to put a splint on your hand to keep the bone in place. You mustn't get it wet, so when you take a shower you'll have to cover it with a plastic bag. Then I'm going to give you a sling. You're going to need to keep your hand as high as possible to avoid further swelling.'

Topping off his little speech with a final "flourish", he appeared perfectly happy to announce a few more items of bad news in a decidedly flippant manner:

'There you go. You can go home now but before you leave the hospital, you should make an appointment. We're going to have to take a look in two weeks' time. If the bone doesn't set correctly, we'll have to operate. And, in any event, even without an operation you should bear in mind that this is going to take a really long time to heal – at least six weeks, if not more.'

In short, the situation was even worse than the Jazz-Girl's initial fears. And she walked out of the room feeling *extremely* disappointed with this junior doctor whose complete and utter lack of bedside manner left much to be desired; it seemed highly unlikely that he had even so much as bothered to read the form which the male nurse had filled in because if he had, he would have immediately understood that this news would be particularly hard for her to hear in her capacity as a "jazz pianist". The idea of undergoing an operation, of having to entrust her precious hand to a surgeon while under the effects of a general anaesthetic, quite simply filled her with dread. As for the thought that she would now be deprived of playing the piano for six weeks… well, that was just inconceivable as far as she was concerned. So it was that, with a heavy heart, she made the appointment and then returned to the waiting room where she sat down for the time it took her husband to come and get her.

A few minutes later, just as she was on the point of leaving the hospital, she heard a by now familiar voice behind her:

'Madame Somerville?'

It was the young male nurse who, upon seeing his patient with her right hand splinted and held up in a sling, enquired in a truly compassionate voice:

'Oh. No. You haven't broken anything, have you?'

'Unfortunately, I'm afraid I have. I can't tell you precisely which bone because the doctor himself was unwilling to tell me. However, according to him, this is going to be a long haul. Six weeks at the very least! Can you imagine? Six weeks without any piano playing? I just don't know how I'm going to cope. And to add insult to injury – literally speaking! – I might even have to have an operation.'

In response, the male nurse laid a sympathetic hand on her shoulder and simply said:

'Madame Somerville, I'm so very sorry. I sincerely hope it all works out for you.'

The contrast with the cold approach of the junior doctor was astonishing. The nurse's kindness touched her right in the heart, with the result that she left the hospital in tears.

Easter Monday...

That day, the Jazz-Girl was in a *really* bad mood. Little by little, she was discovering all the challenges that would now form part of her daily life; overnight, simple gestures had apparently turned into Herculean tasks. How, for example, was she to wash one hand, on its own, without the other one to rub it against? Taking a shower, with her right hand held high and protected by a plastic bag was tantamount to performing an elaborate magic trick in terms of the dexterity it required. As for the pain, it just would not subside. And yet all this physical inconvenience was nothing compared to a much deeper form of suffering which quite simply refused to leave her. This was of course the wound inflicted on her musical soul. How on earth was she to survive for six weeks without being able to play the piano?

In a bid to make up for his initial reaction to her accident, the Jazz-Girl's husband took it upon himself to order a present for her – a superb piano stool to replace her digital piano stool which had been on its last legs (no pun intended!) for many years. Then, with the help of Charlie and Juliet, he made the meal which they were supposed to have eaten the night before.

In spite of her family's best efforts, the Jazz-Girl, though deeply touched by their kind gestures, simply could not manage to shake off her bad mood.

The next day, when her husband went back to work and her children to school, it was even worse. Now she was alone, all alone with her injury. How on earth was she going to manage?

Remembering the charity lunch, she proceeded to inform the organisers that she would probably not be able to play the piano on this particular occasion. Writing an email was, like every other gesture, no mean feat as she struggled to use the mouse with her hand in a splint. That said, in response she received several kind messages of support, which raised her spirits.

Alas, this pleasant feeling was to be short-lived…

She was standing in her sitting room when, without warning, the sight of her piano sent a feeling of intense deprivation shooting through her entire body. It was a feeling that completely overwhelmed her.

Shocked by the violence of her reaction, she endeavoured to get a grip. Surely she was getting this slightly out of proportion? It was time to take a step back and endeavour to have a sense of perspective about what was happening.

As luck would have it, the Jazz-Girl, just like her husband, had been raised in a strict Catholic family, receiving all the notions of Catholic guilt that go hand in hand with such an upbringing. And among those religious values, which had been instilled in her, lay the idea that to give even the slightest importance to one's own personal problems was tantamount to self-pity. So, with this in mind, the Jazz-Girl now attempted to give herself a serious talking to:

You're being completely ridiculous. It's not as if you're a professional pianist. Yes, you're unable to play the piano for six weeks but so what? Is that really your only problem? You've had worse things happen to you and you know full well that much worse things happen in the world every single day.

Unfortunately, this internal monologue failed to come up with the goods. Deep down, the Jazz-Girl was screaming. Ultimately, she realised there was just one possible solution: in order for her to be able to tolerate her injury, she simply had to find a way of playing the piano.

Accordingly, she sat down and began to play with her left hand, rapidly establishing that this was not going to be enough. Consequently, she attempted to play using the three fingers of her right hand – the thumb, the index and the middle finger – which were not covered by the splint. However, this turned out to be impossible. Since the splint was longer than her hand, it prevented her from playing with her three healthy fingers, and this in spite of the fact that, out of desperation, she even tried to play with her hand turned over, her palm facing upwards!

Still seated at the piano, she proceeded to take a good long look at her injured hand in an attempt to understand precisely why she was reacting in this violent manner. Just what exactly was making her feel so very angry and frustrated?

Several answers came to mind. In addition to being deprived of playing the piano for six weeks, she was actually very scared that she might forget her repertoire and she had been working on it for months. She was disappointed not to be able to perform in public; her dream had just been shattered. And she found the idea of a possible operation quite traumatic; three months earlier she had undergone two major operations, for a serious health problem, which had thankfully been successful. However, she was only just recovering and she did not feel ready to go down into another operating theatre quite so soon afterwards, not to mention her ever-present fear of entrusting her precious hand to a surgeon while under the effects of a general anaesthetic.

This moment of reflection turned out to be extremely useful because it led the Jazz-Girl to the crucial conclusion that, in actual fact, one single major concern stood head and shoulders above all the other aspects of her frustration put together. This was, of course, the question of her future as a pianist. In other words, was her hand going to heal properly? If somebody could convince her that she would not be left with any permanent damage, then she could quite probably find a way to cope with the temporary deprivation. On the other hand (again, no pun intended!), the idea of being left with permanent damage was just too much to bear.

It was time to act. Her splint looked primitive and makeshift, as if it came from another era, whereas the current trend was in fact to treat fractures over a short period of time by immobilising the injured bone in a light cast made of resin. The Jazz-Girl knew this because at her children's school there was generally at least one pupil with a broken limb, especially after the winter break when a lot of families went skiing. Only recently, one such pupil had been to her home. A few weeks previously, one of Juliet's friends, Emma, had come round for lunch and been proud to show off her resin sleeve, which she was going to be wearing for the next ten days having just broken her arm, while at the same time going through the traditional ritual of asking everybody to sign it.

It was at this point that the Jazz-Girl decided she needed to get a second opinion for, if she were to do everything within her power to make a full recovery, the first basic stage would be to ensure that she had actually received the right treatment. And in order to do that, she needed to consult a specialist. But whom could she consult? It would have to be someone who came highly recommended but she did not know anyone at all who worked in this field.

Clearly she had no choice but to appeal to any possible contact likely to set her on the right track…

Racking her brains, a physiotherapist friend came to mind so she immediately sent her an email.

Then another idea came to her. Two years previously, a well-known Parisian jazz pianist had broken his wrist. The Jazz-Girl did not know him personally but since his email address was up on his website, she took the liberty of writing to him, convinced that, as a professional pianist, he would surely have consulted the very best doctors for his injury.

Having sent these two emails, she remained firmly glued to the spot, not daring to leave her computer for a second, so as to be able to pounce immediately on the replies!

Three minutes passed – three minutes, which might just as well have been an eternity – and still no reply!

Obviously, this was all perfectly normal. After all, there was absolutely no reason why people should be available just because she had written to them.

Then, completely out of the blue, she had *the* most amazing brainwave – leading her to think that Apollo might just be on board at last. What if she were to contact her piano tuner? François Pradel was doing an increasing amount of work for the Paris concert halls and surely their staff would have the references of the best doctors for treating injured hands. It was, after all, in their interests to look after the musicians who worked for them.

That said, having had this brainwave, the Jazz-Girl was initially in two minds about pursuing the idea. Her piano tuner, if he did have access to these references, could be forgiven for thinking that it would be a tad excessive to give her – a mere amateur pianist – access to them, too.

There again, she *was* really determined to do everything within her power to obtain the right treatment and, in any event, what could she possibly have to lose by simply writing to him?

And so it was that she set about writing her third email of the day on this subject and, since she was now on a roll, no detail went unmentioned.

Clearly laying out all the reasons behind her despair, she spoke of the long hours she had spent working on her repertoire and her fear of forgetting it, of her disappointment at not being able to perform in public, of her feeling of deprivation – so intense that it was as if she were being deprived of a drug, of her fear of long-term damage, and so on and so forth. Then, waiving aside any remaining doubts as to whether or not she should send this letter, she pressed firmly on the appropriate button… and would have crossed her fingers had she been able to do so!

This time, the Jazz-Girl did not have to wait very long at all; François turned out to be the first person to reply, with an email so long that it left her wondering how he had actually managed to write it in the time! It began thus:

"Dear Nina,

I'm so very sorry to hear this. I do hope it is not too serious. What you must understand, however, is that injuries to the hand take a really long time to heal. You're going to have to be very brave.

That said, do not despair, dear Nina. The good news is that you have come knocking at exactly the right door…"

François appeared to have understood everything. Absolutely everything. Her distress. Her despair. Her frustration. As for his re-assuring words – "You have come knocking at exactly the right door" – they caused tears of relief to roll down her face.

Scrolling down, she went on to discover a long list of addresses – so long in fact that she actually wondered whether François had sent her the name of every doctor he had ever encountered in his entire life! Furthermore, as an indication of just how seriously he was taking her plight, he had even included the address of the official Paris Ballet osteopath. Clearly, then, contrary to the Jazz-Girl's fears, her piano tuner was not remotely interested in the fact that she was merely an amateur pianist; the main thing, as far as he was concerned, was to do everything he could to protect her passion, hence his swift, efficient response.

Within this long list of addresses, one in particular caught the Jazz-Girl's eye: that of *La Clinique de la Main* – in other words, there was actually a clinic which was solely dedicated to the treatment of hands. The Jazz-Girl would subsequently learn that there are several of these clinics in Paris but François was advising her to go to this specific one because it was well known for its successful treatment of professional musicians.

Wiping away her tears, the Jazz-Girl responded with:

"Dear François,

I cannot thank you enough for your prompt reply. Your message has cheered me up no end. I am now going to call the clinic for an appointment and I shall let you know the outcome without fail."

§

Obtaining an appointment at the clinic was not, as it happened, that easy. Initially, the receptionist had nothing to offer for at least two weeks, during which time – the Jazz-Girl feared – serious damage could set in if her fracture had been incorrectly treated at the hospital.

She thus found herself with no option but to utter a few "magic words":

'Do you by any chance have a slot for a genuinely urgent case? You see, I happen to be a jazz pianist and I'm due to give a concert in two months' time.'

These words apparently had the desired effect.

'Hold the line, please. I'll see what I can do…

Madame Somerville? Thank you so much for holding. Can you come to the clinic at three this afternoon?'

No prizes for guessing the Jazz-Girl's answer to that question!

A few hours later…

The waiting room at the clinic was full to bursting so the Jazz-Girl was naturally expecting to be there for several hours. The irritated expression on the face of everybody sitting in the room appeared, moreover, to confirm this. Within seconds, this palpable level of collective irritation was to rise even higher because, contrary to her expectations, the Jazz-Girl was called almost immediately. Clearly the clinic had taken heed of her words and was treating her as an urgent case. And for one brief instant she felt a huge surge of Catholic guilt rise within her because, deep down, she knew she was receiving this

VIP treatment for the simple reason that she had seriously exaggerated the truth. But it was too late to do anything about it now and, in any case, she could always go to confession later!

Arielle Moing – a female doctor whose piercing blue eyes seemed to be literally shining with intelligence – accompanied her to the consulting room saying:

'Bonjour, Madame Somerville. I believe you're a jazz pianist. Is that right?'

While slightly apprehensive about how Arielle Moing might react, the Jazz-Girl decided to come clean and explain the reality of the situation, all the while hoping and praying that this doctor, who had so kindly rearranged her schedule to see her, would not be too angry.

In actual fact, due to *the* most enormous stroke of luck (thank you, Apollo!), Dr Moing turned out to be a passionate pianist herself and was therefore extremely understanding of the problem. She even went so far as to reassure the Jazz-Girl that she would be equal to the task by citing the names of all the professional pianists she had treated during her career. She also told the Jazz-Girl how, several years earlier, she had purchased a beautiful second-hand piano from a man who had spent eighteen months restoring it just for her. Concluding on the subject, she said:

'I love jazz but I only play classical music on the piano. I would have absolutely no idea how to improvise and, in any case, at my age it's far too late to learn.'

As the Jazz-Girl handed over her X-rays, she replied:

'You know, it's never too late to learn. I am living proof of that. I started studying traditional jazz, mainly blues, in fact, extremely late on in life. And it's not exactly rocket science. In fact, initially there's just an awful lot to learn off by heart, which is the whole paradox of improvisation. It so happens that I've actually written a jazz method for beginners. If you want, I'll give you a copy of it sometime.'

Dr Moing was more than happy to accept this offer as she began to study the Jazz-Girl's X-rays, following which she gave an explanation which could not have been further removed from that given by the junior doctor at the hospital:

'You've fractured a knuckle – the one just under your little finger. This is why it's going to take a long time to heal. Joints always take much longer. Unfortunately, we're looking at least six weeks and it will be a good year before this accident is completely behind you. That said, the main thing is to focus on the long-term. Recovering the use of your hand, exactly as before, is *all* that matters. And I can guarantee that this will be the case if you do exactly as I tell you. Okay? You need to forget playing at the lunch and look at the bigger picture, which is of course the end result.'

However hard it was to hear some of these comments, they did actually reassure the Jazz-Girl. Arielle Moing was clearly extremely competent in her field – which was just as well really for, when she looked at the Jazz-Girl's splint, the verdict she gave on her colleague's work was utterly terrifying:

'I simply cannot believe that you received this kind of treatment in a Paris hospital. The doctor has done the exact opposite of what he should have done. The bandage holding the splint in place is far too tight and it's tight in all the wrong places. As a result, the part of your hand which should be left free to move is so tightly strapped up that it cannot move at all, whereas the part which should be held firmly in place is actually able to move quite freely. If you keep this splint, you will undoubtedly inflict long-term damage on your hand because it is highly likely to cause permanent loss of mobility. Madame Somerville, by insisting we give you an appointment, you did exactly the right thing.'

Upon hearing these words, the Jazz-Girl felt a shiver go down her spine. The cavalier job of the junior doctor could have cost her her passion. And, quite clearly, had it not been for François Pradel's swift and efficient action, she simply would not have had this narrow escape. Consequently, in that very instant, her gratitude towards her piano tuner increased tenfold. Never again would she see him in the same light. From that point on, he would always be the man who had saved her hand...

'Madame Somerville, is everything all right?' asked the doctor.

'Yes. Yes, I'm fine, thank you. I'm just a bit shaken. You see, you've just made me realise how very lucky I am to be here.'

'Well, like I said, you did absolutely the right thing coming to us. Now, allow me to take care of your hand properly.'

Dr Moing began by removing the splint. Then, concentrating hard on the job in hand (once again, no pun intended), she set about cutting several bandages – all different lengths – while muttering to herself enigmatic comments such as: 'Okay, so this piece is going to be my hem...' Intrigued, the Jazz-Girl was content just to watch. The doctor then showed her patient how to position her hand, wrapped the bandages around it, put on some surgical gloves and dipped her own hands in a bucket filled with a thick white liquid, which she proceeded to use to sculpt what could only be described as a veritable work of art; within the space of just a few seconds, a superb resin glove had formed around the Jazz-Girl's injured hand. This glove looked similar in shape to a boxer's except that it was not closed at the end, so as to leave her fingers sticking out. The mere sight of this modern professional-looking glove alone would have sufficed to reassure the Jazz-Girl. The comments that followed, however, reassured her even more:

'With this glove, if everything goes according to plan, the bone will set properly, which means that you should be able to avoid having surgery. Just to be on the safe side, get your hand X-rayed in ten days' time and come and see me immediately afterwards. If the bone *has* set properly, then I will remove the resin glove. In the meantime, you need to keep your hand in the sling as much as possible and continue to move your thumb, index finger and middle finger. That way, when the time comes, you will only be required to rehabilitate the two fingers – the ring finger and the little finger – which are firmly held in place due to the way I have shaped the glove. Incidentally, the good news is that musicians do not require professional physiotherapy following fractures to their hands. They do their own rehabilitation on their instruments; but we'll cross that bridge when we come to it.'

Who would have thought it? The Jazz-Girl actually left the clinic feeling quite upbeat! The situation was as positive as it could possibly be in the circumstances. On top of which, she had just been actively encouraged to keep three of the fingers on her injured hand moving. And it was her firm intention to do that by – yes, you've guessed it – playing the piano!

With half an hour to kill, before going to pick Juliet up from school, the Jazz-Girl decided to go to a nearby café where she sat down and immediately started to move the said three fingers in a decidedly exaggerated way. This drew the waiter's attention to her resin glove, causing him to enquire:

'Nothing serious, I hope?'

'No, I've broken a knuckle, which in the big scheme of things is not serious at all. It's just that I happen to be a pianist. (*Wow! Those words seemed to be popping out with increasing ease!)* So, when it happened, I was actually really scared for my hand.'

'Goodness, you're a pianist! What do you play, classical music?'

'No, I play blues.'

'Wow! You play blues. That's amazing!'

'I agree. That is, it's amazing when I can play. But with this injury, I shan't be playing very much over the next few weeks, which is actually going to be extremely frustrating.'

In response, the waiter paused for an instant and then, with a teasing grin spreading across his face, said:

'Look at it this way. It's a golden opportunity to live the experience to the full. You play blues, right? Well, now… you're actually going to have the blues!'

The Jazz-Girl promptly burst out laughing, which encouraged the waiter to pursue the conversation with:

'But please don't be sad because I bring you good tidings. Every Sunday, we have a jazz brunch here. You should come. It would do you good.'

The Jazz-Girl was now grinning back at him as she replied:

'You know, with my injury, I'll probably take one look at the musicians and then sit through the brunch plotting their murder because I'll be feeling so jealous that they can play and I can't!'

A few minutes later, when the waiter returned with the espresso she had ordered, he said:

'I've just been to enquire on your behalf. This Sunday, there'll be a saxophonist, a drummer and a double bass player. But there won't be a single pianist in sight. So you'll have no reason to be jealous and, take it from me, it really will do you good to come to the brunch.'

This waiter's unsolicited display of kindness touched her in exactly the same way as the male nurse's considerate behaviour towards her in the hospital had – so much so that she took the firm decision to go to the jazz brunch the following Sunday.

When the Jazz-Girl finally arrived at the school gates, Juliet was delighted to see her mother looking much happier than she had been that morning. The day had indeed not got off to a very good start but now it was just getting better and better – the icing on the cake being that several mothers, upon noticing her injury, approached the Jazz-Girl with offers of help.

As soon as she was home, the Jazz-Girl informed François of her positive news. And, against all odds, as this day drew to a close a genuine feeling of happiness descended upon her, a feeling fuelled by the various reactions of the people with whom she had come into contact – François Pradel's kindness and efficiency; Arielle Moing's willingness to rearrange her schedule to accommodate her because, just like her, she was a passionate pianist and, more importantly, because she was a highly gifted doctor, a genuine artist in her field who knew she could give her the right treatment; the waiter's touching, considerate comments; and the sympathy of the numerous mothers who had approached her at the school gates. So, when all was said and done, this day, having started out under a rather black cloud, had actually turned out to be surprisingly good!

Now, the next day, as if fate had decided to display a touch of black humour, the Jazz-Girl actually had a piano lesson!

Some months previously, on the basis that he "no longer had much to add" to her improvisations, Zach had suggested that she stop taking weekly lessons, advising her instead to take just the odd lesson whenever she felt the need. As luck would have it, a week before her accident she had booked two lessons with him which, in spite of her initial reservations, she eventually decided to maintain. After all, it would do her good to spend some time with another pianist.

That day, the Jazz-Girl used the lesson to show Zach some of the jazz arrangements she had written on her musical notation program. As they listened to her work through the loudspeakers of the computer, Zach checked it out and made a few suggestions. Then, since they had some time left over, the Jazz-Girl turned to him and said:

'I'd really like to play one of my arrangements for you. Why don't we go next door to the piano?'

With a decidedly amused look on his face, Zach enquired:

'You're not going to play the piano with your injured hand, are you?'

'Zach', replied the Jazz-Girl, 'you spent five years coming to the house once a week to give me a piano lesson. *You*, of all people, know that I can be extremely stubborn when it comes to playing blues.'

Sitting down next to her at the piano, Zach made no attempt to contradict her.

Thus it was that she played her arrangement, as well as could be expected, while at the same time asking her teacher to use his imagination whenever she was required to simplify the right-hand riffs and figures.

Once she had finished playing, Zach seemed genuinely surprised.

'You know, I love your arrangement and I have to say that your performance was really quite polished.'

Referring to the time when her hands used to tremble nervously during her lessons, the Jazz-Girl pointed to her right hand and replied:

'That's the whole point of having my hand bound in a resin glove. It makes trembling absolutely impossible. The lengths we artists go to!'

Zach burst out laughing, relieved to see that she had not completely lost her sense of humour in the accident.

The Jazz-Girl then slightly backtracked by saying:

'I am desperately trying to see the funny side but in fact I'm *really* disappointed that I can't play at the lunch. I so wanted to see if I could rise to the challenge. And I felt I was ready.'

Zach endeavoured to console her with:

'There'll be other opportunities.'

'I don't know about that. You know full well that I came to blues extremely late on in life and the opportunities to perform in public are actually few and far between.'

'What if you were to get somebody to play alongside you? You could play with your left hand and another pianist could improvise over the top.'

'I did think about that. But what I really wanted to do was see if I would be capable of playing solo, in front of a hundred people.'

'Well, in that case, why don't you just hit a few chords with your left hand and sing?'

Now on the verge of turning into a stubborn two-year-old, only just managing to repress her increasing desire to stamp her foot and go "Hmmm!", the Jazz-Girl exclaimed:

'But I don't want to sing! I *just* want to play!'

Zach went silent and began to think…

Whenever Zach felt unable to resolve a personal problem, he would draw inspiration from a Japanese proverb – *If something is missing in your life, seek it out among the things you already have* – and this is precisely what he did now. Turning to his former pupil and speaking to her in a tone which, while still compassionate, was now firmer and more directive than before, he said:

'You have a beautiful instrument in your possession. And you don't need to do very much at all to produce a good sound from it. As a left-hander, you have always had an incredibly solid left hand on the piano and, what's more, you currently have three healthy fingers on your right hand. Now, you know as well as I do that, as far as blues is concerned, less is more. Duke Ellington actually proves this to us. Do you remember his piece – "C-Jam Blues" – composed of just two notes?'

'Yes, I do. C and G. That's the one, isn't it?'

'Yes, you've got it. So here's the deal. *You* are going to go away and compose as many pieces as you can with the means at your disposal and next week *I'll* take a look at your work.'

With a wide smile appearing on her face, the Jazz-Girl breathed a huge sigh of relief and replied:

'Zach, it's a brilliant idea. Thank you so much. Now, at last, I know just what to do!'

With that, the lesson drew to a close and the Jazz-Girl stood up to accompany Zach to the door. Barely was she on her feet, however, when she sat down quite abruptly, explaining:

'I'm so sorry, I'm really not feeling too good.'

Unused to seeing her like this, Zach looked horrified as he asked her:

'Nina, are you sure you're okay? Is there anything else in addition to the injury to your hand?'

'No, don't worry, it's just the pain. It made me faint quite a lot when I had the accident and when I got up just then I felt as if I were about to faint again.'

'Are you saying that nobody gave you anything for the pain?'

'Actually, they did! You're absolutely right. At the hospital they gave me anti-inflammatories and painkillers – it's just come back to me – but when I got home I was so angry that I tossed them in the medicine basket and consequently completely forgot to take them.'

Without hesitating for a single second, Zach, who for several years had been coming to her home to give her lessons and therefore knew his way around, went straight into the kitchen returning immediately with her medicine and a glass of water.

A few minutes later, reassured to know that she had now taken her tablets, Zach left to go to his next pupil.

It was then that the potent cocktail of emotions – shock, anger, fear and relief – of the last few days began to catch up with the Jazz-Girl, so much so that she decided to go for a rest. She had only just lain down on her bed, however, when she heard her telephone, which she had left in the study next to the computer, go "ding". Initially, she tried to ignore the text message but, ultimately, her curiosity as to its contents prevented her from relaxing enough to rest. It was, after all, Wednesday afternoon[12], which meant that her children had gone off to their respective extra-curricular activities of fencing and modern dance. And what if one of them were trying to reach her? Mustering up a few remaining droplets of energy, she went to the study, grabbed her telephone and returned to her bedroom to lie down again, where she was surprised to see that the text message was, in fact, from François Pradel.

"Dear Nina,

How are you feeling? I do hope you're okay. I really don't want to tire you out but I felt I must contact you because a pianist has just told me about a certain Bernard Cornier who is apparently a highly reputed specialist at the clinic. Was he the doctor who treated you?"

Once again, François' kind words brought tears to her eyes, so touched was she by the lengths to which he was going to protect her passion. And in spite of the difficulties involved in writing a text message with one hand, she immediately replied:

"Dear François,

I cannot begin to tell you just how touched I am by your message. Doctor Cornier was unable to rearrange his schedule to see me, unlike Arielle Moing who not only treated me but also struck me as being extremely competent. I'm due to see her again in ten days' time and I promise to keep you informed. Thank you so much for your kind, invaluable help."

With that, the painkillers started to take effect and the Jazz-Girl was, at long last, able to rest.

$$\oint$$

Now, like just about everybody else who sets foot on this planet, during the course of her life the Jazz-Girl had known some tough times. And she had always been astonished to discover that these times were not, in fact, all bad because, as a general rule of thumb, they would come bearing unexpected gifts. In other words, surprisingly positive things

---

12 In France, children do not go to school on Wednesday afternoons; this time is kept free for extra-curricular activities.

would arise from the bad times. And such occurrences invariably left the Jazz-Girl with the impression that fate, destiny, the powers that be, or indeed whatever force it is that governs these matters, appeared to be saying: so sorry to have inflicted that upon you. Please accept this by way of a consolation.

Over the days that followed, several unexpected, incredibly positive consequences of her injury were to reinforce this established trend…

$$\&$$

The next morning, taking heed of Zach's advice, the Jazz-Girl sat down at the piano and, using the "means at her disposal", managed to compose four new pieces. One of these pieces was based on a riff she had heard on a record some three years previously. At the time, she had shown it to Zach who had her teased her mercilessly about it. As far as he was concerned, this riff was a pure product of the 60s and belonged, at best, in a film such as *Austin Powers*. That day, however, by playing the riff on a swing rhythm, the Jazz-Girl succeeded in creating an incredibly bluesy sound. It was a sound which was also to be heard in each of her other new compositions – and with good reason. In blues, as Zach had reminded her, less is more or, to put it another way, the silent pauses are as important as the notes, because they play a role similar to that of punctuation in a text. And as she listened to her pieces through the loudspeakers of her computer, having first written them on her musical notation program, she was pleased to observe that numerous silent pauses were quite naturally present in her compositions due to the limitations imposed by her right hand. So, ultimately, to her great surprise, these four pieces were actually making a valuable contribution to her repertoire. As for the riff, she found it very reassuring. She had only ever heard it once, three years previously! And yet this riff had suddenly come back to her when she was at the piano, which she took as proof – if ever proof were required – that music leaves an incredibly strong imprint on the human brain. Consequently, one of the Jazz-Girl's major concerns could now be eliminated: clearly it was highly unlikely that she would forget her repertoire in the space of just six weeks!

This productive morning at the piano was the first of the many "unexpected gifts" which would be bestowed upon the Jazz-Girl as a direct result of her injury. The second was swift to follow...

Saturday 10 April...

It was Charlie's birthday and that year, having just started Russian lessons at school, Charlie asked his parents if it would be possible for the whole family to go to a Russian restaurant for his birthday treat. Since the Jazz-Girl was currently incapable of doing anything much in the kitchen, his parents were more than happy to accede to his request.

Having overcompensated for the fact that with her hand in a cast she required more time than usual to get ready, on this particular occasion the Jazz-Girl was actually ready first, with the result that, for once, *she* was the one waiting for everybody else. Thus, she found herself sitting in an armchair with time to kill. This caused her, once more, to contemplate her hand, trapped – indeed, imprisoned – as it was in its "boxing glove" and, all of a sudden, she was overwhelmed by the same intense feeling of deprivation which had invaded her whole being in the immediate aftermath of the accident. Admittedly, the situation was now as positive as it could possibly be in the circumstances. However, Arielle Moing's words – "It will be a good year before this accident is completely behind you" – were never very far from her mind. Consequently, she continued to perceive her injury – in much the same way as she had from the beginning – as a threat, a barrier to her passion, a cause of *the* most terrible deprivation, since it was rendering her unable to play the piano with all of her ten fingers.

And so it was that the Jazz-Girl, having nothing better to do, decided just for once to dispense with the idea of trying to get the problem into perspective, and totally succumb to this intense feeling which was so invading her. It was, after all, high time to let this deeply negative feeling run its course.

What followed was truly sublime...

By virtue of *the* most extraordinary epiphany, all her negative thoughts suddenly gave way to a radically different perception of her predicament.

In that very instant, the Jazz-Girl was able to see that this temporary deprivation was in fact serving to render her acutely aware of a concept which, while incredibly basic, was nevertheless extremely important: in order to appreciate something to the full, sometimes a period of deprivation is actually necessary.

Obviously, before her accident the Jazz-Girl had been fully conscious of the fact that she derived enormous pleasure from playing blues. It had, however, taken this injury to make her realise that, ultimately, her music provided her with so much more than mere pleasure or enjoyment, for it had apparently become utterly indispensable to her over the years, flooding as it did her very existence with an infinite stream of absolute happiness. Better still, this happiness lay just at her fingertips and, in order to gain access to it, all she had to do was take a mere few steps across her sitting room – something she could do every single day of her life if she so wished.

This crucial realization would enable the Jazz-Girl, from that point on, to view her injury in an unexpectedly positive light. In spite of the fact that it was obviously putting her through her paces, her injury would no longer be her enemy. On the contrary, it would now be her ally because it was serving as a very necessary rite of passage on her musical journey. And the reason she deemed this rite of passage necessary was because it had just made her aware of a fundamental truth, a truth which, unlike her fracture, would never leave her: to have such an immense source of pure bliss at her fingertips was to be extremely fortunate, privileged even, and this in turn was making her realise just how very precious her passion *was* – which she considered, as a result, to be a true heaven-sent gift.

This magnificent transformation in the way in which she perceived her injured hand suddenly gave the Jazz-Girl a burning desire to share the immense joy, which the gift of her passion was clearly bringing to her, with as many people as possible – leading her to take the firm decision that, as soon as her hand healed, she would do everything within her power to achieve this.

The exquisite beauty of this moment appeared to bring time to a standstill, which somehow caused the Jazz-Girl to perceive the world in much brighter colours, so bright in fact that she remained seated in the armchair, quite incapable of moving, firmly anchored in the present moment, savouring every single second of it. And when her husband finally came to tell her that everybody was ready, he was surprised to find her looking "utterly radiant" – before going on to "inspect" her outfit, which made him burst out laughing as he exclaimed:

'Such elegance! Only you could do something like that!'

He was naturally referring to her sling, for the Jazz-Girl, having decided that the sling provided by the hospital was just too ugly for words, had managed to concoct another one out of a long black silk scarf, which matched her outfit to perfection!

Two days later...

Following the sublime epiphany in the armchair, an all-pervading feeling of serene happiness had descended upon the Jazz-Girl. Consequently, she was not expecting to experience another equally magical moment so soon afterwards...

That day, she was in her local chemist when the pharmacist enquired about her hand and then said to her:

'You know, you really did the right thing going to that clinic. The hand is actually an extremely complex part of the human body and it's always better to consult a specialist. This is, in fact, the advice I give to the fishmongers who come in here. You see, when it's market day, sometimes they end up cutting their hands, so they pop in as we're close by. However, I send them straight to the clinic because it is, after all, their profession that's at stake.'

'I have to say,' replied the Jazz-Girl, 'I do indeed feel really lucky to have been treated there – especially as I myself am a bit like the fishmongers in the sense that my hands are particularly precious to me. You see, I happen to be a jazz pianist.'

'Really? Wow! I didn't know that.'

'Well... yes and no. Originally, I'm a translator. But five years ago, I started learning jazz improvisation and just before my accident I was preparing to give a major public performance. That's why I'm a bit frustrated by this injury.'

It was then that the pharmacist, clearly barely able to contain her surprise, looked the Jazz-Girl straight in the eye and exclaimed:

'You took up jazz a mere five years ago and you've already reached a level where you can perform in public?! What are you? Some kind of genius?'

'Me? A genius? I hardly think so. But one thing's for sure. Without a shadow of a doubt, I do have a very intense passion burning within me.'

With that, the Jazz-Girl left the chemist. The tone of surprise in the pharmacist's voice, however, simply refused to leave the Jazz-Girl, causing her to reflect on the long, somewhat bumpy but nevertheless amazing road she had travelled to reach jazz improvisation.

Forty years previously...

Nina was feeling so very happy. She had just celebrated her ninth birthday and for one reason, one reason alone, she had been dreaming of this day for months – the reason being that in this large family of restricted means, a golden rule asserted that each child was allowed a single extra-curricular activity from the age of nine. And since finances were so tight, the chosen activity actually served as a birthday present.

The previous year, Nina's sister had chosen to take ballet lessons. Nina, on the other hand, had always known that she would choose the piano. It had, after all, been really easy for her to make this choice for the simple reason that standing in the sitting room was a small piano, so small in fact that the keyboard spanned just five octaves[13]. To Nina, however, it did not really matter if some notes were missing because, for as long as she could remember, she had regularly been sitting down at this piano to play her favourite songs by ear. Given that she was the only child in her family to take an interest in this instrument, Nina considered it, moreover, to be her exclusive domain, her secret garden. And, in this family of four children – all born incredibly close together within the space of just four years –, it was so important to have that.

The very first piano lesson was an absolute revelation for this little nine-year-old girl. The teacher appeared to give her a magic wand, which in reality was a crystal-clear explanation of how to read music. And the teacher's words, completing as they did the various explanations Nina had previously received from her mother who also played the piano, now appeared to transform all those weird little black and white things on a music score into an extremely easy way for Nina to play her chosen instrument. Consequently, when she got home, in the space of just one short afternoon she learnt to play all of the forty pieces in the book which her teacher had just given to her.

During the course of the next two years, Nina continued to progress in much the same way, that is to say at the speed of an

---

13 The keyboard on a standard piano spans just over seven octaves.

express train, with the result that when she was just eleven years old, the teachers at her primary school asked her if she would be prepared to accompany the singing at the Christmas carol concert. Nina was naturally delighted to accept, especially as standing in the assembly hall was a beautiful upright piano with a full-sized keyboard. Furthermore, since none of the teachers knew how to play this instrument, or indeed any instrument at all, in order to show Nina just how grateful they were, they decided that she should be allowed to stay in during morning playtimes so that she could rehearse. This created some tension among Nina's friends who, because they had to stay outside in the playground while she sat inside playing the piano, were so jealous that they started to give her a really hard time about it. Undiscouraged, Nina took the reaction of her so-called "friends" to be but just a small price to pay for the immense joy that being able to spend even more time sitting at the piano brought to her.

Sadly, a few months later, Nina's piano lessons came to an abrupt end. Her teacher, she later found out, had serious health problems and had unfortunately been obliged to take early retirement. Worse still, in this little village in the north of England no other piano teacher was to be found.

That said, music, it would seem, was not prepared to give up on Nina just like that. Could it possibly be that Apollo was already secretly toiling on her behalf?

It was during this period that the now famous film *The Sting* came out and inadvertently sparked off a worldwide craze for ragtime – the precursor to piano jazz. It was a craze, which swept the planet, to such an extent that practically anyone who vaguely knew how to play the piano started to learn this hitherto little-known genre of music. Obtaining the music scores was, as a result, extremely easy for they were sold absolutely everywhere. During the next few years, Nina thus undertook to learn, all by herself, a large part of Scott Joplin's repertoire and, in doing so, discovered a taste for the syncopated rhythms which characterise the vast majority of this composer's works. What she could not know, of course, is that, rhythmically speaking, this music was actually providing her with the best possible preparation for playing another style of music, a genre which many years later would become her great passion in life but which, for the moment, was content to wait patiently in the wings.

By the time Nina was seventeen, she learnt the good news that a new teacher was now giving lessons in her village and, during the course of the next year, she resumed her classical piano training before, once more, having to give it up. In the meantime, at school she had discovered a passion for languages and it was her dearest wish to study French and German at Oxford University. In order to be able to obtain a place at this great academic establishment, she was required to achieve top marks in her "A" levels and it was therefore time to concentrate on doing just that.

During the years that followed – a year working as an *au pair* in France, two years in Oxford, a year in Germany and a final year in Oxford – Nina, without any access to a piano, was no longer able to play.

That is to say, she was no longer able to play until the day she made *the* most amazing discovery…

It happened during her final year – the year when students traditionally cease to have a ball, and get their heads down to work. As the saying goes, however, all work and no play makes Jack a dull boy – or, in this case, Jill a dull girl – and with this in mind, one Sunday afternoon Nina decided it was time for a well-earned break. As a result, abandoning her somewhat dense revision schedule in the library, she started to wander aimlessly through the corridors of her college. And it was not long before she happened – somewhat bizarrely given that this was actually her third year at the university – upon a part of her college that she had never seen before. It was here that she spotted a door marked "Music Room".

The simple act of pushing this door open enabled Nina to discover a hidden treasure.

In this room stood *the* most magnificent grand piano. A Steinway. It was a truly beautiful instrument, unlike any she had ever seen and, initially, so transfixed was she by this wondrous sight that she found herself quite simply unable to move.

When finally she did sit down to play, the sound seemed unusual, almost alien, to her ears for she found it hard to believe that it was actually possible for a piano to sing so very gracefully; the notes were so clear and yet so mellow.

This amazing pianistic experience had such an impact on Nina that it incited her to take a very important, albeit somewhat outlandish, decision – so outlandish in fact that it was soon to become her standing joke: if ever she were to buy a piano, it would be a Steinway or nothing!

Enquiring about her discovery, Nina learnt that it was a legacy from a former student and the really good news was that it was not exclusively reserved for those studying music. On the contrary, everyone and anyone was allowed to play this piano for free and, in order to secure a slot, a mere signature on the schedule hanging on the door outside was all that was required.

Consequently, during the rest of her final year, Nina would regularly grant herself little breaks to go forth and make music on this beautiful Steinway. And shortly after leaving Oxford she was proud to discover that these breaks had clearly not done her any harm for she had actually managed to obtain a decent degree in modern languages!

A few months later, armed with her new qualification, Nina fulfilled a major personal dream by landing herself a highly coveted translation job in Paris.

From the outset, Nina really loved her life in the French capital – and all the more so when, one year later, she met the man who was to become her husband. Enter Etienne, an international business lawyer.

Shortly after Nina and Etienne were married, the very first digital pianos, called Clavinovas, started to emerge and Etienne decided he would surprise his wife by giving her one such instrument for her birthday.

Upon receiving this wonderful present, Nina, who had not touched a piano for several years since leaving Oxford, took a year of lessons in order to get her playing back up to scratch. And to her great surprise she rapidly reached a level where she could play Chopin waltzes, Bach Two-Part Inventions and Mozart sonatas. Evidently, in spite of her long absence from the piano, she had not lost the ability she had had as a little girl to read and quickly learn to play a piece.

This ability was, however, double-edged in that not only did it reveal a strong point but also a weak one. It was during this period that Nina discovered how easily frustrated she was by the constraints of classical music, which she felt left her no freedom for her own expression. At the same time, deep down she knew that a more talented pianist would be capable of infusing these pieces with just the right personal touch required to make the difference between merely playing a piece and truly interpreting it.

This brought Nina to the conclusion that she had quite probably reached her limits with classical piano. And in any event, it was not actually that hard for her to do away with the great classics because she was rapidly becoming obsessed with another kind of music.

It so happened that when Nina's husband had given her the digital piano, her father-in-law – delighted to learn that she was taking up the piano again and momentarily prepared to overlook his abiding principle of "joyful frugality" – had, in a bid to encourage her, given her *the* most wonderful present: a book of piano blues.

What on earth made him choose that particular book? To this day, Nina still has absolutely no idea. It was not as if her father-in-law were a big fan of blues. On the contrary, he only ever played classical music on his flute. But whatever the reasons behind this mysterious choice, one thing was perfectly clear: Nina literally devoured her new book, to such an extent that, every evening, she would run home from work, drop her bag on the hall floor and immediately sit down at her Clavinova to play her newfound style of music!

Several years were to pass before Nina and her husband were blessed, somewhat later than intended but better late than never, by the arrival of two beautiful children. Having travelled a very long road to come into this world, a handsome little boy named Charlie finally appeared, followed four years later by the exquisitely pretty Juliet. In France, having a boy first and then a girl is generally referred to as the King's choice. As far as Nina and Etienne were concerned, however, whether or not the king approved was actually of little consequence for they themselves were quite literally ecstatic!

Now content to enjoy her new role as a young mother to the full, during this time Nina put her desire to pursue learning piano blues on the back burner, blissfully happy instead to play nursery rhymes for Charlie and, subsequently, to Juliet, whom she would sit, as soon as they were old enough, in the high chair next to her so they could pretend to play along with her.

When Charlie started primary school, just like Nina at the same age he too began to display an interest in the piano. In response, Nina initially placed a sticker on the middle C key, thus giving Charlie the reference point required to learn the pieces of the very first book she had herself been given at the age of nine. This solution kept Charlie happy while she set about looking for a teacher who could give him some proper lessons.

Finding a teacher proved to be somewhat difficult, so much so that Nina was getting really desperate when Ségolène, the mother of one of

Charlie's school friends, offered her the details of her daughter's teacher. For want of anything better, Nina somewhat reluctantly accepted this offer, although deep down she feared that Ségolène's chosen piano teacher would be much too strict and too old school for Charlie. The reason behind this fear was that although Ségolène was a genuinely nice person, she nevertheless came from a world far removed from that inhabited by Nina – a social category whose main problems in life appeared to be how to maintain the family château, the difficulties of organising a lunch for thirty during the hunting season or, indeed, where to obtain decent foie gras at a reasonable price!

Imagine, then, Nina's surprise when in walked Zach. The incarnation of cool! At least that is the message that the various elements of his appearance – floppy hair, a leather jacket, the trendiest pair of jeans imaginable and a crash helmet in his hand – seemed to be conveying. It was practically a foregone conclusion that Zach would rapidly become a true hero for Charlie and that is exactly what happened.

Given that Zach was really good with children, Juliet was also swift to fall under his spell, to the extent that this little four-year-old girl would happily defy her reputation of being exceedingly shy and literally *run* to open the door for Zach when he arrived every Wednesday afternoon to give Charlie his lesson.

As for Nina, who had always sworn that she would never become a helicopter mother, her desire to remain in the background during Charlie's lessons meant that she would generally hide herself away in the kitchen with Juliet, where they would spend the hour baking.

With Zach as a teacher, Charlie made rapid progress but like a lot of boys his age – at the time he was just eight years old – concentration was not exactly his strong point. So whenever this little boy's mind started to wander, Zach would afford Charlie a short break by entertaining him with a mini performance of some well-known classical piece.

Everything changed for Nina the day when, for some reason, Zach decided to switch to another style of music and proceeded to give a cracking performance of a fast and furious boogie-woogie. That day, Nina literally had to force herself to stay in the kitchen because she was counting the minutes till the end of the lesson in order to be able to put a very important question to Zach:

'I just heard you play that boogie-woogie. Do you by any chance teach blues?'

'Yes, of course I do.'

For Nina, there was no "of course" about it because it was the first time she had ever met a piano teacher who taught both classical music and jazz. Consequently, she was extremely surprised to discover that jazz was in fact Zach's first musical discipline, indeed his speciality.

The next week, Nina took a trial lesson. It was a lesson that was to change her relationship with the piano and music forever.

The crucial point came when Zach showed Nina the sheet music of a famous jazz standard. In contrast to a classical music score, here there was no bass clef. In other words, nothing was written for the left hand. As for the right hand, this was reduced to a simple melodic line composed of single notes – or to put it another way, completely devoid of any chords or double notes – which had intriguing little "codes" written above the treble clef such as Fmaj7, C7 and Bb6. With disarming simplicity, Zach then went on to explain:

'These "codes" all relate to specific chords. Each one of these chords consists of four notes. When you improvise on the piano, you can play these notes wherever you wish to on the keyboard and in whatever order you wish.'

While Zach's explanation was indeed simple, to Nina it constituted *the* most extraordinary revelation. From that moment on, never again would she consider the keyboard of her instrument to be a long line of black and white keys, for it was now divided into groups of four notes which she could organise and reorganise in whatever way she saw fit. Furthermore, as she listened to Zach's explanation, these groups of notes seemed to start dancing before her very eyes, as if to reinforce the vital message they were sending her: from that day forward, they would be providing her with a profound, possibility infinite, source of new melodies.

A few weeks later, a place freed up in Zach's schedule enabling Nina to start taking weekly lessons with him. During the first of these lessons, Nina, just like the vast majority of pupils who had gone before, confessed to Zach that while she was really keen to discover jazz improvisation, she did not actually feel capable of improvising herself for, in spite of the revelation of the first lesson, the subject continued to be something of a mystery to her.

Zach was swift to reassure her, dispensing with any myths surrounding the subject in one fell swoop by enlightening her as to the wonderful paradox which forms the basis of jazz improvisation:

'The best jazz musicians are usually the ones who have learnt the greatest number of chords and musical phrases by heart. Take it from me, in the beginning there is just an awful lot of information to commit to memory and if you have a good memory, I can assure you, you can do it.'

Fortunately, this was indeed the case. Nina happened to be blessed with an excellent memory, of the type that could easily put an elephant's to shame, and during the next few months this memory would serve her well – as would another trick she had up her sleeve. It turned out that jazz improvisation was not quite the alien concept she had at first thought, in that the entire process (of reading something on a page – in the case in point, the chords – and then transforming it mentally in order to produce something different on the keyboard) revealed itself to be startlingly similar to that of translation. So, in fact, here she found herself on very familiar territory. And thanks to the head start afforded to her by these two considerable advantages, together with Zach's excellent pedagogical skills, Nina progressed in absolute leaps and bounds.

Delighted with her rapid, completely unexpected progress, Nina also began to discover just how much she loved jazz improvisation. Whereas classical music had indeed left her with a feeling of frustration, an unfulfilled gap, as if she had somehow missed the point, the freedom of expression that came with jazz improvisation filled this gap perfectly, thus forever eliminating all her frustrations of the past. In short, Nina had at last found her great passion in life and such was her enthusiasm for it that a very dear friend decided to give her a lovely new name.

And so it was that Nina became quite simply known to all as the Jazz-Girl.

When all was said and done, then, it would seem that the tone of utter surprise in the pharmacist's comment – "You took up jazz a mere five years ago and you've already reached a level where you can perform in public?!" – was actually justified for, when the Jazz-Girl had first started taking lessons with Zach, she had not been expecting to progress so quickly nor indeed to go so far. On the contrary, she had merely hoped to understand the basics. And now here she was, just five years later, complaining because she had been deprived of playing in public whereas the fact of the matter was that to have reached this stage proved, beyond all doubt, that she had far exceeded her wildest dreams with regard to jazz.

More significantly, this simple comment by the pharmacist made the Jazz-Girl realise, not before time, that she should perhaps recognise the presence of a force that had evidently been guiding her for many, many years...

Clearly, in view of the numerous obstacles standing in her way – the lack of a teacher in her village, the lack of time during her studies, the lack of an instrument over long periods of time –, the Jazz-Girl could so easily have gone through life without ever discovering her passion for improvisation. Music, however, in the manner of *the* most faithful of friends, had categorically refused to abandon Nina, from the time she was a little girl –who, before she had even taken so much as a single lesson, would sit down quite spontaneously to play the piano – right up until she became a fully-fledged Jazz-Girl who had finally found her true passion in life. Thus it was that every time an obstacle had steered her off course, music had come looking for her in many different disguises – the worldwide craze for ragtime, the discovery of the magnificent Steinway, the surprise presents (a digital piano and a book of blues) and, to top it all, the perfect teacher who happened to be right under her nose for he was already coming to her home once a week to give piano lessons to her son.

In short, in spite of all the various obstacles, music had clearly continued to make its presence felt until such time as the Jazz-Girl had finally been able to find her true vocation. This observation enabled her to appreciate for the very first time the scope of a force for which she would from now on have the greatest respect – the force in question obviously being that of the very power of music itself.

And to think that the simple question which had provoked this entire analysis had been put to her as a direct result of her injury. Who would have thought it? When first she had heard the sharp crack as her hand hit the pavement on that fateful day of her accident, never for one second could she possibly have imagined that this apparent disaster would lead to such intensely rewarding moments of reflection.

The next day, the Jazz-Girl had the second piano lesson, which she had booked just before her accident.

Pleasantly surprised to discover that she was in much better shape than the previous week, Zach began by checking the four new pieces she had composed. Then, since he had no corrections to make, she suggested that they use her new compositions as a basis for a four-hand – or, in this case, a three-and-a-half-hand! – jam session on the piano.

Sitting down at the piano, she explained to Zach:

'Since these pieces only use the middle and bass octaves, I thought you could use the high notes to improvise.'

In response, Zach faked the look of an authoritative teacher and retorted:

'Sorry, but it just doesn't work like that. I am going to play exactly where I want to.'

Flashing him the wickedest of grins, the Jazz-Girl pretended to threaten him with her gloved hand in the manner of a boxer.

'I think it's probably best if I stick to the high notes,' was Zach's wise conclusion.

And with that they embarked, just like in the good old days, on a joyful jam session at the end of which another surprise lay in store for the Jazz-Girl. When she listened to the recordings they had made, she discovered to her great delight that she was playing with much more precision than usual. Admittedly, the means at her disposal were substantially reduced but she had apparently compensated for this shortfall by making optimum use of what she had. As a result, against all logical expectations, it now appeared that her injury was actually causing her piano playing to improve!

$$\oint$$

The big day was fast approaching. In two days' time the Jazz-Girl was due to return to the clinic and if the X-ray confirmed that the bone had set properly, then Dr Moing would remove her resin glove.

The Jazz-Girl was really desperate for this day to come; while perfectly aware that in the case of a fractured joint ten days was actually a relatively short time to wear a cast, she was nevertheless in a hurry to have the cast removed for she felt that her hand, imprisoned in its glove, could scarcely breathe. And that was not all. There was actually another reason for her impatience: *every* single person, upon noticing her gloved hand, seemed to feel obliged to recount his or her very own fracture story – and *this* was beginning to drive her completely crazy!

It turned out that the "been there, done it all before, even got the T-shirt to prove it brigade" divided into three distinct categories…

Now, the Jazz-Girl was more than willing to recognise the fact that she should not be too hard on the members of the first category for these were the people who would tell her their story out of a simple wish to express their sympathy: 'I totally understand. It's a real pain when it happens. I clearly remember when I broke my…'

In contrast, the people belonging to the second category were not quite so nice for, when talking about their past accidents, they seemed to have just one aim in mind, which was to raise the meaning of the term "competitive spirit" to a whole new level. These were the type of people who generally view life as a permanent Olympic Games in which, whatever the situation, only one thing counts, and that is going for gold. Thus it was that they would adopt the most sneering voice possible to say something along the lines of: 'Ten days? A tiny little fracture? That's nothing! You should hear what happened to me. Never one to do things by halves, when I broke my leg in three places, a few days later I had another accident and broke one of my arms and my nose!' Conclusion: quite clearly, single fractures were for wimps.

The people who told this type of story in their achingly superior voices seriously irritated the Jazz-Girl, leaving her as they did under the impression that she had somehow failed at the university of fractures and should try and do better next time.

Thank goodness, then, for the third category, which was reserved for one man and one man alone – a man named Olivier. Good old Olivier. His unique story saved the Jazz-Girl from the deadly boredom of all the rest!

It was lunchtime and the Jazz-Girl was on her way to school to pick up Juliet when she noticed Olivier, a neighbourhood acquaintance, out walking his dog.

Since the Jazz-Girl knew that Olivier was going through some difficult times at work, when he enquired about her gloved hand she endeavoured to underplay the problem.

'Yes, unfortunately it's a fracture. But at least it's nothing serious. In a few weeks it should all be behind me.'

In spite of her best efforts, however, Olivier, who was evidently relieved to talk about something other than work, appeared to want to pursue the subject:

'But it's really annoying. On top of which, I do believe you play the piano, don't you? Surely it's a bit of a tough call.'

'You're right. It is a bit tough. But like I say, it's only temporary.'

'Yes, I hear what you're saying, but I really do understand how hard it is. You see, when I broke my arm...'

Oh no, thought the Jazz-Girl. *Please. Not that. An umpteenth broken bone story! Lord, give me strength!*

Swift to apply the strategy which she had been obliged to develop with a view to concealing the profound feelings of boredom which all of these stories provoked in her, the Jazz-Girl immediately switched into "actress" mode. Thus, she was now faking an intensely interested expression, which she had recently so cultivated to perfection that she actually considered her performance to be worthy, at the very least, of a best actress Oscar!

As luck would have it, Olivier had broken his arm just six weeks prior to his wedding and although he had now been married for at least twenty years, he proceeded to recount the whole experience as if it had occurred only yesterday, sparing the poor Jazz-Girl no detail whatsoever as she desperately tried to hold back the yawns.

'Can you imagine how difficult it was? I was absolutely good for nothing. Poor old Sophie! She had to do all the wedding preparations.'

'It must have been truly terrible.'

'And then there was my mother-in-law who kept giving me a really hard time about it: "What on earth were you thinking of? How could you have gone and done something quite so stupid?" As if I would have done it on purpose!'

'Ah, mothers-in-law, hey?'

'To make matters worse, during the weeks leading up to the wedding my doctor was not even sure if he would actually be able to remove my cast in time for our big day!'

And so it was that Olivier pursued his story, recounting every last detail of every single medical consultation, all the while putting his heart and soul into creating such a sense of suspense that the Jazz-Girl seriously began to wonder if he himself knew how it would end. To marry with his arm in a plaster cast or not to marry with his arm in a plaster cast, that was the question!

This all went on for a good few long and very tedious minutes until, in an attempt to add a dramatic touch to the imminent conclusion of his story, Olivier decided to stop walking in order to announce:

'And then, three days before the wedding...'

At this point, he paused for further dramatic effect whereupon his dog, clearly irritated at having his walk interrupted, appeared to roll his eyes to heaven. As for the Jazz-Girl, who was by now beginning to fear she would be late for Juliet, she just wanted to scream at him: *Olivier, for God's sake, get to the point, spit it out, man!*

Olivier, however, was keen to take his time:

'And then, three days before the wedding... just three days before the wedding... (*she could now practically hear a drum roll*) my doctor... managed... to remove the plaster cast!'

'Phew!' replied the Jazz-Girl, relieved not so much for Olivier and Sophie's wedding photos as for Juliet who was waiting for her.

With the story now finished, the Jazz-Girl thought they would at last be able to continue on their way. Sadly, however, it appeared that the story was not in fact over. Barely had they taken three steps when once again Olivier stopped walking. The dog now looked even more irritated than before. As for the Jazz-Girl, who was forcing herself to be slightly more discreet, deep down she genuinely sympathised with Olivier's faithful friend.

Ever keen to increase the dramatic effect, on this occasion Olivier looked deep into the Jazz-Girl's eyes as he asked:

'But, Nina, can you imagine what a handicap it was on our honeymoon?'

The Jazz-Girl was at a complete loss as to how to respond, which unfortunately only encouraged Olivier to reiterate his question:

'Can you picture it? Can you – truly – picture it?'

Now on the verge of exploding, the Jazz-Girl wanted to shout: *No! No! NO! How on earth can you expect me to picture you on your honeymoon? Olivier, please, I'm begging you, finish your story once and for all. Otherwise I'll be late for school!*

Fortunately, she managed to refrain from reacting in this manner just in time because it was precisely then that Olivier's story took a most unexpected turn:

'Imagine, Nina, just for one second... There I was, on my honeymoon, with absolutely *no* mobility whatsoever in my right hand. On my honeymoon! Imagine the sheer and utter frustration of it!'

Now desperately trying to repress a serious need to burst out laughing, the Jazz-Girl was convinced that she saw the dog give her something resembling a wink for, clearly, he had just noticed the mischievous twinkle which had spontaneously appeared in her eyes, doing little to conceal her newfound curiosity. Had Olivier really just said what she thought he had? Could it be possible that this man, an upright citizen of the elegant sixteenth arrondissement of Paris, who went to church every Sunday and whose children attended the best private schools in the country, could it actually be possible that he was about to reveal to her, right here in broad daylight, the full extent of his sexual frustration on his honeymoon? Would he be providing her with as many details as when he had told her about each and every one of his medical consultations: the long torrid nights he had planned on spending with the eminently delectable Sophie, nights of which he had been deprived due to a complete and utter lack of mobility in his right hand? Olivier's story suddenly had a wonderfully salacious air about it with the result that the Jazz-Girl was in more of a hurry than ever to discover its dénouement!

Unfortunately, Olivier was still intent on taking his time as once more he repeated the question:

'But can you *really* imagine my frustration, Nina?'

Here, the Jazz-Girl had no other option than to remain silent, her only possible answer being: *Can I imagine? Don't you realise that my imagination has just gone into overdrive?*

Despite her silence on the subject, Olivier remained undeterred. In order that the Jazz-Girl concentrate properly on *his* answer to *his* own question, he now placed a hand on her shoulder and, looking her straight in the eye with an intensely solemn expression, said:

'What you have to understand is that Sophie and I are both passionate golfers. And for our honeymoon we had booked into a superb hotel in Mauritius, right next to a large golf course. But with no mobility in my right hand, I was unable to play for the entire week. So, you see, that is precisely why I can understand all your frustration about the piano. Let's face it, a passion is after all… a passion.'

And it was on that profoundly philosophical final note that Olivier concluded by saying:

Now, Nina, you mustn't let me hold you up. I hope it all works out for you. I'm off to walk Johnny.'

The Jazz-Girl allowed a few seconds to elapse, until Olivier and his dog were well out of sight, before succumbing at long last to one highly explosive fit of laugher, during which it occurred to her that she might just have been living in France for too long; clearly, she was beginning to react exactly like the French who, if the myth of the stereotype is to be believed, naturally assume that absolutely everything is related to sex. It was high time for her to think about a possible stay in her native country with a view to curing this problem!

𝄞

The big day had finally arrived and, as instructed, the Jazz-Girl went to get her hand X-rayed just before her consultation with Arielle Moing, who greeted her by saying:

'Oh hello. You're the jazz pianist, aren't you?'

'I am indeed. And since we're on the subject, I'd like you to have this. It's a copy of my jazz method.'

This gesture clearly moved the doctor who paused for a moment before saying to her patient:

'You know, I really am extremely touched. You have no idea how many times patients promise to bring things but never actually do. But you, well, you didn't forget. This is most kind of you. I look forward to using your method and, by way of a thank you, this consultation will be on me.'

This pleasant start to the proceedings set the tone for what followed: upon studying the new X-rays, Dr Moing was pleased to inform the Jazz-Girl that the bone had set correctly and that an operation would therefore be unnecessary. The Jazz-Girl felt immensely relieved to hear this – and even more so when Dr Moing announced:

'The next step is to remove the resin glove. Then I shall bandage your ring finger and your little finger only, which means the rest of your hand will be a lot freer. That said, if you are happy to continue wearing the glove, you could keep it for a bit longer. It's as you wish.'

'No, no, I'd prefer you to remove the glove, please,' replied the Jazz-Girl who just couldn't wait to get rid of it.

In the seconds that followed, however, she found herself bitterly regretting this decision.

In order to remove the resin glove, Dr Moing reached for a tool which strangely resembled a pizza cutter, except that this appeared to be a really dangerous version of that innocuous kitchen utensil; when she turned on the power, the circular blade started to spin at a terrifying pace, and the noise it made – that of a pneumatic drill – was even scarier. What if the doctor were to slip with this dangerous weapon? All of a sudden, the idea of wearing her resin glove for the rest of her life struck the Jazz-Girl as being a much more sensible option than having it removed, but it was too late. In the light of this, she placed her hand firmly on the table, turned her head the other way and closed her eyes, at which point she heard Dr Moing say:

'Don't move, now, Madame Somerville.'

Don't move? There was hardly any risk of that. The Jazz-Girl's profound feelings of fear were currently doing a fine job of keeping her absolutely frozen to the spot!

All her fears were banished, however, when a few seconds later her hand had been successfully freed from the glove and she was relieved to observe that the doctor had actually managed to remove the resin cast without removing any of her fingers into the bargain!

That said, while reassured to see her hand all in one piece, the Jazz-Girl nevertheless had a shock. Her hand was still black and blue and extremely swollen. Furthermore, it was as if it no longer had any strength in it.

Dr Moing, for her part, was thoroughly optimistic:

'This is all quite normal, Madame Somerville. Your hand is likely to remain swollen for at least another month. But don't worry, it will all come right in the end.'

Dr Moing then showed the Jazz-Girl how to take care of her hand over the next few weeks. Every day, she was to cover the healing knuckle with an anti-inflammatory patch and bind the ring finger and the little finger together with a compression bandage to stop them from moving. As for her other fingers, they were now completely free and, just like on the previous occasion, the doctor encouraged the Jazz-Girl to move these fingers as much as possible, this time adding:

'As long as you don't exert too much pressure on them, you can even play the piano with these three fingers if you wish to.'

At this point, the Jazz-Girl chose to remain silent, not daring to say that this was something she had been doing ever since her accident!

Upon leaving the clinic, the Jazz-Girl felt quite simply euphoric. For one thing, she had managed to avoid having an operation. Better still, the treatment over the coming weeks was going to make a huge difference to her daily life. Now that she was allowed to remove her bandages to take a shower, the balancing act of holding her hand high above her head would be a thing of the past. And she would also, at long last, be able to savour the delicious pleasure of being able to wash both hands by rubbing one against the other!

So delighted was she by all this good news that the Jazz-Girl desperately wanted to let everybody know immediately. However, in her opinion, one person deserved to be informed as a matter of priority and that person was, naturally, François Pradel. She therefore proceeded to write a long email detailing all her good news and expressing her immense gratitude towards him. François, for his part, was particularly delighted to learn that she would now have more freedom on the piano and this incited him to conclude his equally long reply with a touching mini-prescription: *"Two pentatonic scales, three times a day."*

Relieved and thrilled to know that the worst was now behind her, during the course of the next few weeks the Jazz-Girl continued to send regular progress reports to François; as far as she was concerned, letting him know just how grateful she felt towards him by thanking him for his invaluable help was the very least she could do.

To her surprise, the Jazz-Girl would systematically receive, almost immediately, long replies from François, replies which she truly loved reading. To observe her tuner at work on her piano was to witness pure poetry in motion and this poetry, which revealed his inner sensitivity, came across in his writing too. It was during this time that she also discovered her tuner's innate kindness. He never ceased to encourage her by regularly congratulating her on her determination to overcome her injury. Above all, however, in François Pradel she detected an unusual capacity to display an abundance of that rare quality known as empathy. And it turned out that there was a good reason for this. One day François confessed to her that he had indeed initially reacted to her injury as if it were his own for the simple reason that he suffered from a personal deep-seated fear of something happening to his hands.

Just like the Jazz-Girl, François also genuinely loved their written exchanges. At the time, he did not know that his English client was a qualified translator and had therefore been trained to write in French. He thus found himself surprised to discover the style of her emails which, according to him, were "so beautifully written, genuinely moving and yet full of comic touches". As a result, he would go to great lengths to reply in a literary style, which in the long run gave him a taste for the art of writing itself.

This period saw the emergence of a rather unusual relationship between these two piano enthusiasts, a relationship that, due to its epistolary form, was in fact unique both for François and the Jazz-Girl. The Jazz-Girl took this to be yet another positive consequence of her injury.

What she could not yet know was that one last surprise lay in store for her...

One month later, during the third consultation, Arielle Moing confirmed to the Jazz-Girl that it would no longer be necessary for her to wear the anti-inflammatory patch and the compression bandage all the time; she was now to use them only when she felt the need.

So the time had finally come to start rehabilitating her ring finger and her little finger. The good news was that the Jazz-Girl would, as promised, be able to do all her rehabilitation on the piano, the golden rule being that she should stop playing whenever her fingers hurt for she would otherwise put herself at risk of having chronic arthritis in her hand later on in life. This potential threat incited her to take the doctor's advice very seriously indeed.

Impatient to rediscover the pleasure of being able to play the piano with all of her ten fingers, when the Jazz-Girl initially began the rehabilitation process she was in fact terribly disappointed to find that her fingers would start to hurt after just one short half hour of playing – the time she usually required to warm up. Necessity being the mother of invention, however, over the days that followed the Jazz-Girl radically changed her approach by learning to savour every last second of her precious half hour at the piano. As a result, she began to play each note as if it were her last and was astonished to observe that her playing was once again improving. It was on that basis that she suggested to the organisers of the charity lunch that she play for half an hour during the pre-lunch drinks. Her performance would be a lot shorter than planned but this would be better than nothing.

Overjoyed to have risen to the challenge against all odds, on the day of the lunch, when the Jazz-Girl played the piano, she felt as if she were floating around in a bubble of pure musical bliss.

As for the organisers, so delighted were they to see her play that they literally showered her with compliments on her performance. The comments coming from one man in particular were of the type that the Jazz-Girl would never forget:

'You know, I just want to say that I *really* enjoyed your performance. I love blues and I know an awful lot of people who play it. When *you're* at the piano, however, it's a whole different ball game. You play body and soul. And you exude so much joy that it's really contagious. I felt extremely happy watching you. It was as if you were enveloped in a veritable halo of light. So, thank you.'

What a truly magnificent reward for all her efforts! This man had unwittingly granted the Jazz-Girl her greatest musical triumph to date; his compliments proved, beyond doubt, that she had indeed managed to accomplish her mission – the one on which she had set her heart during the sublime moment of reflection in the armchair: to share with others all the joy which the heaven-sent gift of her passion unfailingly brought to her.

Clearly, Apollo had kept the best surprise for last.

&

In conclusion, when all was said and done, the injury to her hand had actually served to remind the Jazz-Girl of some really valuable lessons, repeatedly illustrating the basic fact that life is full of surprises and that, generally, unexpectedly positive things arise from the tough times.

Surely, moreover, *the* most amazing surprise of this entire incident had to be the wonderfully paradoxical nature of its very outcome. This initially devastating blow, which the Jazz-Girl had logically presumed would hinder her progress in music, had in reality done just the opposite, spectacularly propelling her on her way to the extent that she now clearly defined herself as a "jazz pianist" because on several occasions this very appellation had involuntarily popped out, until such time as her subconscious had managed to will her towards a much more conscious acceptance of the truth.

Gone then were her numerous doubts and hesitations: her fear of messing up a performance, of being faced with an audience who did not like her music or, worse still, of being overcome with stage fright. Thanks to her injury the Jazz-Girl presently felt a burning desire, like never before, to perform in public and thereby communicate to others the immense joy that her music regularly brought to her. Consequently, the next time she was to receive a request to play, she would not hesitate for a single second to give as her answer one absolutely enormous resounding YES!

Keith Jarrett

It was around this time that the Jazz-Girl and her piano tuner began to forge a solid friendship with a world-famous American musician, a giant among giants in the music business – which explains why the story that follows is, and really must remain, completely confidential. To put it another way, just to be absolutely clear, this friendship has always been kept one hundred per cent Top Secret. Indeed, it is so very clandestine that even the artist *himself* does not actually know about it…

That morning, the Jazz-Girl had an appointment with François Pradel and the prospect of seeing him for the first time since her accident was slightly overwhelming her; his invaluable help of the previous weeks meant that she now saw him in a completely different light so she was not preparing to receive "just" her piano tuner. On the contrary, she was about to come face to face with the man who had totally understood the crucial implications of this accident for her, the man whose empathy had struck her as being truly exceptional, the man who had quite simply saved her hand from long-term damage. How would she ever be able to thank him enough for going to such lengths to preserve her passion in order that she might now enjoy this passion to the full?

When he arrived, François did indeed begin by asking her all about her injury and the progress she was making regarding the rehabilitation of her hand.

Then he proceeded to tune the piano, which one hour later was as good as new.

It was at this point that the Jazz-Girl started to brace herself for a few moments of excruciating embarrassment: she was about to test her piano in the presence of her tuner.

Obviously, she had complete faith in François' work. However, just to be on the safe side, she generally did a little test while he was still there. And although it made perfect sense to do this – indeed, some would deem it absolutely necessary – the presence of her tuner, a man who these days worked mainly for world-famous pianists, intimidated her somewhat. The bottom line was that, however many times the Jazz-Girl had been complimented on her progress in jazz improvisation and on the fact that to be performing in public after just five years of lessons constituted a rare accomplishment, deep-down she knew, only too well, that her level of playing had to be something of a joke compared to the pianistic skills of the artists with whom François regularly rubbed shoulders. So, in spite of her increasingly burning desire to perform in public, playing the piano in front of this man still posed a major problem for her. And that day, as if the situation were not already sufficiently pressure-laden, just as she was on the point of placing her hands on the piano keys, her tuner, albeit unwittingly, actually managed to up the ante…

François was in the process of preparing the invoice when, suddenly, he shook his head, let out a deep sigh and then ripped up the bit of paper saying:

'Nina, I'm so sorry. I've made a mistake. I'm going to have to prepare another invoice. Please forgive me. The thing is, I'm a bit stressed out. In fact, to be totally honest with you, I'm suffering from one enormous bout of stage fright. You see, I've just been informed that next month I'm going to be tuning a piano for Kète Ja-RAIDE.'

Upon hearing this, the Jazz-Girl was at a complete and utter loss for words. Clearly, given the way her tuner had made this apparently momentous announcement, he must have accepted an assignment for someone really big, an assignment which terrified him so much that presently, even here in her home, he was in a real state about it. She therefore desperately wanted to show him that she sympathised but, in reality, she did not have the foggiest clue as to what or whom he was referring and in the end, she decided it would probably be better to come clean and admit this:

'I'm really sorry, but I have *never* heard of that pianist,' she replied, somewhat emphatically.

With an incredulous look on his face, which did little to conceal his extreme surprise, François enquired:

'You mean to say you've never heard of Kète, Kète Ja-RAIDE?'

Quite suddenly the penny dropped. Phew! What a relief!

'Ah, you mean Keeeeith, Keith JA-rrett!'

'Yep. That's the one. Kète, Kète Ja-RAIDE. Apparently, he's really difficult, *very* demanding.'

'Well, yes, I can completely sympathise with you about your stage fright. But at the same time, it must be wonderful to meet such great artists. And just think of the compliment it is to your work. They have chosen *you* to prepare *his* piano. Isn't that amazing?'

There was nothing for it. François now seemed more preoccupied with his mispronunciation than anything else as he endeavoured to say the name properly – "Keeeef" – before going on to give the Jazz-Girl a slightly embarrassed smile.

As for the Jazz-Girl, she was feeling absolutely mortified by her blunder and immediately set about trying to rectify the situation:

'I'm so sorry. I admit that I didn't understand you straight away but that is only because you said the name with a really lovely French accent.'

Then, in an attempt to reassure him further, she pursued the subject with:

'You know, there really is no shame in having an accent. I've been living in Paris for nearly thirty years now and you, with your ear, are perfectly well placed to hear that I still have a slight accent when I speak French.'

A conversation ensued during which they discussed language learning and the fact that the Jazz-Girl's children were completely bilingual because she always spoke to them in English while her husband spoke to them in French.

François then turned his attention back to the preparation of the invoice while the Jazz-Girl proceeded to test the piano – an exercise which in the current circumstances looked likely to be about one thousand times more excruciating than ever before. A highly gifted "piano tuner supremo" was already present in the room – an ace among aces who was doing an increasing amount of work in prestigious concert halls for internationally renowned pianists such as Daniel Barenboim and Martha Argerich. And now, to make matters worse, the name to beat all others was hovering directly over the piano – the name of the king of jazz improvisation. *The* Keith Jarrett! Mister Köln Concert himself!

Once the Jazz-Girl had finished playing her piece, she declared the piano absolutely perfect. Her piano playing, on the other hand, had been quite the opposite. Utterly shameful! And as usual after a terrible performance of this kind, she suddenly felt really small.

Now it was François' turn to try to rectify the situation. He loved blues and, with his habitually kind manner, would always go to great lengths to encourage his client, regularly congratulating her on the progress she was making.

'That was great. It's very different from the blues pieces you generally hear. And I have to say, I thoroughly enjoyed what you just played.'

Touched by his tactful approach, the Jazz-Girl relaxed, thanked him for the compliment and explained:

'The reason it sounds different is because it's a jazz arrangement of the theme from a Mozart piano concerto. I've just written it.'

François liked the idea so much that he actually took a copy of the piece away with him when he left.

Keith Jarrett on the other hand was not – it would seem – ready to leave. On the contrary, his presence appeared to linger on in the room long after the departure of the piano tuner and this was but a mere harbinger of things to come…

𝄞

It was the month of July and the beginning of the school holiday.

With the Jazz-Girl's husband away on a ten-day business trip and their son on a two-week sailing course in Brittany, the Jazz-Girl decreed that she and Juliet should treat themselves to a girls-only trip, suggesting, much to the delight of her then ten-year-old daughter, that Juliet choose their destination.

Juliet's first choice turned out to be Tokyo so her mother naturally had to point out the impracticalities of this initial suggestion:

'I'm sorry, darling, but Tokyo is much too far. We are only going away for a few days. How about somewhere in Italy, or even France? You know there are some very beautiful places to see in this country alone.'

Taking heed of her mother's advice, Juliet then suggested Cannes, the reason being that a few weeks earlier she had really enjoyed watching the film festival with her mother as, together, they had admired the stars ascending the mythical staircase in their designer gowns.

Here, Juliet's mother was in two minds. While she had no wish to pour cold water on all of her daughter's travel plans, she nevertheless felt obliged to point out the following:

'I'd love to take you to Cannes, Juliet, but are you sure you really want to go? There's not much to see, you know. We'll end up spending all our time on the beach, in the pool, shopping and going to restaurants.'

As this point, Juliet flashed her mother a look which appeared to say something along the lines of, "You've just described paradise on earth to me and you're asking me if I really want to go?"

Then, lest there be any doubt, just to make sure the message was *absolutely* crystal clear, she completed it with one almighty, resounding utterance of that particular monosyllable which the youth of today use to such effect:

'Duh?'

So that settled it. It was a definite "yes" as off they set for a few days of living it up like princesses in swanky Cannes!

Upon their arrival, they decided that they should enjoy the princess theme to the full by paying a visit to some other princesses in the region – or, at any rate, by paying a visit to their official residence! In other words, they booked an excursion to Monaco which, as it was due to take place on their last day, would enable them to end their stay in style.

On the day of the excursion, the weather was absolutely superb – the clear bright southern light rendering the sublimely beautiful Côte d'Azur even more spectacular than ever.

Once in front of the palace, the Jazz-Girl and Juliet were highly amused to observe the changing of the guard, for that is just what it was, literally speaking; in contrast to the one they had witnessed some years previously in front of Buckingham Palace, at eleven o'clock sharp one solitary soldier emerged from within the Monacan Palace to replace the other solitary soldier who had been standing outside on duty for the last few hours! Trying hard not to laugh for fear of appearing disrespectful, they then went on the official tour of the palace interior before settling down for lunch in the restaurant located on the square outside. Here they marvelled not only at the absolutely magnificent sea view but also at the quality of the food – fresh grilled fish accompanied by Mediterranean vegetables – which was surprisingly good given that they had chosen *the* most tourist-y spot of the entire principality to have lunch!

Now on a roll with the princess theme, on the way home they decided to make a stop in order to tour the famous Fragonard perfume factory where their guide, a young polyglot from Poland, proceeded to tell the group, in several different languages, all about the work of a master perfumer – known to those in the trade as a professional "nose".

At this point, the Jazz-Girl's mind began to wander, leading her to fantasise about a profession which, although it did not actually exist, she nevertheless decided she would like to create, for here she started imagining herself becoming a professional "ear" whose role it would be to test the pianos which her tuner prepared in the various concert halls of Paris before the pianists came along to give their respective verdicts. This would enable her to spend her life playing some of the finest pianos known to man while at the same time rubbing shoulders with some of the world's greatest musicians. The ultimate dream! And quite obviously, that is precisely what it was: a wild dream – which would never be anything more than a mere figment of her imagination.

That said, in the minutes that followed, the Jazz-Girl was to receive a call regarding another wild dream of hers, one which had been coursing through her mind for some time. Furthermore, unlike the far-flung notion of becoming a professional "ear", here, it appeared, was a dream that she might just be on the point of fulfilling…

The Jazz-Girl and Juliet had just completed their tour of the perfume factory and were in the gift shop when the Jazz-Girl's telephone rang. It was her husband, who was ringing to tell her that one of his colleagues – *the* events' organiser of his law firm – would be contacting her over the next few days to find out if she would be prepared to play at a reception that the firm was intending to hold the following September.

Talk about the definitive OMG moment! This call completely stopped the Jazz-Girl in her tracks. And to think that she had vaguely raised this idea at her husband's office party without imagining for one single second that somebody might actually take her up on it…

A few months previously...

Christmas was fast approaching and the Jazz-Girl's husband had just received an invitation to the office party – a habitually sumptuous affair to which the "spouses and significant others" of all those who worked for the Paris branch of this major international law firm were traditionally invited.

That year, the firm had decided to throw a theme party and, as far as the Jazz-Girl was concerned, the theme in question could not have been more appropriate for it was – yes, you've guessed it – blues! Better still, the invitation came with the following sartorial instruction: "Dress code: 20s style."

Now it so happened that the Jazz-Girl really loved the fashion of this era. Consequently, she threw herself wholeheartedly into creating her look by procuring a beautiful flapper dress, a pair of vintage shoes, a cigarette holder and a headband with a feather in it. In order to complete her look, she asked her hairdresser, Ivan, to cut her bob much shorter, à la Louise Brooks. Once she had picked Ivan up off the floor – for here it should be pointed out that Ivan, upon visualising the potentially severe result, had actually fainted at the suggestion! – she managed to persuade him to lop at least a couple of inches off her hair and, with that, her look was indeed complete.

That Friday evening, as she waited for her husband downstairs in the large reception area, the Jazz-Girl was immediately struck by the fact that everybody appeared to be in particularly high spirits. She also found it hugely entertaining to observe the visual transformation in the lawyers who were beginning to come down in their various outfits – a striking contrast to their usual sober attire.

She was then somewhat surprised to notice Anna, one of the partner's wives, arrive wearing jeans, trainers and a T-shirt! Turning to Anna's husband, Thomas, the Jazz-Girl jokingly asked:

'Don't you think it's great that Anna has managed to give a whole new meaning to the term "20s style"?'

Thomas responded by winking at Anna and then, feigning resignation, looked at the Jazz-Girl and said:

'Yeah, she got it all wrong. She thought they meant 2020!'

At that point, Anna burst out laughing as she proceeded to produce a superb dress together with full accessories from a suit cover, while swiftly disappearing upstairs to change in her husband's office.

Evidently, everyone was more than happy to enter into the spirit that night!

A few minutes later, the Jazz-Girl's husband came to get her and together they walked towards the majestic reception room where the party was being held.

Just in front of the entrance stood a large basket filled with all manner of accessories – bow ties, cigarette holders, feather stoles and hairbands – for those who had been too busy to prepare an outfit. As each couple approached the entrance, a photographer took pictures of them standing in front of a white screen and, by dint of some technological magic trick, the resulting photograph showed 1920s Paris in the background! Inside the reception room, the disc jockey was creating just the right mood by putting on traditional jazz records. And the whole setting was completed by the projection of silent movies on all of the four walls.

It was a truly wonderful evening, throughout which the Jazz-Girl felt absolutely ecstatic – so much so that, during a conversation with the office managing partner, a man to whom she privately referred as the Big Boss, she found herself unable to refrain from expressing her complete and utter undiluted enthusiasm, as she said:

'Richard, I simply cannot thank you enough. This is one fabulous party! And I just want you to know that I am completely in my element. You see, I really love the 20s, not to mention blues, which I love even more.'

'Why, thank you, Nina,' replied the Big Boss. 'It's so good to hear that. Could I ask you to repeat those comments to Maria and Flavie? They've organised the entire evening and I'm sure your positive feedback will make them very happy too.'

Given that as a general rule of thumb it is always better to do as the Big Boss asks, the Jazz-Girl was more than happy to comply with his request as she went in search of the organisers and once again expressed her enthusiasm for the evening:

'Maria, Flavie, please allow me to thank you most profusely for this party. It's truly exceptional. '

She then went on to explain that blues happened to be her great passion in life which was just one of the reasons why she was having such a good time.

A conversation on this latter topic ensued and, after a few minutes, the Jazz-Girl enquired:

'By the way, just out of curiosity, did you think of bringing in any musicians for the evening?'

'Yes, we did,' replied Maria. 'But, unfortunately, we didn't manage to find any in time.'

It was at this precise moment that the Jazz-Girl found herself in that situation which happens to us all at some time or another. Indeed, she herself had already been there on several previous occasions so, unfortunately, she knew the scenario only too well. It was the one in which she was about to be carried away by the party atmosphere and consequently talk far too much. At such times, the words would just seem to keep on popping out independently of her brain which would, in contrast, be doing its serious best to send her the warning signals required to put a very necessary brake on all free-flowing verbal activity.

And so it was that, casually throwing caution to the wind, she dropped the following gem into the conversation:

'What a shame! It's a *real* shame that you didn't come to me. You see, I myself happen to be a blues pianist.'

To this, Maria replied by simply stating:

'But, Nina, you don't seem to understand. We don't actually *have* a piano here on the premises.'

Now, with all the confidence she had recently gained due to the consumption of one or two (possibly nearer five!) glasses of Champagne, the Jazz-Girl was hardly likely to allow herself to be deterred by a tiny little detail such as the complete and utter absence of any appropriate instrument for playing blues, for she was currently on a roll and there was absolutely no holding her. In fact, it would be safe to say that presently she was feeling truly invincible. And this in spite of the fact that her inner voice had just switched to red alert mode and was desperately screaming loudly and clearly at her: "No, no, *no*!! Please, just don't go there!" Sadly, there was nothing for it. The Jazz-Girl continued in a manner which was even more assured than ever, as she asserted:

'You know, it's actually really easy to hire a piano for an evening. On top of which, a grand piano is such a beautiful instrument that it definitely adds to the elegance of any reception room. You should also bear in mind that I work with other musicians so I could bring in a guitarist and a saxophonist as well, should you be interested.'

'Really?' replied Maria. 'That's so good to know. We're always on the lookout for new ideas. And I do like your suggestion very much. It's different. In fact, it's quite original. So, thanks, Nina. Thank you very much. We'll be in touch in the near future.'

As she walked away, the Jazz-Girl began to wonder just *what* precisely had possessed her to make such a ridiculous suggestion! She knew only too well that she would be utterly incapable of performing in front of her husband's colleagues for the simple reason that she had known them all for many years and, while they were always really nice in a social context, she was also well aware that the lawyers' world was anything but meek and mild. This meant that if ever she were to mess up such a performance, her husband's colleagues would never let him, or her, forget it. The scene was already playing out before her very eyes. Every day they would send her husband links to clips on YouTube showing child prodigies performing superb blues improvisations quite probably from the tender age of two. In such circumstances, they would take the joke for a real spin. Why, oh why, had she just not kept her big mouth shut?

Endeavouring to reassure herself, the Jazz-Girl decided that her husband's law firm was highly unlikely to hold another blues-themed reception in the near future because their approach was to vary the types of entertainment they laid on. Furthermore, Maria had quite probably said she would contact her out of mere politeness. Yes, surely that must be it. Consequently, reasoned the Jazz-Girl, the chances of this conversation ever giving rise to anything at all were very slim indeed.

A few months later…

By the time the Jazz-Girl took her husband's call, as she stood outside the perfume factory in the South of France, her attitude was radically different. In the meantime, she had had her accident and this unfortunate incident had served as a powerful reminder that, in life, it is impossible to know what lies around the corner, and that it is therefore extremely important to enjoy whatever the present brings. Regarding her piano playing, she was thus more motivated than ever before – driven by a burning desire to share her music and highly unlikely to refuse the slightest opportunity to perform in public. And it has to be said that here she was indeed looking at a truly wonderful, golden opportunity…

Eager to have a maximum amount of information at the ready, on the way home from the excursion the Jazz-Girl called the piano tuning department to enquire about the possibility of hiring a grand piano for an evening; although she had casually asserted at the office party that it was "really easy" to do this, in reality she had no idea whether it was even possible! The pleasant voice was swift to reassure her, however, by duly giving her the rates, including transportation and tuning, of the various instruments available for hire.

The next day, upon her return to Paris, the Jazz-Girl received a call from Maria who concluded their long discussion by asking the Jazz-Girl to send in a demonstration of her work together with a detailed proposal. In a bid to strike while the iron was hot, the Jazz-Girl immediately prepared an email in which she pointed out that, while any grand piano would do, a Steinway would be a definite asset. She also included the details of her piano tuner, explaining that if she were to be hired for the evening, it would be good to have François Pradel on board because he knew her demanding ear like nobody else.

Once she had finished writing her email, the Jazz-Girl could hardly wipe the smile off her face. The idea of spending an evening playing blues on a top-quality piano in the sumptuous setting of this prestigious law firm was nothing short of a genuinely magical dream. Furthermore, if ever her recommendations were to be accepted, she would find herself performing in the best conditions possible, of the type usually only granted to world-class musicians, for here it should be pointed out that any professional concert pianist who *owns* a Steinway actually *has* a Steinway concert piano placed at his or her disposal wherever he or she performs in the world. As for the absolute crème de la crème, these pianists even go so far as to tour with their personal piano tuner in tow. So, arguably, the Jazz-Girl did indeed appear to be setting somewhat grand terms and conditions for her future piano bar performance. That said, "nothing venture, nothing gained" being her general mantra, she was prepared to go to whatever lengths were necessary to make a success of this evening, which for the time being was merely a concept – a suggestion, which remained to be confirmed since several question marks currently loomed over it...

The initial crucial hurdle would be for the events committee to give its approval regarding the demonstration of the Jazz-Girl's music. Next, it would be up to the Big Boss to accept the general idea. And, finally, the proposed package would have to fit in with the set budget.

Given, then, the numerous hoops through which her proposal had yet to go in order for it to be taken on board, the Jazz-Girl sincerely believed that the chances of obtaining a green light on this were actually very slim indeed.

In reality, however, the first stage was accomplished with relative ease: the four members of the events committee gave a rapid and definite thumbs-up to the Jazz-Girl's demonstration by writing to say how much they had genuinely enjoyed it. As for the two remaining conditions – approval from the Big Boss and the question of the budget – since these were beyond her control, all that remained now was for the Jazz-Girl to set about preparing her repertoire.

A few days later, the Jazz-Girl left Paris to spend the rest of the summer in Normandy with her daughter and her son (who had just returned from his sailing course), the plan being that her husband would join them there for weekends until such time as he began his annual leave in August.

During this period, the Jazz-Girl proceeded to work on a full and complete repertoire. Still in the process of rehabilitating her hand, further to her accident, she found herself obliged to work for relatively short periods of time, with an anti-inflammatory patch on her hand and a compression bandage wound around her little finger. In spite of these restrictions, however, it was an intensely creative period for her. That year, Normandy was experiencing an unusually hot summer. Indeed, the weather was more of the type to be found in the South of France. Consequently, every afternoon she would seek refuge from the heat and go inside the house to immerse herself in her private, secret world of jazz. And so it was that, methodically and assiduously, she went through all the standards she had studied with her teacher and, in addition to these, she learnt a whole new set of pieces with a view to creating a repertoire lasting several hours.

In parallel, she completed her preparation by learning several relaxation techniques specifically chosen to combat stage fright, just in case!

Upon her return to Paris the following September, the date of the reception was duly confirmed and it was at this point that Keith Jarrett decided to resurface...

For a few days now, the Jazz-Girl had been broaching, somewhat tentatively with family and friends alike, the subject of the musical adventure that lay before her. And whenever she did so, she would generally be met with a question which she found extremely unsettling:

'Do you think you'll get stage fright?'

Far from Paris, in the comfortable cocoon of the ivory tower that was in fact her Normandy cottage, the Jazz-Girl had felt quite confident that she would be able to tame her stage fright sufficiently to pull off her performance at the reception. Two essential factors lay at the base of her confidence. First of all, musically and mentally speaking her preparation had been extremely thorough. Secondly, it was not as if she were being asked to give a concert performance. On the contrary, all she was required to do was play background piano bar music in a large reception room which would most likely be full of lawyers either talking business development with each other or, failing that, consulting their mobile phones to keep an eye on their latest deals. In other words, her "public" was, at best, only vaguely going to listen to her piano playing and this was something she found extremely reassuring.

That said, it would only take the mere mention of the dreaded words "stage fright" for her to find herself completely paralysed with fear – patently aware of the enormity of the challenge facing her.

Consequently, in an attempt to control the sheer and utter feelings of terror that would at such times rise within her, the Jazz-Girl grew accustomed to responding with an air of exaggerated confidence, desperately hoping that the outward display of such a sentiment would enable her to feel the same inwardly. And it was this very tactic she chose to adopt when *the* question arose once more during a conversation with some friends who apparently had no qualms whatsoever about giving free rein to their thoughts on the subject:

'Nina, it's great that you're going to perform in public but how on earth will you cope with stage fright?'

'Yeah, let's face it, accepting to perform in front of your husband's colleagues is really quite something!'

'I know I couldn't do it...'

'Me neither. You're taking one hell of a risk, you know. All I can say is good luck to you!'

Thanks a bunch, guys, thought the Jazz-Girl. *That's just soooo what I needed to hear. Nice one!* Then, endeavouring to get a grip, she said to herself: *Come on, Nina, you can do this. You're equal to the task.*

And so it was that, in "confident Jazz-Girl mode", she gave the following reply:

'What you have to understand is that stage fright is just not an option for me. It doesn't even figure in my vocabulary. Performing in public is all about concentration. And when I concentrate on each chord as it appears, the rest actually follows quite naturally.'

Now on a roll, she decided to reinforce the point with increasing amounts of conviction – the very opposite of what she was really feeling deep down within her:

'And in any case, all I have to do is sing the notes to myself as I'm about to play them and that way I know that I can produce precisely *the* sound I wish to hear on the piano.'

In response, her friends all chorused excitedly:

'Brilliant! It's bloody brilliant! That's *exactly* what Keith Jarrett does!'

In the face of such an absurd comparison, the Jazz-Girl burst out laughing, concluding:

'Well, there you go. If it's good enough for *the* Keith Jarrett, then I see no reason why it shouldn't work for *the* Nina Somerville!'

𝄞

A few days later, the Jazz-Girl called the piano tuning department to talk about the forthcoming event and explain to the pleasant voice precisely why the stakes were so very high:

'My husband's law firm is due to hire a Steinway from you for a reception at which I shall be playing. Do you think it would be possible to book François Pradel to tune the piano on the day? I know that asking for my personal tuner might seem a bit over the top but it would really help me to have him on board. The fact of matter is that he knows my ear like the back of his hand and I want to do everything within my power to make a success of the evening. You see, I'm going to be playing in front of all my husband's colleagues and I'd really hate to harm his career by messing up the evening with a poor performance!'

Genuinely amused by the situation, the pleasant voice started to laugh as she replied:

'Don't worry, Madame Somerville. I'm on the case and I'll get back to you just as soon as I have an answer.'

Barely had the Jazz-Girl hung up when she received a call to confirm that François Pradel had indeed been booked to tune the piano on the day of the reception.

Shortly afterwards, François sent her the following message of support:

"Dear Nina,

I'm utterly thrilled to know that I have been chosen to prepare the piano for your special evening. Rest assured, I shall work twice as hard as usual to provide you with a piano that would make Keith Jarrett jealous ☺!"

There he was again! In fact, these days the American icon never seemed to be very far away…

𝄞

The big day was now approaching. Unfortunately, however, it appeared to be doing this at something of a snail's pace. Worse still, during the week leading up to it, hitherto unknown quantities of adrenalin started to flow through the Jazz-Girl's veins, entire kilos melted off her frame through sheer nervous energy, and hours of sleep became something of a rare commodity.

Thankfully, the day of the reception finally arrived and having over the course of the previous days depleted a lifetime's worth of stress, the Jazz-Girl now felt remarkably calm. She was ready.

It was early afternoon when the law firm rang her to confirm that the piano had been duly delivered and that she could come in to rehearse.

Half an hour later, upon her arrival, she was accompanied to an absolutely sumptuous reception room which opened out onto a magnificent garden.

Once she saw the piano, she felt completely at ease, as if she were at home. Eager to test it out, she set to work immediately.

She had only just begun, however, when she became aware of the presence of another person in the room. As she looked up from the piano, she saw a face which was very familiar to her. It was François Pradel, grinning from ear to ear as if he were just as excited as she was at the prospect of this evening.

A disc jockey then arrived and began to set up his equipment while the caterer started to cover the tables with pristine white cloths.

Suddenly, there was so much traffic in the room that the Jazz-Girl decided to retreat upstairs to her husband's office in order to leave François to work in peace.

One hour later, she came back down again.

François had almost finished and was cleaning the piano, making it gleam resplendently, when he asked her *the* question:

'Do you think you'll get stage fright?'

Remembering the conversation with her friends, she started to laugh as she responded with:

'Definitely not! Everything is going to be just fine because, according to my friends, I happen to apply exactly the same tactics to my performances as Keith Jarrett does to his!'

She then went on to explain why she had made this comment, before admitting that in reality stage fright was a real problem for her but somehow, whenever she sat at the piano, she felt quite calm and this feeling was inspiring her with confidence.

François confessed that he felt exactly the same. As she had witnessed at their previous meeting, the mere thought of being booked to tune for a major artist such as Keith Jarrett would suffice to leave him filled with fear. When seated at the piano, however, as master of all he surveyed, it was he and he alone who called the shots and this feeling would usually serve to radically eliminate any feelings of nervousness.

This brief exchange with her piano tuner, a man whose passion for the king of all instruments was equal to hers, did the Jazz-Girl an enormous amount of good. As a result, when she sat down to continue her rehearsal she discovered that her fingers suddenly seemed unusually sure of themselves on the keyboard. Keen to preserve this newfound confidence for her performance that evening, she thus took the wise decision to cut her rehearsal short; having played for just ten brief minutes, she left the law firm and went home to get changed for the reception.

𝄞

At precisely seven o'clock she returned, eager to enjoy every last second of this long-awaited evening. It was an experience that was to turn out to be truly magical on every single level: the piano was an absolute gem – a shining example of musical perfection; the acoustics

of the reception room were excellent; as for the buoyant party mood…
well… this apparently served to heighten the Jazz-Girl's playing.
Consequently, that night she gave what could only be deemed, by a
very long chalk, to be her best performance to date; she played every
single note as if it were her last and even the most difficult passages
of her arrangements, which had always posed a problem during her
numerous rehearsals, now seemed to flow.

As agreed with the organisers, she performed for three sessions,
each lasting three-quarters of an hour, and during the breaks the
compliments just kept on coming: from the caterer, the disc jockey,
her husband's colleagues and ultimately the Big Boss himself! As for
the Jazz-Girl's husband, in his case no words were actually necessary.
Beaming a smile at her every now and then from across the extremely
crowded reception room, he spent the entire evening wearing a look
of immense unbridled pride that said it all.

By the end of the evening, completely transported by the amazingly
positive reaction of her "public", the Jazz-Girl found herself floating
around, somewhere high up in the sky, on a large white cloud of
musical euphoria.

The next day she had the immense pleasure of receiving several
messages of thanks from the law firm, which she took as clear
confirmation that the events of the previous evening must have been
real after all!

Eager to share her joy, she wrote to her piano tuner to express her
sincere thanks for his superb preparation of the piano, before going
on to tell him all about her wonderful musical adventure which she
described as a moment of pure unadulterated bliss, rendered all the
more magical due to its very ephemeral nature.

Keith Jarrett, on the other hand, was apparently anything but
ephemeral! On the contrary, it appeared that he was quite determined
to stick around as once again he popped up in the Jazz-Girl's life…

When François Pradel replied, having first congratulated her
profusely, he could not resist concluding his message with the
following tease:

*"Before you know it, the concert halls will be queuing up to book
you. Do keep me informed so I can invite Keith!"*

That did it. There was nothing for it. It was time to face facts. Keith
Jarrett had never ceased to make his presence felt – from the time
François had last come to tune the piano, right up until the day of

her extraordinary musical dream. And now he was back again. So it seemed that the Jazz-Girl had no other option but to welcome him into her inner, private circle. In fact, it appeared that it was the very least she could do given that this giant of the music industry had now become so much a part of her life that apparently they were already on first name terms, for had not François quite simply referred to him as "Keith"?

And that, dear readers, is precisely how the king of jazz improvisation, *the* Keith Jarrett, Mister Köln Concert himself, became from that day forward the *official*, albeit virtual, friend of the Jazz-Girl and her piano tuner; a very dear friend who was to make regular guest appearances in their written exchanges and who would subsequently provide them with an infinite source of hilarious running jokes.

Furthermore, it is important to acknowledge that Keith Jarrett had the immense honour of becoming their special friend, their music buddy if you will, long before these two piano enthusiasts actually became friends with each other.

However, should you wish to find out just *how* the Jazz-Girl and her piano tuner managed to make the transition from their essentially professional, albeit amicable, relationship of service provider and client to one of true friendship, well, for that all you have to do is simply keep on reading...

The Night the Piano Sang Out of Tune

In response to a cry for help which she had recently received from her guitarist friend Benjamin, the Jazz-Girl was working hard to put together a repertoire solely comprised of love songs – "Blue Moon", "Plaisir d'Amour", a jazz version of "Bella figlia dell'amore" from Verdi's *Rigoletto*, and many, many more.

A few days previously, the owner of a large restaurant had approached Benjamin to see if he would be prepared to play at the forthcoming Saint Valentine's dinner. Now, while Benjamin was generally delighted to accept any "gig" that came his way, the problem with this particular request was that he would have been required to play for five hours non-stop – a true marathon, in other words – and irrespective of whether or not *he* felt up to it, he was practically certain that his fingers were not. Benjamin had therefore made the following suggestion: he would bring his digital keyboard along so that the Jazz-Girl could fill in with some piano blues whenever he needed to take a break.

Given her increasing desire to perform in public, the Jazz-Girl was, for her part, utterly delighted to have received this request and, entering wholeheartedly into the spirit, decided that it would be a good idea to include a tango[14] in her repertoire, the idea being to create just the right mood for the numerous lovebirds expected at the dinner by performing this piece with her guitarist friend at the beginning of the evening on a slow sensual rhythm.

By the time their pre-dinner rehearsal drew to a close, the Jazz-Girl and Benjamin were starting to feel rather pleased with themselves, if not a tad smug. They'd nailed the tango in a single take and were confident that, with this particular performance, they

---

14   You can listen to this piece on my YouTube channel. Just enter: Nicky Gentil.

would be sure to create, from the very outset, one hot atmosphere that night!

Or so they thought…

In actual fact, the temperature cooled down somewhat dramatically before it had even had time to rise, when the owner of the restaurant took it upon himself to pour cold water all over their best-laid plans, by announcing the day before the dinner that he no longer wanted the pianist or, more specifically, the keyboard; it was his considered opinion that the small space required to accommodate this instrument could be put to better use by squeezing in one more table with a view to receiving yet another intertwined couple.

Quite clearly, he had missed the basic point that to squash clients together like sardines was not necessarily the best way to create a romantic atmosphere!

Oh well, never mind. His loss, thought the Jazz-Girl.

On the other hand, she had to admit that it was slightly her loss too; she had really been looking forward to playing that evening.

Her disappointment was, however, to be short-lived because her husband, in order to console her, had a surprise up his sleeve: a reservation for an operatic dinner for two.

$$\text{\clef treble}$$

The Jazz-Girl and her husband had discovered the Bel Canto restaurant a few years previously – an establishment that employed trained opera singers whose role it was to perform great operatic arias, accompanied by a professional pianist, in between serving the clients.

Consequently, that night, any lingering regrets that the Jazz-Girl may still have had about her own performance being cancelled were now about to be eliminated by the glorious music of Verdi, Mozart and Offenbach.

From the moment they entered the restaurant, the Jazz-Girl and her husband could tell they were in for a wonderful evening. As on previous occasions, they were immediately struck by the splendour of the décor. A perfect expression of the magical mood of a night out at the opera, the large room – with its mezzanine level, its Murano chandeliers and its plush walls draped with sumptuous velvet costumes – looked more like a theatre than a dinner venue.

On the ground floor, an absolutely superb grand piano took centre stage.

It was indeed a truly exquisite evening. The singers put on an excellent performance, accompanied by an exceptionally gifted Chinese pianist whose playing sang gracefully due to a particularly light and delicate touch.

Towards the end of the evening, once the opera singers had performed their final song – "Brindisi" from Verdi's *La Traviata*, with the entire restaurant singing along and raising glasses of Prosecco – the pianist, a Chopin specialist, began to play some of the great Polish composer's waltzes.

For her part, the Jazz-Girl found herself savouring every last note of this performance. Although she herself had given up classical piano many years previously, she always took great pleasure in listening to others interpret it, never ceasing to marvel at the contrast between the sound of this particular genre and jazz; to her, it was as if, depending on the type of music being played, the piano had the capacity to be two completely different instruments.

Then something quite strange began to happen: a somewhat surprising auditory experience...

While the Jazz-Girl continued to enjoy the pianist's superb performance, at the same time she began to notice that certain notes in the middle octaves of the piano were *just* beginning to go out of tune; the said notes appeared to have slightly lost their unison and were now producing the dreaded meowing sound. That said, she wondered whether this might not be but a mere figment of her imagination, for could it really be possible for her ear to detect such slight discrepancies when she was seated so far from the piano? Admittedly, she had often heard of sound engineers and piano tuners whose hearing was so precise that they were capable of detecting the slightest imperfection in the sound of an instrument, even in a large concert hall, but she also knew full well that such professionals were legendary in the music industry, revered as a breed apart, as the sound elite.

And so it was that the Jazz-Girl, adopting an exaggeratedly self-satisfied look, proudly announced to her husband that he should feel honoured because he happened to find himself in the presence of a legend! She then went on to explain the reason behind her irony: she *just* could not believe it possible for her to detect, in the manner of a professional, slight imperfections in the unisons when she was seated so far from the piano. Indeed, as she and her husband were on the mezzanine level, they were actually as far away from the instrument as it was possible to be.

Her husband, on the other hand, took her assessment seriously because he was well aware that numerous professionals – musicians, piano tuners and music teachers alike – had often remarked on the rare precision of his wife's hearing. He was, moreover, used to joking that his wife came equipped with bat's ears, an expression which had always made their children laugh when they had been of an age to take it literally.

It was on the basis of her husband's reaction, that the Jazz-Girl became curious to see if she might just be right about the state of this instrument. And the only way to find out for sure would be for her to test it...

In the past, the Jazz-Girl and her husband had noticed that the musicians in the Bel Canto restaurant were generally delighted, and even quite touched, whenever clients approached them with questions because it meant they were taking a particular interest in their performance. Consequently, they had no qualms about going up to speak to the pianist as they were on their way out.

There were now only about ten clients left and the pianist was in the process of tidying her sheet music away. The Jazz-Girl spent some time talking to her and congratulating her profusely on her performance, before going on to explain that she herself was a pianist but, in her case, of the jazz variety. She then started to question the classical pianist as to the piano and the frequency of the tunings and finally she plucked up the courage to ask her if it would be all right to play something.

To her great delight, the classical pianist said yes.

The Jazz-Girl sat down at the piano and began to play her blues arrangement of "Auld Lang Syne". It was the perfect piece for testing the unisons in the medium range of the keyboard. She knew precisely how these notes should sound when the piano was in tune, especially as it was this very piece that she would generally use to check the state of her own piano. In fact, so accustomed was she to this particular exercise that she was by now capable of playing the piece blindfold – which was probably just as well in the circumstances...

Barely had she begun when an elderly man walked past the piano declaring, loudly and clearly, in what could only be described as an utterly scathing tone:

'It's hardly the delicate touch of the Chinese pianist, is it?'

The Jazz-Girl felt as if she had just received *the* most enormous kick in the teeth.

Objectively, she knew this man was entirely right. Her touch on the piano would never hold a candle to that of the professional pianist. On top of which, she was well aware of her technical limitations and had never claimed to be a virtuoso. Be that as it may, she also knew what this man apparently did not: that jazz playing requires a very different technique and *that* includes a very different touch. So, while she was more than happy to accept the veracity of this man's comment, she was actually very angry about his behaviour. The bottom line was that it was extremely tactless of him, downright rude in fact, to have uttered this comment out loud in such a way as to be sure she would hear it.

Determined not to be put off by his insensitive words, the Jazz-Girl carried on playing and actually just got better and better; as any live performer knows, anger can actually help a musician to let go on his or her instrument which, in turn, heightens the performance. And as she continued to play, she also continued to remind herself of her golden rule…

Over the years, the Jazz-Girl had worked hard to overcome the crippling stage fright which had struck her in adulthood. Consequently, she had come up with a set of rules which she now only needed to repeat to herself before playing in public, in order to pull off a performance. These rules were astonishingly simple, pretty basic even, such as: *take your time, concentrate on every bar, of every piece, right down to the very last note, beware of the pieces you know you can play blindfold, don't allow yourself to be carried away by the music –* this last comment being a reference to a classic trap, a sure-fire way to mess up a performance. She had other key phrases up her sleeve but among all the little pieces of advice she would regularly give herself, a golden rule reigned supreme: *whenever you play in public, you have to leave your ego behind, preferably at home.*

This last rule was the product of several disappointing incidents to which she had been witness in some of the Paris jazz clubs. On more than a few occasions she had been utterly dismayed to observe certain members of the public behaving in a really disrespectful manner. These were the type of people whose sole aim, once in the club, was apparently to sneer unreservedly at the various performances of the highly gifted jazz musicians present. This type of behaviour would leave her perplexed as to why these people had actually gone to the trouble of purchasing a ticket. It would also cause her to reason that if major artists such as these had to put up with disparaging comments from the public, then she should just accept that this was something that went with the territory and therefore cast aside all ego-related concerns by trying to avoid taking any negative comments too personally.

There was, however, one slight hitch. That night, her ego, unaware that she might actually play, had apparently followed her to the restaurant and was now bitterly regretting its unintended transgression!

Be that as it may, the Jazz-Girl somehow managed to bring her fragile ego under control just long enough to wind up her performance. And once she had finished playing, to her genuine surprise, all those present – clients and staff alike – burst into rapturous applause.

Observing the scene from above, Apollo was smiling. He was almost satisfied with his work, but not quite. He too had been extremely irritated by the elderly man's insensitive behaviour and whenever he toiled to organise a wonderful evening for the music lovers of this planet, he was not prepared to allow one of his children to leave under a cloud of disappointment. At times like these, he would have dearly loved to be able to call upon the services of a God designated to inflict punishments upon people who were so very rude. To his utter dismay, however, no such God existed because, understandably, none of his colleagues had any wish to take on the job!

Fortunately, Apollo knew just how to take care of the members of his family, something he generally did with extraordinary strength and power. And so it was that, in order to help his little Jazz-Girl forget the words of the elderly man once and for all, he undertook to lavish her with two wonderful gifts which came in the form of two quite unexpected compliments.

As the applause subsided, the classical pianist took the Jazz-Girl completely by surprise by heaping praise upon her:

'That was truly magnificent. Thank you so much. I really envy you. I do wish I could play like that. I would genuinely love to be able to play jazz but I am quite incapable of it.'

Next, it was the tenor's turn to congratulate her. He came charging back into the room, flashing a teasing smile at the classical pianist on his way, to exclaim:

'I just knew it. I was convinced it wasn't our pianist playing. She would be quite incapable of playing like that. That was really wonderful. Bravo!'

The restaurant pianist accepted these comments with good grace. And she could indeed afford to be generous because her performance had been nothing short of superb.

The Jazz-Girl, for her part, was utterly delighted to receive such compliments from two professionals; by complimenting her like this, the tenor and the pianist seemed to be saying that they considered her to be one of them, regardless of the discrepancies in their respective levels of talent and the types of music they chose to interpret.

As for Apollo, he was at last beginning to feel satisfied. Thanks to these compliments, his little Jazz-Girl was now blissfully happy, especially as she had also just received a third gift into the bargain: the results of her test...

The fact of the matter was that by daring to play the piano in the operatic restaurant that night, the Jazz-Girl had not actually been intending to display any particular pianistic skills. She had, on the contrary, simply wished to find out if she were putting the ear, with which Apollo had blessed her at birth, to good use. More specifically, she had wished to find out if she had managed to accomplish, just for once in her life, that which the mythical, legendary ears of the music industry accomplish on a regular basis: an accurate assessment of the piano's sound from a distance. And that evening, it was this very rare auditory experience that constituted in her eyes – or in this case in her ears! – *the* best reward possible.

The thing is, it had only taken her a short performance to confirm that she had indeed been absolutely right about the state of the piano. In the medium range, practically all the notes were starting to lose their unison. Consequently, this instrument could have benefitted from a visit from François Pradel because it actually required quite a bit of work doing on it.

And so her simple conclusion was that while the opera singers with their sublime voices, and the highly gifted pianist with her exquisite playing had together provided *the* most superb entertainment for the entire duration of the dinner, that night the piano, for its part, had all the while been singing out of tune.

The Incredible Story of the Piano
Life Saver

From time to time, in addition to his usual job of tuning, François Pradel would be required to perform a more specific task on the piano. And it was generally on these occasions that the Jazz-Girl would discover *just* how surprising the piano tuning profession could be.

Such was the case the day her tuner decreed that it was time to clean the instrument's interior. That morning, upon his arrival, he announced:

'Okay, so, today I'm going to have to borrow your vacuum cleaner and I shall also be needing a duster.'

Wow! It really is true, thought the Jazz-Girl to herself. *There are men walking this planet who know about the existence of such objects. What's more, here is a man who even wants to borrow them so he can actually use them. Un-believable!*

Even more surprisingly, it turned out that François had a *very* precise idea as to the type of duster he required. The first one was rejected on the grounds of being "too soft and fluffy", causing the Jazz-Girl to produce an entire sack load of dusters so that he could choose one for himself. François eventually found just what he was looking for and, pulling the chosen duster lengthways and widthways, he then proceeded to go into raptures about the quality of his find:

'Oh yes. Oh yes. This one is absolutely perfect! The cotton is slightly abrasive which is *exactly* what I want. You know, in actual fact, I'm only going to need to tear off a little strip but… the material is such good quality… Would it be okay if I were to keep this duster?'

It was just getting better and better! Clearly, François did not use dusters on an exceptional basis; on the contrary, he wished to keep this one precisely because he regularly had recourse to this household item!

Now genuinely amused by the unlikely scene that was playing out before her eyes, the Jazz-Girl responded with:

'Seriously? You want me to make you a present of a cotton duster? You know, I think I can run to that. After all, we in the Somerville family can be really quite generous when we want to be!'

Taking the teasing in good part, he flashed her a wide smile, which encouraged her to continue by casually announcing, as if it were the most natural thing in the world:

'Actually, it's hardly surprising that the material is such good quality. You see, whenever I want to create a stock of dusters, I just go and rip up a few of my husband's shirts.'

Upon seeing the wide smile rapidly disappear from François' face, the Jazz-Girl surmised that her tuner was now, in all likelihood, concerned about the potential survival of the elegant black cotton shirt he was wearing that day, which incited her to qualify her words with:

'Obviously I mean the shirts that are wearing out. Rest assured, your duster is most definitely *not* the product of some violent marital dispute.'

These words had the desired effect; her piano tuner visibly relaxed to the extent that, as a mischievous glint appeared in her eyes, she found herself quite unable to refrain from muttering under her breath:

'At least not that one, anyway...'

Clearly unsure as to quite how he should take these comments, François decided it was high time to get down to the serious business of cleaning the piano's interior.

The first step was to take the instrument apart, which he did by removing the frame of wood surrounding the keyboard in order subsequently to remove the action[15]. So far, so good – the Jazz-Girl had already seen him do this whenever he did the voicing. The next step, on the other hand, was somewhat less reassuring. François placed the action – slightly too far away from the piano for the Jazz-Girl's liking – on the large table situated in the dining area of the room. And that was not all. Without so much as batting an eyelid, he then proceeded to remove all the piano's keys, while at the same time coolly announcing his professional plans: he was considering doing a year's training at Steinway & Sons, Shanghai, and was keen to have the Jazz-Girl's opinion on this.

15 See footnote on page 10 for a definition of the action.

Try as she might to take an interest in his future, she was in fact somewhat distracted by the immense surge of panic currently rising within her for her piano, her treasure, her baby, had just been dismantled into a thousand little pieces, which were now scattered all over her sitting room! Could he not see that she was really struggling to maintain a semblance of self-control? What if he were to make a mistake and put the keys back in the wrong order?[16] As a result, she got out her camera and started to take photographs of the various parts of her piano, in the bizarre belief that a mere visual record would somehow guarantee a positive outcome when it came to putting all these parts back together to form one single instrument!

It was now the piano tuner's turn to be genuinely amused by the situation and he leapt at the chance to retaliate:

'Just imagine if I were to be called out now to deal with a concert hall emergency.'

Observing the look of horror appear on his client's face, he immediately backtracked with:

'If it's of any reassurance to you, I can tell you that I have *never* received an urgent request when cleaning a piano's interior.'

As with her words to him a few minutes previously, these words too had the desired effect – the Jazz-Girl visibly relaxed. They ultimately had a similar consequence, for her tuner could not resist adding:

'But it would be funny, wouldn't it?'

One all!

In addition to the sheer entertainment value of their banter, from a musical point of view the morning turned out to extremely enlightening for the Jazz-Girl. François used the opportunity to teach her all sorts of things about the internal workings of her instrument, taking the time to show her precisely what happens inside a piano whenever, on the outside, the simple act of pressing down a key is performed. This, in turn, enabled the Jazz-Girl to observe that her piano, even when completely dismantled, was a genuine work of art.

One hour later, with the instrument's interior now thoroughly clean, the tuner put all the bits of this sophisticated jigsaw puzzle back together and, once again, a beautiful piano proudly embellished the Jazz-Girl's sitting room with, thank goodness, all the keys in the right order! He then set about tuning it and by the end of the morning the piano was absolutely perfect, as good as new. Furthermore, the Jazz-

16　All the keys are actually numbered.

Girl now also understood precisely why cleaning its interior had been necessary; the touch was consequently much lighter.

This type of additional work was something François would carry out about once a year but one day he was obliged to do a specific job on the piano once and for all.

It was a job that would turn out to be unique – in every sense of the word!

$\oint$

The Jazz-Girl's piano had been stable for a good while now, staying resolutely in tune for several months at a time. Consequently, François had decided to take it to the next level by exerting additional pressure on the tuning pins with a view to exploiting the instrument's full sound potential.

It was during this period that the piano began to sing with a sublimely pure voice, giving rise to compliments from all those heard it, including from a little girl of just ten years old.

Madeleine was one of Juliet's friends. And just like the majority of children who came to the Jazz-Girl's home, Madeleine, upon seeing the piano for the very first time, asked if she might be allowed to play something.

For her part, the Jazz-Girl was always more than happy to comply with this request for the simple reason that she found it reassuring to see that the children of this particular generation, growing up, as they were, in a world of screens, with their main concerns revolving around Facebook, Snapchat and Instagram, were also actually capable of taking an interest in an acoustic instrument which from an aesthetic point of view remained firmly anchored in the nineteenth century.

Past experience had taught the Jazz-Girl that what really interested members of the younger generation was the visual spectacle provided by the instrument's interior. With this in mind, she opened the grand lid of her piano and removed the music stand.

As for Madeleine, she sat down and, despite the fact that she had given up her piano lessons two years previously, gave an absolutely perfect rendition of "Für Elise".

Once she had finished playing, Madeleine, her eyes now wide open with surprise, proceeded to express herself on her performance... in the jargon of the moment!

It should at this stage be pointed out that this extremely well brought-up little girl – the pure product of an upper-middle class family – had just discovered the word "like" and apparently, she genuinely believed that to insert this word into every single sentence was the coolest thing imaginable.

And so it was that she proclaimed at the top of her voice:

'Like, it's amaaaaaazing!'

Next, she looked at her fingers as if she were not quite sure that they belonged to her hand, played a few notes and explained:

'Like, *all* I'm doing is this...'

Then she paused to point to the piano's interior, thereby indicating that she was indeed referring to the emerging sound, and exclaimed:

'And, like, the piano does *that!*'

Rounding off her comments in style – that is to say, her own particular style! – she subsequently managed to concoct a sentence which could not have been further removed from the Queen's English:

'Like, it's so kinda, well... like!'

The Jazz-Girl remained silent, content simply to smile at Madeleine, so moved was she by what she had just witnessed, for whatever this little girl lacked in verbal elegance, it was safe to say that the sheer poetry of this unique moment more than compensated for it. The fact of the matter was that the Jazz-Girl had become quite accustomed to seeing children take an interest in her piano, but with Madeleine it had been different; here, for the very first time, a child had actually commented on its sound. And Madeleine's magical reaction spoke volumes, not only about the incredible ear she clearly possessed but also about François' remarkable work. The piano was quite simply superb and was to remain so for six wonderful months.

Towards the end of this period, the piano started to go very slightly out of tune. There was no hurry. The Jazz-Girl could have waited. Nevertheless, taking into account François' guiding principle of "a little and often", she decided to book an appointment.

And besides, she herself, in her eagerness to maintain the intensely pure sound of the last few months, also preferred to act sooner rather than later.

Then, a week before her appointment, a strange phenomenon occurred. Practically overnight, the piano went completely out of tune. What a pity! Her tuner would not be able to hear the sublimely beautiful sound which had recently so graced her playing.

As far as François was concerned, the situation was much more worrying. When he tested the piano, he got quite a shock – a shock which he made no attempt to conceal from his client.

Shaking his head in frustration, he said:

'Nina, it's not right that the piano should sound like this. It must have got damp inside. I've done everything I can to stabilise it but I cannot do anything about climate-related issues. They're down to the room in which the piano stands.'

He then proceeded to give her a more precise explanation of the problem. It was in fact the wood forming the soundboard[17], which had become slightly damp and consequently more pliable. This, in turn, was causing the strings to loosen, resulting in the piano going out of tune.

In his view, it was time to monitor the room in order to clarify the specific cause of the damage. High levels of humidity, even if they remained stable, would be really bad news for the piano. Fluctuating levels of humidity would be simply disastrous.

The Jazz-Girl could scarcely believe her ears. Her tuner's comments were raising questions which she most definitely had no wish to address. Had Monsieur X been right all along? Was the room all wrong for the piano? If so, this would mean that her piano would never stay in tune for any length of time. It was an eventuality that she just could not bear to contemplate.

Once he had finished tuning the piano, François advised the Jazz-Girl to buy a hygrometer. Having vaguely looked at a few on the Internet, however, she rapidly abandoned her search. After all, her piano was back in perfect shape and since she had absolutely no wish to face facts, she decided to treat the recent problem incurred as a mere "minor" setback!

$$\oint$$

A few days later, the Jazz-Girl had an appointment with Zach (who in addition to being a piano teacher happened to be a highly accomplished saxophonist), having recently booked him for several

---

17 The soundboard is the plate of wood – beneath the strings on a grand piano and behind them on an upright piano.

sessions so that she could record some of her work. Over the previous weeks together they had chosen and rehearsed several jazz standards, Zach completing her improvisations with solos on his saxophone. And now, given that the piano had just been tuned, they decided that it was the perfect time to make the recordings.

That day, musically speaking, they were both on extremely good form. They started out well and just went up from there, every piece they played sounding better than the previous one. So much so that for a good two hours they barely spoke, content to communicate, in the manner of true jazz musicians, solely via facial expressions: a nod to say "last grid, then we wrap it up" here, a smile to say "wow, isn't this great" there.

Unfortunately, however, towards the end of their recording session, a small black cloud began to emerge on the horizon, tainting the euphoric atmosphere as it did so…

During the final takes, the Jazz-Girl began to detect slight imperfections in her piano. Two notes had apparently lost their unison and one of the base octaves sounded higher than it should. She could only agree with François. Something was indeed very wrong. Her piano should just not sound like that so soon after having been tuned.

And yet, still she did not want to believe it. As she played her last piece, she started to reassure herself. Surely she could put this all down to fatigue. Yes, that must be it. She was getting tired and this was quite probably modifying her perception of the sound.

Sadly, her state of denial was to be short-lived for it was not long before she received crystal-clear confirmation of the problem…

Once they'd finished recording, the Jazz-Girl noticed that Zach too was suffering from that deliciously healthy kind of tiredness that habitually follows a successful musical performance – accentuated in his case by the respiratory exertion required for playing the saxophone. Consequently, she offered to make some coffee before he left.

As she went into the kitchen to prepare it, Zach sat down at the piano and started to play a few bars of soft jazzy music. Usually she loved hearing him play but on this occasion she was horrified by what she heard. Even when standing relatively far away from her instrument, she was able to detect serious imperfections in its sound!

As soon as Zach left, the Jazz-Girl, who was now starting to panic somewhat, grabbed her phone and called the piano tuning department. The pleasant voice, realising that her client was clearly quite worried, offered her an appointment for the next morning – the very first slot of the day. Anxious as to how François Pradel would take this, the Jazz-Girl immediately sent him a text message to forewarn him, but this message went unanswered. Evidently, he was not very happy about being called back so soon. On the other hand, she had no choice. Her piano clearly had a problem, a major problem as it turned out, for during the next few hours it went completely out of tune. She simply could not believe it. Just how was it possible for her piano to be doing this? It was, after all, an extremely valuable top-quality instrument that had the good fortune to be regularly maintained by a highly talented tuner – a true artist who was one hundred per cent devoted to his profession.

$$\oint$$

The next morning, the Jazz-Girl began by offering her sincere apologies to François Pradel:

'I'm very sorry to have called you back so soon but the piano has turned into what I can only describe as a veritable house of cards.'

'A house of cards? That sounds really bad.'

'I agree. Yesterday, two notes lost their unison. Then suddenly a whole lot more appeared to follow suit.'

François sat down at the piano and did a few tests. Then, shaking his head in frustration, he turned to the Jazz-Girl and said:

'You're right. At least five octaves have gone out of tune. Nina, the last time I was here I told you that this is quite clearly a humidity-related problem. Have you bought a hygrometer?'

In her obstinate refusal to believe the humidity theory, she replied:

'No, I haven't, because as far as I'm concerned a top-quality instrument such as mine should stay in tune. And if the piano is this fragile, then the only possible explanation is that there is some kind of technical defect. In that case, it's up to Steinway & Sons either to replace it or to repair it. And my question to you is at what point do we have recourse to the guarantee? You see we've no time to lose. We need to identify the problem just as soon as possible because the guarantee is only valid for another eighteen months.'

Clearly irritated by his client's blatant refusal to accept his diagnosis, François tested the piano once more and, this time, making no effort to conceal his anger, raised his voice considerably to exclaim:

'Nina, I'm telling you, your piano should just *not* be doing this! I cannot see any technical defect whatsoever! This problem is *so* obviously humidity-related. And what *you* must understand is that *I've* done my job properly. In fact, I've spent far too long on your piano and, frankly, I've better things to do with my time!'

To say that the Jazz-Girl was thoroughly taken aback by these comments would be a gross understatement. She was not at all used to seeing François behave in this manner and, shocked by the violence of his reaction, she only just managed to refrain from saying: "I too have better things to do with my time!" She had, after all, spent an awful lot of time – and money, as it so happened – on the maintenance of her piano. Having had it tuned extremely frequently, she too considered that she had done all that was required of her and she was now highly concerned about the poor results arising from all their efforts. Furthermore, for François this was just one piano among many others, whereas for her it was much worse; this was her one and only piano, her treasure, her baby. Had she made a terrible mistake in buying this piano and, consequently, wasted a colossal amount of money on the pursuit of her wild dream?

Endeavouring to take some of the heat out of the situation, she paused to draw breath and then said:

'Please allow me to make myself extremely clear. Not for one second am I questioning your work. On the contrary, it was precisely with a view to making you understand just how much I value the finesse of your tuning and voicing that I sent you all those messages over the last few weeks, describing the sublimely pure sound which you have given to my piano. And I must say that, out of a personal regard for you, I felt really ill at ease about having to call the piano tuning department to complain yesterday. That is why I sent you a text message to forewarn you. I just felt so bad about it.'

These words seemed to have the desired effect. François calmed down and immediately started to reassure her:

'Nina, you did absolutely the right thing by calling. If *ever* there is a problem, you mustn't hesitate to let us know.'

Encouraged by his comments, the Jazz-Girl decided that it was now time to come clean about her true fear.

'You know, there are actually two reasons why I didn't buy a hygrometer. First of all, when I looked on the Internet there were so many of them that I just had no idea which type to choose. Secondly, and more importantly, I confess I have a real mental block about a possible humidity-related problem; if it turns out to be true, if the climatic conditions of this room are not right, then the piano will never really stay in tune. And then what will I do? It's not as if we can change the room. So, you see, this is why I'm clinging for dear life to the hypothesis of a technical defect and in any event we have to check this out because, as I told you, the guarantee is going to expire quite soon.'

'Well, the only way to eliminate the possibility of a humidity-related problem is to have a hygrometer,' replied François as he went on to advise her about the type she should buy.

Somewhat wearily, the Jazz-Girl noted the reference down, realising as she did so that she suddenly felt utterly exhausted. The fact of the matter was that the last few months had not been at all easy for her. Despite her "all's well that ends well" attitude, her accident – which had threatened to deprive her of her passion – had worn her out. Her hand was only just getting better and now her piano, her source of absolute musical happiness, was itself sick. So her passion was yet again under threat.

And in that instant she suddenly felt so tired of the entire matter that she now desired only one thing: to rid herself of the problem for good. Thus it was that she came up with a radical solution that shocked them both:

'You know, to be completely honest with you, I'm beginning to wonder whether, ultimately, this is just not the piano for me. When it starts going all over the place like this, I sometimes think that I would be better off buying something more basic – the type of piano that is less expressive but more solid and therefore less likely to go out of tune so easily. What do you think? Do you have any thoughts on this? Could you recommend a piano that would be more suited to my needs?'

She was now on the verge of tears and bitterly disappointed; her musical dream, which had started out in the manner of an idyllic fairy tale, was currently turning into a nightmare. In addition to this, she was under the distinct impression that François was no longer willing to support her in her quest for a perfect sound. His angry outburst had left her reeling.

This, however, was to overlook her tuner's innate sensitivity. Her unexpected words had produced a deeply pained expression on his face. And silence reigned for a good few minutes as, pensively, he contemplated the piano. Then, very softly, he began to play a beautiful piece of classical music.

Once he had finished playing, he looked her straight in the eye and said, in a voice laden with emotion:

'Nina, I'm begging you, please do not sell your piano. You have a magnificent instrument in your possession. We need to identify the problem and then, I promise you, I'll find a solution.'

Utter relief descended on the Jazz-Girl as she heard these comments; François appeared at last to be back on board with his kind, reassuring manner.

Fearing that she might now actually burst into tears, she left the room and against her better wishes ordered a hygrometer.

$$\text{\clefG}$$

Two days later, the piano was once again out of tune.

Worse still, during the week that followed, the hygrometer confirmed the precise nature of the problem; the humidity levels in the room were fluctuating at an alarmingly high rate and it was actually really easy to understand why. At the time, Paris was in the throes of one of the wettest springs on record. On the other hand, each heavy bout of torrential rain would generally be followed by a burst of brilliant sunshine. Now, it so happened that the Jazz-Girl's sitting room was south-facing; in other words, it was directly exposed to the sun at the hottest time of the day. As a result, the high level of humidity created by the rainfall would drop dramatically whenever the rain stopped and the sun came out. In short, it was the worst-case scenario for her instrument; in such conditions, even the world's most solid piano would struggle to stay in tune.

As far as the Jazz-Girl was concerned, there was only thing for it: she would just have to learn the basics of piano tuning herself in order to be able to correct the unisons, or at any rate the worst offenders, in between appointments with François.

With this in mind, she sat down at her computer and started to watch a lesson on YouTube.

Barely two minutes later, however, she totally abandoned the idea, for it had only taken this short time to cure her of the ridiculous notion that she might actually be capable of even so much as the basics of piano tuning. The bottom line was that the initial stages alone were extremely complex, technical and far beyond anything the Jazz-Girl was capable of comprehending. Furthermore, in parallel to the lesson, several warnings had flashed up on the screen; when amateurs attempt to tune their own piano they generally do more harm than good, which in turn renders the professional's job even more difficult.

At a loss as to what to do next, the Jazz-Girl stood up and stared vaguely out of the window – torrential rain was once again drenching the entire city – and there she remained, for a good while, simply contemplating the sky which, due to its incessant water-pouring, almost appeared to be rubbing it in; yes, her piano did indeed have a humidity-related problem!

Then as she continued to observe the large raindrops that were so generously watering the streets of Paris that night, a very simple but nevertheless brilliant idea quite suddenly dropped into her mind: if she were to be at all successful in her pursuit of a solution to the piano's problem, quite clearly she should start at the very beginning, by attempting to understand the problem properly.

So, for the second time that evening, she sat down at her computer but on this occasion entered just two words: pianos-humidity.

One little click on the mouse was all it took for the computer to produce several hundred thousand answers. However, only one of them was of any real interest to her – the very first one – which simply read: Piano Life Saver.

Curious to know more, she clicked on the link and immediately began to read.

The home page displayed the following explanation: "Ideally a piano should be in a room with a stable temperature and a permanent humidity level of forty-two per cent." In other words, it would be almost impossible to create ideal conditions for a piano.

In response to this, an American company had invented the Piano Life Saver – an ingenious system providing stable conditions for the instrument regardless of its environment, to be fitted, in the case of a grand piano, directly under the soundboard.

Surprisingly, this piece of equipment, whose noble mission (to save the life of a piano) was undeniably sophisticated, operated in a manner that was almost childlike in its simplicity; there was a bar to heat and dry the soundboard whenever it became too damp, and a water box to humidify the soundboard whenever it became too dry. A piano protected in this way from any fluctuating external factors could thereby stay in tune for longer periods of time.

As she read this information, the Jazz-Girl found herself in two minds – both intrigued and a tad sceptical. Could it be that, due to a mere click on the mouse, she had accidentally managed to stumble upon a magical solution, a perfect cure for all her piano's ills? If so, why had she *never* heard of this piece of equipment? François Pradel himself had never once mentioned it. So was it just some kind of tacky gadget? After all, the very idea of fitting an electrical device onto a beautiful grand piano did seem a bit like sacrilege.

Eager to have the pianist's view on this, she clicked on the "Client Feedback" heading and was interested to discover that the people who described their instruments before having a Piano Life Saver fitted could have been talking about her own, so similar were the problems raised.

Still bearing in mind the guiding principle that she should err on the side of caution, she then decided it was time to leave this website; all the information she was reading had after all been posted by the manufacturers of the system and it was important that she avoid being too easily influenced by the effective work of their marketing department; clearly, information from another source was required.

Pursuing her research, she managed to find a list of Paris tuners qualified to install Piano Life Savers. Interestingly, two of them worked for extremely prestigious piano dealers. A further website displayed a list of world famous pianists who used and recommended the system. And last but by no means least, one of Steinway's major competitors asserted that, in the case of pianos destined for countries with a tropical climate, the guarantee would be valid *only* if a Piano Life Saver were fitted.

Once again, she tried to remain cautious, reminding herself of the golden rule which she and her husband would regularly repeat to their children: "It's not because you've read something on the Internet that the information is actually true."

And yet, even if she were only to believe just half of what she had read, she had to admit that the arguments in favour of having a Piano Life Saver installed on her instrument were extremely convincing.

It was time to approach François Pradel for a professional opinion on the matter but this posed her with a major problem. His words – "I've got better things to do with my time" – were still ringing in her ears and she feared that her many questions would just end up irritating him even more.

Evidently, a diplomatic approach was required. Calling him was quite clearly out of the question. And even if she were to send him an email, given the current mood the mere sight of her name – "Oh, no, not her again!" – would probably annoy him to the point where he would decide to ignore the message.

In the end, however, sending an email did appear to be her best bet...

In order to show him that she did not intend to take up too much of his time, she thus wrote in the "Subject" box: "Just a quick question, please..." Then in an attempt to make him understand that she was not being difficult but that she was in fact deeply disappointed by the recent temperamental behaviour of her piano and that action was therefore required, she began her message in the following manner:

"Dear François,

I'm so sorry. It's me again. I'm compelled to write to you because the piano's recent problems continue to be a major source of disappointment. To put it another way, to me if feels as if cold water has just been poured all over my musical dream. As a result, I have started to look for a solution and am now taking the liberty of contacting you for your professional opinion on this matter..."

In spite of all her efforts at diplomacy, however, her email went unanswered and since the summer vacation was fast approaching, she decided not to chase the matter up. All issues relating to the piano would now just have to wait until her children went back to school in September.

Early July...

The Jazz-Girl and her daughter were on the second day of their girls' trip to Cannes. According to the locals, it was a bad summer – which actually translated into the wonderfully pleasant temperature of twenty-eight degrees and bright sunshine every day. In other words, the weather was just perfect after the Parisian monsoon, and their little break in the South of France was doing them an absolute power of good.

That morning, Juliet and her mother went on a guided tour of Cannes' old quarter and upon agreeing that they had thereby fulfilled their cultural "duty" for the day, they then decided to spend the afternoon at the hotel swimming pool.

In order to justify the indulgent treats she was planning on having at dinner that night, the Jazz-Girl began by swimming several lengths. Then just as she was settling down in a deckchair to read, her telephone rang. Presuming it would be her husband, she was surprised to see François Pradel's name flash up on the screen:

'Hello, Nina, how are you?'

'Oh hello, François. Actually, I couldn't be better. I'm on holiday in Cannes and I'm currently sitting by the pool, which is where I intend to stay for the rest of the afternoon, so life is pretty good!'

'In that case, I'm truly sorry to have disturbed you. When can I call you back?'

Kicking herself for having made him feel ill at ease, she immediately set about rectifying the situation:

'No, no, not at all, I'm on holiday, so I have all the time in the world. Just give me a minute. I'm going to move away from the pool so as not to disturb the people who are resting... Okay, I'm in a quiet spot now. Fire away! I'm all ears.'

'Well, first of all, I'd just like to say that I have lots of good news for you...'

Some months later, François would explain why he had taken so very long to reply to her email. The fact of the matter was that her reference to "cold water" all over her dream had had an absolutely devastating effect on him, causing him to fear that her passion had somehow been damaged, or even broken. Worse still, he believed it was entirely his fault. As a result, he had resolved to do whatever he could to sort out her piano's problems, beginning by gathering a maximum amount of information.

Naturally, this telephone conversation was not the time for going into such details; at this stage he was content merely to discuss the practicalities with her...

It turned out that he, himself, had the training required to install a Piano Life Saver and had indeed fitted the system on various types of pianos during his career. That said, these pianos were in the care of other tuners so he had had no means of monitoring their progress subsequent to his installations. This meant that, despite the many convincing arguments for fitting such a system on her piano, he had no way of guaranteeing that it would actually solve the problem and it was for this very reason that he had never raised the subject with her.

Apart from his slight reservations, what followed was incredibly positive. He had just learnt to fit the system onto a piano with strips of industrial Velcro, which meant that he would no longer be required to drill holes in the beams of wood under the soundboard. So, if ever she wished to sell her piano, for whatever reason, it would be possible to remove the entire system without leaving any trace of it behind. Finally, he had spoken to the technical director of the piano tuning department who had duly confirmed that installing this equipment would not have any adverse effect on the guarantee of her instrument.

Together, they took the time to weigh up the pros and cons: the system was quite costly and installing it would require an entire morning's work. On the other hand, it appeared that the cost would rapidly be amortised because, in theory, the piano would subsequently not require such frequent tuning.

And so it was that, slowly but surely, the Jazz-Girl and her tuner came to the conclusion that the Piano Life Saver option was definitely worth a shot.

As far as the Jazz-Girl was concerned, everything was now perfectly clear. Consequently, she was somewhat surprised when François spontaneously expressed an apparently lingering doubt:

'You know, Nina, I really hope that we *have* found the right solution. I would so love to get it right for you, once and for all.'

In that instant, she was able to detect a slight tone of sadness in his voice and she was rather taken aback by the fact that this man, usually so sure of himself when it came to anything to do with pianos, now seemed slightly cautious and hesitant. With this in mind, she said:

'Rest assured, François, I am convinced that if there is one person who can resolve my piano's problems, it's you.'

It was then that François decided to reveal the true source of his concern:

'Nina, you need to know that there is actually a specific reason why we will always have to work together on a very regular basis.'

'Really? What would that be?'

"It's your ear. You happen to hear things with an extremely rare form of precision so, whatever I do to your piano, however much I work on it, the likelihood is that you will always be able to detect tiny little imperfections which other people simply cannot hear.'

So, once again, it was back to the problem of her ear and, once again, François' comments intrigued the Jazz-Girl…

Admittedly, she was used to receiving compliments on her ear and this from as early as she could remember. Her mother, for example, would still proudly boast about how her younger daughter had spoken fluently from just eighteen months of age and subsequently revealed how good her ear was, due to an impressive capacity to imitate other people's voices, entertaining in the process all those around her! Indeed, at the time, the linguistic and auditory skills of young Nina had so impressed her parents that they had even had an unexpected effect on one of her siblings. Nina's elder brother, then aged four and jealous of his sister's verbal prowess, had responded by going on a silent protest, thus reducing his vocabulary to the two words which were essential for his very survival: "min" and "daddin" – his own special way of saying mummy and daddy!

Subsequently, during her school years every music teacher had systematically commented on her ear.

However, in spite of all these compliments and in spite of her more recent, and somewhat surprising, auditory experience at the Bel Canto restaurant, the Jazz-Girl had up until now remained sceptical about the subject, and with good reason.

To her, two specific factors had always flown in the face of the assertion that her ear might actually be something special. Firstly, she did not have perfect pitch, far from it in fact. Secondly, if her ear was so very good, why oh why did she still have a slight accent whenever she spoke French, even though she had now lived in France for more years than she had ever lived in England?

Receiving this type of compliment from François Pradel was, on the other hand, different and about to do away with her scepticism on this subject once and for all. After all, here was a man who lived in a land almost entirely populated by bats! In other words, the vast majority of people with whom he came into contact – highly talented colleagues, the best pianists in the world, top-notch sound engineers – were all blessed with exceptional ears.

So, ultimately, if anyone were in a position to classify her ear as being something out of the ordinary, it was indeed her piano tuner –

which meant it was probably high time she stop being sceptical and just accept it.

She therefore replied:

'I agree, my ear *is* what it is: a problem factor. And, unfortunately, there is absolutely nothing we can do about it. On the other hand, it's precisely because of my demanding ear that I was truly able to appreciate the sublimely pure sound you gave to my piano at the beginning of the year. You see, the thing is, you have shown me the extraordinary capacity of my instrument and now I just want to be able to enjoy that capacity to the full.'

And so it was, on that particular note (no pun intended), that they finished their long telephone conversation, which had ultimately proven to be extremely beneficial. They had examined the piano's problems, and the solution envisaged, in great detail. They both felt reassured about the situation. And, all in all, it appeared that everything was at last perfectly clear between them.

Better still, by the end of this call they knew that their working relationship was stronger than ever, for the Jazz-Girl and her tuner were now united like never before in their quest for a perfect sound. All heated exchanges would consequently be a thing of the past. Never again would they argue about her piano.

Three months later...

As she removed the Piano Life Saver from its box, the Jazz-Girl noticed a sticker attached to the cable with the following instruction on it: "Warning: the Piano Life Saver must remain switched on at all times. Avoid sockets that are controlled by a light switch."

When François Pradel arrived, she therefore began by telling him:

'I'd like you to install the system in such a way as to be able to plug it in over here, please. I've checked out the socket and can confirm that it is not linked to any of the light switches. So, in theory, there should be no problem. However, what you need to know is that I have absolutely no influence whatsoever over the activities of our resident ghost!'

Now, in all fairness, it has to be said that the instinctive reaction of the vast majority of service providers, upon finding themselves in the home of a client who talked freely about her resident ghost as if every home naturally had one, would most likely be to exit the premises at lightning speed to avoid spending the morning in the presence of a suspected mad woman!

Such was categorically not the case with François Pradel. On the contrary, his eyes were literally shining with excited curiosity as he enquired:

'You have a ghost? Seriously? Wow! I *really* love hearing things like this. Please tell me all about it!'

'Indeed we do. We actually share our home with a ghost. Generally, he likes to make his presence felt via the telephone; he has a very distinctive ring – precisely two and a half times – and the screen is completely blank; it doesn't even say "Private Number". As for the summer, well, that's a whole new ball game. This is the season when he decides to diversify his activities. Sometimes he'll spontaneously turn on all the lights in the sitting room. So you see, we can only conclude that he particularly favours electrical devices, hence my fear regarding the Piano Life Saver. That said, he's not a scary ghost. Actually, we all, parents and children alike, really love having him around.'

The joyful, slightly wacky, if not a tad surreal, nature of this anecdote set the tone for the rest of the morning...

In order to fix the system under the piano, François was mainly required to work lying down. And when he was not lying down, the Jazz-Girl and her tuner found themselves both sitting on the floor underneath the beams of the piano, with a view to determining where best to place the various parts of the system to ensure that it would be able to do its job properly while remaining as discreet as possible. During this time, they also took the opportunity to discuss their respective music projects, which they did in a remarkably relaxed manner – as if working together while sitting on the floor underneath a piano was something they naturally did every day!

All things considered, their ease in this unusual situation was not actually that surprising; the fact of the matter was that these two piano enthusiasts just happened to feel really happy whenever they came near this, the king of all instruments. And that included whether they be sitting or standing at its keyboard, working on its interior or, as in this case, underneath its beams! Indeed, as far as they were concerned, this beautiful musical cocoon, whose roof was none other than the soundboard of a superb grand piano, could not have provided them with a better setting in which to work.

Two hours later, the system was in place and the Jazz-Girl and her tuner were proud to declare it an aesthetic triumph; the Piano Life Saver was barely visible.

Unfortunately, the same could also be said of the sitting room floor – for it was now strewn with packaging, tools and spare parts. Lurking in the middle of all the mess lay the manual, which they had omitted to read! They thus went through it very quickly to ensure that they had not forgotten anything and discovered, to François' great surprise, that for best results it was advisable to wait for a month before tuning the piano. And to think that, for years, he had been installing and tuning at one and the same time! Be that as it may, since he was in no particular hurry to leave, he offered to tune the Jazz-Girl's piano there and then *and* to come back one month later to do it again.

By the end of the morning, the Jazz-Girl was feeling extremely optimistic; she had just taken a major step towards her ultimate goal of stabilising her beautiful piano once and for all.

Or so she thought…

François regularly liked to claim that the Jazz-Girl's piano had a soul – a temperamental soul – which required some taming. This would really make the Jazz-Girl laugh for to her it was obvious, as she would on such occasions remind him, that the piano just happened to resemble its owner! As luck would have it, she was currently about to discover that the Piano Life Saver was also endowed with a rather strong, temperamental personality, which it was to waste no time in revealing – by playing a little trick on them!

Barely had her tuner left when the Jazz-Girl discovered that her piano now had two additional sounds. Whenever she played the high notes, she could hear the kind of crackling noise a radio sometimes makes. As for the bass and medium range notes, they were accompanied by a swishing sound akin to that of a snare drum brush. Her disappointment was profound; the whole point of the Piano Life Saver was to preserve the pure voice of her instrument but it turned out that this particular piece of equipment was doing the exact opposite!

Repeatedly, she ventured under the piano to take a look at the soundboard in order to determine whether any parts of the Piano Life Saver had moved, for this could indeed have explained the interference, but every time she did so, everything seemed perfectly in place. Frustrated, and somewhat perplexed, she felt as if she were in the classic situation of a schoolteacher who knows the pupils are up to mischief but who, upon turning round to identify the culprits, sees nothing but a classroom full of children who are apparently as good as gold.

Initially, in the knowledge that François was due to return in a month's time, the Jazz-Girl endeavoured to put up with the interference. After a few days, however, her ear could no longer tolerate it and she therefore decided that she had no option but to contact her tuner. This she did, while desperately endeavouring to retain her sense of humour because, by now, seeing the funny side seemed to be the only thing left to do.

Consequently, she found herself writing a message that began thus:

"My dear François,

Regretfully, I once again find myself in the unfortunate position of bringing you bad tidings regarding the piano. The thing is, it would appear that my Piano Life Saver has been delivered complete with its own inbuilt radio and drummer! Is this something that usually happens? Or have I just stumbled upon a rare model?

To put it another way, I am currently encountering two problems. Allow me to explain…"

A few hours later, she was utterly dismayed to read his reply:

"Ohhhh, Nina! I would so have loved to have got it right but clearly it's just been a complete and utter waste of time!"

So that was it? They were to deem it "a complete and utter waste of time" and call it a day, there and then? She could scarcely believe it!

Then, scrolling down, she read the following…

"Now, listen up, because there are actually two possible, and very plausible, explanations for this. The most likely one is that the ghost has taken up residence in the Piano Life Saver. In that case, an exorcist will be able to sort it out in a jiffy.

On the other hand…"

Upon reading her tuner's first "plausible" and "most likely" explanation, the Jazz-Girl burst out laughing. The piano may indeed have been fragile at times but it appeared that their respective senses of humour were firmly intact and, better still, the problem was not that serious.

It turned out that the Jazz-Girl had been on the right track all along. François explained that if any wires were touching the soundboard, they could actually cause interference with some of the notes on the piano. He assured her that he had taken particular care when installing the equipment, especially because if any client were to detect interference it would indeed be her. Unfortunately, however, something must have moved subsequent to his departure.

He therefore advised the Jazz-Girl to gently entice the wires away from the soundboard and, if need be, insert pieces of material between the wood and the said wires in order to keep them in place. He concluded by saying that he would totally understand if she did not wish to attempt this herself, in which case he would pop round to do it.

The next morning, the Jazz-Girl decided to give it a go by venturing once more beneath her instrument. And as she did so, she could not help but smile at the absurdity of this situation, which was currently seeing her spending more time on the floor under the beams of her piano than actually sitting at its keyboard!

Although none of the wires seemed to be touching the soundboard, she nevertheless separated any wire that came close by placing disposable dusters between the said wire and the wood. It so happened that this particular type of duster, which François had rejected when cleaning the piano's interior, on the grounds that it was too "soft and fluffy", actually provided the perfect solution; precisely because it was soft and fluffy, akin to cotton wool, once in place it did not move.

Then she sat down to play the piano…

And, bingo! Her instrument had just recovered its beautifully pure voice. The Jazz-Girl immediately sent a triumphant message to François in which she jokingly offered to become his assistant. He replied by saying he was delighted to start his day with such good news!

One month later…

The big day had finally arrived; François was coming back to tune the piano. In other words, it was the moment of truth for the Piano Life Saver; the system had had time to settle down and was now about to prove, or not, its worth by helping the piano stay in tune.

That day, the Jazz-Girl was genuinely looking forward to seeing her tuner. The last time he had been, they had had a really good time installing the equipment and since that day several utterly hilarious exchanges had flown between them regarding the various teething problems incurred, which had now, thankfully, all but been resolved.

It was, therefore, in a somewhat buoyant, upbeat mood that she opened the door to let him in and consequently had something of a shock. Ashen and painfully thin, François was unrecognisable – a shadow of his usual self, as if he had somehow left his musical charisma at home that day.

This stark change in François' appearance left the Jazz-Girl deeply saddened. Clearly, something was very wrong.

And while her tuner was as polite and charming as usual, she was also under the distinct impression that he just wanted to focus on the task at hand with a view to leaving as soon as possible.

Presuming he might be in need of sustenance, she left the room to prepare a cup of coffee for him, which she then silently placed on a little table next to the piano. François too remained silent, thanking her with a mere nod.

In the normal course of things, her tuner would start off by giving a mini concert – an exquisite performance of a few classical pieces in order to make his diagnosis. That day, however, confirming her initial impression that he just wanted to focus on the task at hand, he immediately got down to the job of tuning.

It was the same thing once he had finished; he did not play his usual pieces. Instead, he lingered over just one note – the G of the middle octave – playing it repeatedly. The Jazz-Girl was at a complete loss as to what was happening. Even from where she was sitting in the study, she could hear that this note was now perfectly in tune. So why keep on playing it? It was as if he simply did not have the energy to play anything else.

When the Jazz-Girl returned to the sitting room, François had already put his jacket back on, clearly indicating that he was ready to leave.

For her part, although she felt so very sorry to see him like this, she just could not bring herself to ask the obvious simple question: "François, are you all right?" This was not only because however well they got on with each other their relationship was nevertheless limited to that of service provider and client, but more significantly because he looked so fragile that she feared the mere utterance of such words might actually cause him to break down. And so it was that she found herself with no choice but to accompany him to the lift in silence.

When they arrived on the landing, it was in a weary voice that François said:

'You will let me know about the piano, won't you?'

Endeavouring to adopt a kind reassuring tone, she replied:

'François, of course I will. It's the very least I can do.'

The Jazz-Girl then returned to her piano where she remained for barely half an hour; François had left a trace of his sadness behind him, which in turn made her feel too melancholic to play.

Be that as it may, never one to abandon her musical treasure for too long, during the days that followed she took every opportunity to play her newly tuned piano, observing in the process that François' worrying state had not in any way affected the finesse of his work. Furthermore, while it was far too soon to declare victory, the Jazz-Girl was nevertheless able to detect several indications that the Piano Life Saver was starting to do a good job; her instrument was the same unflinching model of perfection every single day, its voice worthy of a concert hall piano.

Eager to communicate this initial good news to her tuner, the Jazz-Girl wrote up a detailed report. It was the type of email that would normally have received a long and equally detailed reply. On this occasion, however, François' answer was reduced to just two words: "Thank you."

Upon receiving this, the Jazz-Girl's heart sank. Clearly, something was wrong, very wrong indeed.

A few weeks later...

Christmas was fast approaching and the Jazz-Girl, wishing to thank François for all he had done for her, decided that she should send him a present. After all, over the last twelve months he had saved her hand!, quite superbly prepared the piano for the lawyer's reception, and recently gone way beyond the normal call of duty to resolve her own piano's problems.

Initially, she thought she might have a bottle of Champagne delivered to the piano tuning department's office. At the last minute, however, she changed her mind, thinking it would be more fun to send her tuner a Christmas pudding for, indeed, this slightly more original present had always gone down well when her children had been at primary school and of an age to want to bestow gifts upon their teachers!

The pudding came in a beautiful presentation box but she nevertheless took the time to give it some of her personal gift-wrapping treatment. She also wrote a long letter to François, in which she expressed her heartfelt thanks for all his invaluable support and help, concluding with instructions as to how he should prepare the pudding for consumption.

Upon arriving at the post office, the Jazz-Girl suddenly found herself riddled with doubt; her present looked quite ridiculous. A pudding… when he had saved her hand? Just *what* was she thinking?

In the end, however, she posted it to him anyway, while at the same time reassuring herself: it was the thought that counted and, in any event, no present on earth would ever be worth a hand!

Monday 23 December…

It was the Jazz-Girl's birthday.

The previous day, her husband and children had taken her to a restaurant on the banks of the Seine to celebrate but they had waited until the day itself to give her their presents which, that year, were all related to music in some form or other.

Her children gave her a beautiful little silver brooch in the shape of a treble clef. As for her husband, he produced a superb leather case for her sheet music and he also had a surprise up his sleeve: a four-hour lesson with an extremely well-known jazz pianist. The Jazz-Girl was absolutely ecstatic; this pianist just happened to be the man who had played at the very first jazz concert she had ever attended when she had started taking lessons. It was a wonderful present and her pleasure upon receiving it was, moreover, testimony to the huge progress she had made. In the past, the idea of working and improvising on the piano with this giant of the music industry would undoubtedly have filled her with terror. That day, however, the idea quite simply filled her with joy.

And so it was that, early that afternoon, she happily abandoned her Christmas preparations – closing the door behind her on the numerous presents to wrap and suitcases to pack – in order to set off across Paris in the direction of the Jazzman's home.

The Jazzman lived in an utterly charming house, which bore a strange resemblance to a New York brownstone! For her part, the Jazz-Girl never ceased to be amazed by the fact that, even after having lived in Paris for so many years, it was still possible to discover such beautiful architectural treasures.

She was warmly welcomed by the Jazzman's wife who accompanied her to the music room in the basement where the Jazzman, or the "Maestro" as his wife liked to call him, was duly waiting for his pupil. Standing right in the middle of this small, soundproofed room was a beautiful upright century-old Bechstein.

In the manner of a great artist, great in every sense of the term, the Jazzman, a true showman when on stage, was actually incredibly humble in his daily life and shy to the point where the Jazz-Girl was under the impression that *she* should be the one to put him at his ease and not the other way round.

Be that as it may, the afternoon turned out to be extremely rewarding for her. The Jazzman gave her lots of invaluable advice about technique, showing her how, by merely making a slight change to the position of her hand, she could completely transform the sound of a riff or a left-hand accompaniment. He also shared a few tricks for dealing with the vagaries of performing in public. And, to top it all, he was even willing to make a recording with her – something he rarely ever agreed to do with a pupil.

On the pretext that nothing could equal the freshness of a first take, it turned out that the Jazzman preferred not to rehearse. The Jazz-Girl was therefore about to press "record" when suddenly he stopped her to offer his sincere apologies – claiming that he never played very well when recording!

Endeavouring to suppress a smile at the idea that this great pianist could possibly play in a way that was anything other than exceptional, she pressed the button of her small recording machine and they proceeded to perform several four-hand improvisations.

Had the Jazz-Girl had a spare hand to pinch herself, she would most certainly have done so! Playing alongside this giant of the jazz scene was taking her way beyond her wildest musical dreams. Fortunately, however, she managed to keep both hands on the piano all the way through, miraculously managing to give a performance worthy of her usual level of playing, even though that level remained tiny, minute in fact, compared to that of the Maestro, for such was his genius at jazz improvisation that he might just as well have come from another planet. That said, whatever the differences between their respective levels, the Jazz-Girl was simply delighted to have several recordings to take home, which she would later treasure as a magnificent souvenir of her extraordinary afternoon.

She had indeed spent an incredible few hours with the Jazzman and, evidently, he too had enjoyed the session for, when the next pupil arrived, he invited her to stay and sit in on the lesson. Thanking him profusely for the offer, she nevertheless declined the invitation for her family was expecting her at home.

The Jazzman thus accompanied her to the door and gave her *the* most appropriate birthday present imaginable – a beautiful record he had made some years previously of several of his own compositions, which all just happened to be on the subject of the Entente Cordiale!

The Jazz-Girl was now on her way home and, for some time, the taxi had been stuck in a traffic-jam on the Place de la Concorde. Impatient to enjoy the highlights of her afternoon playing jazz, she asked the driver if he would mind her listening to the recordings while they waited. He duly obliged by switching off the radio and, at the end of the journey, he surprised her by expressing his special thanks for her "wonderful mini-concert"! It turned out that, over the last few days, his clients had done nothing but talk non-stop about their Christmas preparations, so he was delighted to have been afforded a bit of light relief in the form of a "pleasant, bluesy interlude", thereby enabling him to end his day "in style"!

It was a truly magical moment for the Jazz-Girl, who considered his compliments to be yet another great birthday gift.

When at last she arrived home, her husband and children were ready and waiting to conclude what had been a most memorable day, with a meal comprising her favourite things: a sushi platter, a bottle of vintage Champagne and a cake, made with the darkest chocolate imaginable and decorated with a serious number of candles! Raising a toast to her family, she proudly proclaimed that she had just had the best birthday of her life. And even though this made her children fall about laughing, swift to remind her that she was in the habit of saying this every year, on this particular occasion, she happened to believe that it was true.

Later that evening, just as she was about to fall into bed in a blissful state of musical euphoria, the Jazz-Girl suddenly decided to take a look at her emails.

Of the fifteen unopened messages, all mainly advertising, only one really caught her eye. François Pradel had sent her a message marked: "What a surprise!!!" Clearly, he had received the pudding.

Upon opening the email, she was delighted to discover a long, extremely touching letter, which began:

"Dearest Nina,

What an amazing surprise when I went via the office last Friday! A present for me!! Un-believable!!! How can I ever convey to you the immense joy I felt upon receiving it? As I opened the parcel, I just felt so touched and even now, having unwrapped it, I still feel genuinely moved. You see, the thing is, I truly love surprises; whenever I see a present, I revert to being a five-year-old. On top of which, December 25 happens to be my birthday, so your timing just couldn't have been better! I intend to put the pudding under the tree and, on Christmas day, I shall open it once again so that it can be MY birthday cake – against, I hasten to add, the better wishes of all those who shall be celebrating this most important event with me ☺!"

Upon reading these words, the Jazz-Girl felt reassured. Quite clearly, the thought *had* counted. And the mere idea that her piano tuner was going to have a Christmas pudding as his birthday cake genuinely made her laugh. But above all, she was truly happy to deduce, from François' overall tone of undiluted enthusiasm, that he was once again his exuberant and vivacious self; any feeling that something might be wrong could now be cast aside. It was great news. And a wonderful way to end the day; the icing on the cake – or, as it turned out, the pudding!

Tuesday 24 December…

The Jazz-Girl was feeling rather anxious about her piano. She and her family were preparing to set off for the Christmas holiday and during their ten-day break their flat would not be heated. In other words, her instrument was about to be subjected to some quite tough environmental conditions. Worse still, the damp, unusually mild weather of the past few weeks had now given way to a cold, dry spell. Consequently, the humidity levels in the room were on the verge of dropping somewhat dramatically. In short, the Piano Life Saver was to undergo a major initial test. With this in mind, just before they left, the Jazz-Girl took the time to top up the humidifier's container with water, carefully tending to her piano as if it were some kind of delicate plant that might become thirsty. Then she closed the grand lid of her beautiful instrument and crossed her fingers.

As they stood facing the traditional mountain of suitcases, presents, cases of wine and bottles of Champagne, the Jazz-Girl and her family also found themselves faced with the same question that arose faithfully, every year, at exactly the same time. Would they actually succeed in squeezing everything into the car?

As in previous years, they *just* managed it – the only person lucky enough to travel without anything perched on his knees being the Jazz-Girl's husband, which was fair enough really considering that he was at the wheel!

And so they set off, duly squashed together like a family of joyful sardines, in the direction of Normandy.

The holiday did them an amazing amount of good, their days filled as they were with lengthy walks on the beach, trips out to sea whenever the weather permitted – in other words, come rain or shine as far as the Jazz-Girl's husband was concerned! – and long slow meals with family and/or friends, all enjoyed before the glorious spectacle of a roaring log fire.

Consequently, by the time they returned to Paris at the beginning of January, they were all four of them on extremely good form.

The Jazz-Girl was utterly delighted to discover that the same could also be said of her instrument. In spite of the harsh living conditions, her piano was exactly as she had left it, perfectly in tune – clear confirmation that the Piano Life Saver was indeed doing its job properly. Erring on the side of caution, however, just to be absolutely sure, she decided to wait a few days before informing François Pradel, with the result that he actually managed to get in there first; a couple of days after her return she received a message from her piano tuner conveying his very best wishes for the New Year and concluding with the following thought:

"I start this year filled with hope for your piano. Please give me your feedback whenever you can."

The Jazz-Girl duly replied with a long letter detailing the many positive effects of the Piano Life Saver, both on the piano, which now seemed to be staying resolutely in tune (like never before, in fact), and on the pianist! At last she had the sound for which she had been longing. And precisely because every single note was so very pure, she was striving to play each and every one of them as gracefully as she possibly could. In turn, she concluded by sending him her very best wishes for the New Year.

Once week later, François wrote back to her, this time to say that while he was delighted to hear that the piano was at last stable, he nevertheless felt a tinge of regret: their appointments would, as a result, be less frequent.

The Jazz-Girl felt exactly the same. She was going to miss his regular visits. She loved their endless discussions about hammers, strings and unisons. And with whom else could she possibly have this type of conversation?

It so happened that these two musical spirits need not have worried because, from that point on, they were going to stay in touch differently; it was around this time that the Piano Life Saver became the perfect excuse for them to write to each other on a more regular basis about their passion for the king of all instruments and just how important this passion was to them. Consequently, their epistolary relationship, which had begun around the time of the Jazz-Girl's accident, now started to grow and flourish...

Their written exchanges took on a specific style and form; in the manner of two heroes from a Balzac novel, the Jazz-Girl and her tuner would go to great lengths to write using language that was as poetic as it was literary. And that was not all. Each had an equally specific way of signing off, using a formula that was completely devoid of any name. While she would write: "*With my very best musical wishes*", he would sign off with: "*Your most dedicated piano tuner*".

What a wonderful paradox! They thus found themselves using highly sophisticated modern means of technology – computers and mobile phones – to return to a time-honoured, old-fashioned form of communication. In short, via a string of emails and text messages, they would send letters to each other which were so long they could practically have been mistaken for novels!

The intense nature of the subject matter of these letters – their shared passion for music and pianos – was thankfully tempered by the tone of their writing, which happened to be dominated by a golden, and in this case unwritten, rule: everything had to be as funny as possible, which was just as well because it was around this time that the Jazz-Girl and her tuner discovered they shared exactly the same sense of the absurd, thus giving free rein to an abundance of running jokes. As for the source of these jokes, well, it was none other than a number of world-famous pianists! Their best "mate" Keith had obviously been a regular guest star in their letters for a good while now; in fact, mentioning this particular pianist was practically an obligation. However, during this period, nobody, literally nobody, was spared. All the greats – Herbie, Daniel, Hélène, Martha[18] – and many, many more got a look in, as if the complicity arising from their shared passion somehow authorised these two musical spirits to make jokes about everyone and anyone else, while they themselves remained quite untouchable, strictly off limits!

It was during one particularly moving exchange that François confessed to the Jazz-Girl just how much he loved their correspondence. So much so, in fact, that whenever he received one of her letters, he would immediately put down his tuning lever (which was really saying something!) and go and find a quiet corner to sit down and read. With this admission, he seemed to be encouraging her to write to him. At least, that was her interpretation of it, which was why she chose to write back immediately with the anecdote of the moment...

One day, the Jazz-Girl noticed that the "drummer" had returned to the piano and was lurking somewhere among the high notes. Duly armed with a box of disposable dusters, she thus ventured once more under the soundboard, convinced that she could swiftly solve the problem; after all, she was by now an "expert" on the matter! Surprisingly, however, this somewhat makeshift but nevertheless effective solution of the past did not appear on this occasion to be working. Try as she might, the more she separated the wires from the soundboard, with what was an increasingly thick layer of dusters, the more the drummer persisted. And while he was undeniably playing in tempo, what she actually wished to do was play solo! Since it was Sunday morning, she was playing with the grand lid of the piano firmly closed, just as she did every weekend, so as to keep the volume down and avoid disturbing the neighbours too much. Nevertheless, fearing that her dissonant attempts to test the piano might, despite all her precautions, give rise to complaints from the inhabitants of her building, after half an hour or so she abandoned her efforts to sort out the problem, concluding that she was going to have to contact the piano tuning department about this.

The next day, in a bid to kill time while she was waiting to call the pleasant voice, the Jazz-Girl decided to play the piano. Given that

18   Keith Jarrett. Herbie Hancock. Daniel Barenboim. Hélène Grimaud. Martha Argerich.

her neighbours had already left for work, this time she opened the grand lid and there she immediately discovered the source of the interference which, it turned out, had absolutely nothing whatsoever to do with the Piano Life Saver. It had, in fact, all been caused by one little piece of sheet music that had slid inside the piano and trapped itself between the strings of the high notes!

In the knowledge that this anecdote was most likely to give François a huge laugh, the Jazz-Girl took her time to write it up, exaggerating as she did so *all* the details. Naturally, once she had sent it she was expecting to receive an extremely swift reply – not to mention the endless teasing that would undoubtedly ensue!

But in fact, to her great surprise, her letter went unanswered. Literally overnight, her self-styled "most dedicated piano tuner" simply ceased to write to her.

François Pradel's silence saddened the Jazz-Girl. She sorely missed their written exchanges. Worse still, this abrupt change made her fear, once again, that her piano tuner might just be in distress.

A few weeks later...

The winter holiday was fast approaching and the entire family was feeling disappointed; the Jazz-Girl's husband, *the* main skier among them, had just announced that he would be required to remain in Paris for professional reasons.

As a result, the Jazz-Girl was dragging her heels to prepare the numerous items of equipment traditionally required for their departure on a ski holiday, in her view tantamount to moving a circus! To add insult to injury, she was also suffering from a genuine feeling of frustration. A friend had asked her to translate a document and yet still he had not bothered to send it to her – this despite the fact that he knew she was going on holiday in three days' time.

And so it was that, in this agitated frame of mind, a mixture of both disappointment and frustration, the Jazz-Girl switched on her computer and noticed that she had actually received an email. Had her friend finally bothered to send in the document?

As luck would have it, he had not. Swiftly, though, it was of little consequence to her, for the simple reason that the email in question looked so much more interesting. At six o'clock in the morning her piano tuner had sent a long letter entitled: "At last, some news!"

François Pradel began his letter by thanking the Jazz-Girl for her hilarious anecdote about the piano which, he acknowledged, had given him a really good laugh. He then went on to apologise for his long silence, adding that he hoped he had not upset her in any way; it was just that he had been very busy.

The letter continued in what should, in the normal course of things, have been an optimistic tone. François had an amazing amount of good news regarding his career and was now on the verge of fulfilling his wildest professional dreams.

That said, the more the Jazz-Girl scrolled down to read, the more perplexed she felt, for the simple reason that the numerous positive aspects of this letter appeared to be eclipsed by an all-pervading sense of weariness, as evidenced by François' repeated use of the words "tired", "busy" and "preoccupied".

When finally she got to the end of the letter, she understood why: her piano tuner happened to be going through a major personal crisis. He confessed that he had thought long and hard about sharing this news with her for fear it might affect the joyful nature of their epistolary exchanges, which he truly wished to preserve. He so loved their banter and now he needed it. He concluded by saying that the coming months were going to be very tough for him but that he would always be on hand to serve her in his role as most dedicated piano tuner.

François Pradel's letter left the Jazz-Girl feeling really sad. On top of which, she now found herself faced with an extremely difficult task. How on earth was she to reply to him? Deep down, what she really wanted to do was express her sorrow and sympathy regarding his situation and tell him that she would be happy to listen if ever he needed to talk. It seemed only natural to her to wish to do this. After all, when she had suffered the devastating fracture to her hand, he had so helped and supported her. And then there was all the extra work he had done for so many months in order to resolve the numerous problems incurred on her piano.

There again, she felt she clearly had no option but to respect his request: he really loved their banter and now he needed it.

With this in mind, desperately seeking to find the delicate balance required, the Jazz-Girl began, somewhat tentatively, to write back to him.

But it was not long before her fears were confirmed; it was nigh on impossible to attempt to write funny anecdotes about the piano while at the same time expressing just how sorry she was to hear his bad news. Clearly, the two subjects were thoroughly incompatible and every time she tried to write, a profound feeling of unease appeared to descend upon her. The fact of the matter was that she was simply incapable of faking joy in her reply and so she just gave up on writing to him, deciding it would be better to take some time to think things over.

𝄞

Two days later, she sat down at the computer and, this time, a letter just seemed to write itself.

"My dear François,

Thank you so much for your letter, which I read, as you can no doubt imagine, with mixed feelings. Naturally, I was delighted and thrilled to hear all your amazing professional news. Your success is well deserved and I am so touched that you trust me enough to share this news with me before it is actually official.

There again, I cannot deny that I was really sad to read of all your woes. It must be so hard to be torn between the feelings of absolute joy, which surely go hand in hand with the dizzy professional heights you are currently scaling, and the feelings of despair arising from the trials and tribulations of all that is happening to you outside the workplace.

Regarding your concern that your personal crisis might somehow affect the spirit of our letter writing, please allow me to reassure you on this point...

Never forget that our "banter" is fuelled by our shared passion for that incredible instrument that is the piano, and in my view a passion is quite simply untouchable for I genuinely believe that one does not really have any control over such matters. To put it another way, we are extremely privileged to carry a passion within us; it's akin to receiving a beautiful, heaven-sent gift.

And I confess that, in my slightly wackier moments, I secretly like to harbour the belief that this gift has been sent to people like us directly from no other than the God of music himself – Apollo!

So you see, François, it is my firm belief that our shared love of pianos will always guarantee the hilarious, joyful nature of our written exchanges; whatever else happens, I promise you this will remain unaffected.

More importantly, in the coming months it is your very passion which will ensure you hang on in there throughout all that life is about to throw at you because this is to be your source of strength, stability and happiness.

Hopefully, by now, my words will have managed to reassure you and allay your many doubts and fears because what I would really like to say to you is this: don't you think it's about time we faced facts? Quite clearly, the Piano Life Saver has recently been working very hard to sow the seeds of a friendship between us and true friends can talk about anything, the good and the bad.

On that basis, should you ever need to offload, please know that you can count on me to be there to listen.

I'm sending this letter, as ever, with my very best musical wishes to you.

Your newfound friend,
Nina."

Now, the Jazz-Girl had not forgotten that François was in the habit of reading her letters just as soon as he received them, a habit which came not without its impracticalities. In the past, she had even received text messages referring to this very issue:

"Ohhhhh, Nina, I'm sitting in the Metro reading your letter. It's quite simply un-put-downable! But because of you, I've now gone and missed my stop!!! Grrrrrr..." or: *"Ouch! I've just bumped into a lamppost. I'm reading your letter while walking towards the Opera!"*, to quote but just two examples.

On this particular occasion, however, the Jazz-Girl wanted François to take the time to read her letter in peace and quiet, which is why she decided to wait a while before sending it. So it was not until after midnight, upon her return home from a last night out with her husband before her departure to the Italian Alps with their children, that she read her letter one more time before at last pressing "send".

Her strategy paid off. The next morning, François read the letter in the calm surroundings of his flat and, deeply moved to learn that the Jazz-Girl was willing to offer him her support, decided that he was now ready to confide in her by revealing the true nature of his woes.

𝄞

The Jazz-Girl had just arrived at the ski resort when, in what could only be described as an intensely poignant moment, she received a long emotional letter from her piano tuner.

That said, touched as she was to receive this letter, from a technological point of view the timing could not have been worse. The hotel was perfect – paradise on earth – apart from one slight detail: the Wi-Fi area was restricted to a tiny space just in front of the reception desk and the connection appeared to function on a somewhat random basis! Compounding the problem, the Jazz-Girl's mobile phone – so archaic that according to her children even a dinosaur would not be seen dead with it! – did not actually afford her any access to her emails.

However, any slight technical obstacle would prove to be of very little consequence in the light of their epistolary relationship, which was now about to demonstrate just how very strong it was; since the Jazz-Girl had never managed to master the art of skiing, during that week she was in fact quite free – in between long walks taken in the snow and various sessions spent in the pool – to support François via some of the longest text messages ever written!

And that is how a beautiful friendship began to grow between these two musical spirits…

Ultimately, it was actually really easy for them to become friends – the main characteristic of their friendship being an almost childlike form of sincerity for which there was a very simple explanation. They had met in a context that required absolute authenticity at all times; given that each was blessed with an extremely rare form of hearing, it would have been quite impossible for either of them to pull the wool over the eyes of the other regarding the piano. And now their musical authenticity was quite naturally transforming into friendly sincerity.

$$\textlarger{\oint}$$

Upon her return home from her ski holiday, François invited the Jazz-Girl to have lunch with him as a token of his gratitude for all her support.

That day, they were both genuinely looking forward to seeing each other. In reality, however, the lunch began very badly and only narrowly avoided turning into a complete disaster.

The fact of the matter was that the Jazz-Girl and her piano tuner felt extremely uncomfortable. While communicating via letter-writing had been so very simple, they were truly dismayed to find that talking to each other, in the cacophony of a jam-packed brasserie, without so much as a piano in sight to reassure them, was anything but easy.

Thankfully, the Piano Life Saver took it upon itself to come to their aid…

It so happened that the Jazz-Girl had brought along a present for her newfound friend – a book, hailed as being the "wackiest book of the year" – which had really made her laugh. She now handed it to him, explaining that its author had a genuine sense of the absurd, similar to that which peppered their letters.

François responded by thanking her and then, having taken the time to look at the book, turned to her to say:

'You know, as far as I'm concerned, your best joke by a long chalk was the one about the Piano Life Saver!'

The Jazz-Girl remembered it only too well. That day, she had just completed a particularly successful recording session with her guitarist friend Benjamin. In her subsequent euphoria, she had sent one of the recordings to François to enable him to hear the positive effects of the Piano Life Saver on the sound of her piano. And, in order to communicate all her enthusiasm on the subject, she had concluded her letter with the following question:

"I have to admit, so utterly delighted am I with the results of the Piano Life Saver, that I am now considering ordering one for my digital piano. What do you reckon?"

François had replied to this message with:

"A Piano Life Saver on a digital piano? Nina, you do make me laugh. I'm sitting in the Metro with tears streaming down my face. I'm trying really hard to contain myself but it just makes me laugh all the more!"

It was during this lunch that he explained precisely *why* he had found this particular joke so very funny. Clearly, no colleague would ever have dared to make it because among fellow members of the profession it would have been deemed just too obvious. On the other hand, to his knowledge, it had *never* occurred to anyone outside of the profession to make this joke. Except for her. Which was but one of the many reasons why he generally liked to refer to her as a "unique phenomenon"!

This conversation enabled them both to relax; they were back on *terra firma* – the wonderfully safe and secure territory of their shared passion for music. Consequently, they began to feel sufficiently at ease to communicate as naturally and sincerely as they had during their written exchanges with the result that, by the end of the lunch, these two epistolary friends were able to drop the "epistolary" for they were now quite simply firm friends. Full stop.

$$\text{\Large\Clef}$$

To conclude on the story of the Piano Life Saver, it turned out that this astonishing piece of equipment had one last little surprise in store for them: good reason to invent nicknames…

As they got up to leave the brasserie, François made a confession that was, to say the very least, surprising:

'You know, for a long time, I really used to dread my appointments with you. You have *such* an amazing capacity to detect the slightest change in any note that your ear terrified me. As a result, I even started to adapt my tuning techniques. So, you see, today I actually attribute part of my professional success to your ear because, thanks to you, I have discovered that there are many different ways to tune a piano. Above all, I am truly delighted that the Piano Life Saver is proving to be so effective. The thing is, I thought I was just *never* going to make it with *you* and *your* piano!'

The Jazz-Girl could scarcely believe her ears. And to think that, during all those appointments, when she had felt so utterly intimidated in the presence of this handsome man, the piano tuning profession's answer to Hugh Grant and, more importantly, a highly gifted artist – so sure of himself when seated before a piano and so utterly capable of tuning for some of the world's greatest concert pianists –, to think that this man had actually been scared of tuning for her, a tiny, little, unknown, obscure blues pianist! The very thought appeared quite absurd.

And so it was that the next time she had an appointment to get her piano tuned, she simply could not resist writing the following:

"My dearest, most dedicated, piano tuner,

This is just to inform you that, as from today, you can officially begin to tremble, for you have just got yourself an appointment with, what is by your own admission, THE most demanding ear of the entire planet! Does this ring any bells? Tuning Keith's or Martha's[19] piano is, by comparison, absolute child's play. Can you guess about whom we are

19 Keith Jarrett and Martha Argerich.

talking? Are you getting warm? Lest there be any doubt, allow me to confirm that your fate has just been sealed: next Friday, you are to tune the piano belonging to none other than that most scary of bats!"

Not wishing to be outdone, François fired off his reply at breakneck speed:

"No worries! The serial fixer is ready to face the enemy!"

These newfound names appealed to them so much that they actually decided to adopt them. After all, their dual appellations – Jazz-Girl/scary bat, and most dedicated piano tuner/serial fixer – could not have provided a more fitting reflection of the very duality that formed the basis of their friendship: an intense, shared passion for music firmly held in check by an extremely healthy dose of self-deprecation!

And so it is, dear readers, that the incredible story of the Piano Life Saver finally draws to a close. Who would have thought it? This piece of equipment, whose original function – to save the life of a piano – was already very noble, had in addition revealed some quite amazing qualities. It had a personality, not to mention a sense of humour. And once it realised that by working so effectively it might just prevent two musical spirits from seeing each other as frequently, it had gone to great lengths to provide them with extensive subject matter for their written exchanges, thus enabling them to take the necessary steps to become friends.

That said, it is important to remember that behind the Piano Life Saver's most unusual powers, there no doubt lies a much stronger force – for can not this incredible story actually be deemed to be a rather magnificent example of the inestimable power of music itself?

Whatever the answer to that question may be, one thing is absolutely certain: thanks to the help of this apparently quite magical piece of equipment, the various efforts deployed by the Jazz-Girl and her most dedicated tuner to stabilise the piano had been more than generously rewarded – way beyond anything they could ever possibly have imagined!

Post-scriptum

Just for the record: the moment I finished writing the original version of this story in French, all the lights suddenly switched on in our kitchen. It was the month of April and as if the ghost were sending me a message:

"I don't just do lights in the sitting room and I don't just do them in the summer!"

Was he ultimately trying to tell me that HE is the one who calls the shots?

François Pradel's Fabulous Faux Pas

I t would be fair to say that the Jazz-Girl was in a bit of a state on that gloomy winter's evening. Once again, her anxiety levels appeared to be scaling dizzy heights, something that happened *every* time her husband took a long-haul flight. And that particular night, he was on a flight home from a business trip on the West Coast of America.

While fully aware that her reaction was totally irrational, try as she might, she just could not get a grip. In addition, the stress brought about by "rush hour" at home was not exactly helping. In other words, it was the time of day when she would find herself performing the delicate juggling act of preparing the dinner, supervising the homework, signing the numerous forms which her children's school seemed to love sending to frazzled parents, while, at the same time, desperately searching for answers to the existentialist questions which her teenage son would generally put to her at precisely that moment when it would be so much better *not* to raise such questions.

Then, just as she was starting to feel that, in spite of everything, she was actually managing to bring the multitasking under control, her telephone decided to get in on the act. A "ding" announced the arrival of a text message. It was from a friend, asking her if she would mind dropping off his children at school the next day. Barely had she completed her answer when she heard another "ding". Clearly it was going to be one of those evenings…

This second message came from François Pradel, who was in need of a favour.

"Dear Nina,

I've just written a letter to a British colleague. Do you think you could take a look and correct the English for me?"

With this request, François was actually giving her an opportunity to combine her two passions – music and words. Consequently, she leapt at the chance to help him, reasoning that working on this letter would take her mind off things, possibly calm her down a bit and might even serve to keep her entertained after dinner.

At that point, she did not have the slightest inkling of just how much this letter was going to keep her entertained that night…

Impatient to set to work, the Jazz-Girl finished eating as quickly as possible, leaving her children to finish their meal in their own time and asking them to clear up afterwards. As she walked out of the room, they only just managed to refrain from jumping for joy and shouting: "Yesssss!" They were both beginning to get somewhat fed up with their stressed-out mother and tidying up the kitchen would be but a small price to pay for a bit of peace and quiet.

Settling down comfortably in an armchair, her computer on her lap, she opened the email and began to read. The letter was addressed to a London-based concert technician, Martin Sixmann, who was somewhat more experienced than his Parisian colleague and had the enviable job of managing the pianos of some of *the* most prestigious concert halls in London. François had met him a few months previously in Paris and wanted to ask him for some advice.

Now, this letter struck her as rather surprising, for several reasons…

First of all, in spite of the odd mistake, François had actually managed to maintain his usual, touching, poetic style of writing. Admittedly, no native English speaker would have adopted such a style for a professional letter. However, the Jazz-Girl decided not to change it because she found the writing quite charming. And since these two tuners already knew each other, she came to the conclusion that the tone of this letter, with its slightly "exotic" French touch, would really appeal to the London tuner.

As she continued to read, making a few corrections here and there, she stumbled upon a second surprising aspect of the letter. When François talked about the technical aspects of his profession, he was capable of writing some absolutely perfect sentences:

"I know a lot about mechanism and voicing. I feel comfortable with my knowledge, but comfortable is not enough for me. I want to know more."

Unbelievable! The Queen of England herself, had she been, in addition to everything else, a trained piano tuner, could not have worded it more beautifully. It was as if François was, at times, so inspired by his profession that he would suddenly become master of everything – including of a language, which he did *not* actually completely master.

By this point the Jazz-Girl was increasingly of the opinion that her piano tuner really had done rather well to write such a letter. However, she had yet to discover the contents of the final paragraph. Things generally come in threes and it turned out that François had saved the third surprising aspect – the best – for last.

Suddenly, she happened upon a sentence which absolutely leapt off the page. It seemed to have taken the entire letter for François to get down to the real nitty-gritty of the subject. That said, the subject itself was now somewhat different – nothing to do with pianos. In fact, it could not have been further removed from pianos. As for the nitty-gritty, suffice to say that the nitty turned out to be pretty, well… gritty!

In a disarmingly casual, relaxed manner or, to put it another way, with a complete and utter lack of inhibition, the Parisian tuner had concluded his letter to his London colleague by coolly stating:

"I now feel ready to go all the way with you."

Hmmm… A single entendre, if ever there was one, thought the Jazz-Girl to herself. The Queen would most definitely *not* be amused.

The Jazz-Girl, on the other hand, was. In fact, she was beyond amused as she proceeded to collapse into uncontrollable fits of laughter which, once they started, just would not stop. Ah, the French! Ultimately, they were all the same. She had now been living in France for nearly thirty years and not for the first time did she have the impression that she was in a situation worthy of a Woody Allen film – although even this talented filmmaker could probably never invent scenes as funny as those which life in France regularly brought her. In short, the stereotypes appeared to be true. The French were evidently obsessed with carnal pleasure and clearly, whatever the circumstances, they were always up for it. After all, what did it matter if the context happened to be that of a Franco-British professional relationship? *Au contraire. Vive l'Entente Cordiale!*

Endeavouring for the second time that evening to get a grip, the more the Jazz-Girl thought about the parting shot of François' letter, the more any attempts to regain her composure actually made matters worse, now causing her imagination to go into overdrive as several hypotheses about the situation began dropping into her mind.

Was her tuner a closet homosexual? Not, frankly, a very likely contingency given the serious number of female conquests he had under his belt (in a manner of speaking). And she should know for, in her newfound role as confidante, she was generally the first to be informed of his latest success story with the female section of society. On the other hand, his choice of words had come across as pretty direct, so it appeared that she could not rule out the possibility of him choosing the safe haven of his profession to come out of the closet. And in that case, could this mean that he was trying to sleep his way to the top?

This line of reasoning, in turn, incited the Jazz-Girl to question her interpretation of the rest of the letter. Had she had actually understood it correctly? Should she go back over all the sentences in which François had described the various ways he handled his "tuning lever" with a view to detecting a figurative meaning, a hidden message, or even some kind of thinly veiled love declaration?

As she desperately tried to calm down, the Jazz-Girl decided she should use her, by now, very fertile imagination in a more constructive manner – her first priority being to protect François from any threat of legal proceedings for sexual harassment. This she was keen to do as much for him as for her. Otherwise, who would tune her piano? And after thinking long and hard about the matter, she came to the conclusion that she should act in a manner which is usually strictly forbidden by the translation profession. In other words, she took it upon herself to invent an entirely new sentence:

"I now feel ready to complete my knowledge of piano tuning techniques and, in order to do this, would like to be able to observe you at work."

It was then up to her, as a self-respecting translator, to explain the linguistic error to François, especially as she knew that he was intending to write to other colleagues in English. She thus racked her brains to find an elegant and diplomatic way to make him aware of his mistake. However, it appeared that her hitherto vivid imagination had run out of steam because it failed to come up with the goods, resulting in her cutting to the chase by actually writing:

"My dear François,

I've nearly finished correcting your letter and thank goodness you came to me for help. Personally, I thought you were doing quite well. That is until I got to the sentence – "I now feel ready to go all the way with you" – which just happens to read as an open invitation for your British colleague to have sex with you. Not sure that's quite what you had in mind. Unless, of course, you feel particularly close to him!"

Adding a final flourish, just for good measure, she signed off with a bright-yellow winking emoji followed by an equally bright-yellow seriously unsubtle thumbs-up!

So, not quite as elegant and diplomatic as she had hoped...

Then, having added the final corrections, she sent the letter off to her tuner while smiling at the thought that, on this occasion, she had quite probably saved his career.

What François could not know was that, on this occasion, he had actually saved her or, at any rate, her evening. By asking her to correct this letter, he had pulled her out of the doldrums and given her, into the bargain, a deliciously uncontrollable fit of laughter.

That night, the Jazz-Girl, now thoroughly relaxed thanks to her linguistic adventures, slept very peacefully. Yes, her husband was on the plane, but her anxiety had all but disappeared due to her subsequent mirth.

The next morning when she got up, she was still wearing a big smile on her face. A smile which became even brighter when, one hour later, her husband arrived, safe and sound, just in time for breakfast.

The following year...

Once again, François Pradel required a favour from the Jazz-Girl. This time he had to write a report, for the same London-based colleague Martin Sixmann, assessing a piano which together they were going to prepare for a particularly demanding French concert pianist. Given the highly complex, technical nature of the subject matter, the Jazz-Girl suggested that François come round for a working lunch so that they could write up the report together. This turned out to be a good move because it meant that he was on hand to explain the technical problems to be resolved, enabling her to translate them more easily into decent English – decent being the operative word!

A few days later, the London tuner arrived in Paris and François sent the Jazz-Girl the following text message:

"*Dear Nina,*

Thank you so much for your help. It's proving to be invaluable. Martin Sixmann arrived at the concert hall about an hour ago and the technical report is enabling us to make smooth and rapid progress with the piano."

Upon receiving this message, the Jazz-Girl, for whom the linguistic error of the letter was forever etched on her memory, found herself quite simply unable to resist the temptation to reply:

"My dear François,

Thank you for your message. I'm really delighted to hear that my work on the report is such a help to you both. Have a nice day. And be sure to behave yourself with that Martin Sexy-Man☺!"

The following message came back immediately:

"Martin Sexy-Man! Nina, you do make me laugh. Behave myself? Don't know about that! What I can tell you is that he's just in me and we're having a really fantastic time together!"

This time there was no mistaking it. François' explicit words seemed to say it all – rendering the Jazz-Girl utterly speechless. And it must be said, dear readers, that being of a naturally talkative disposition, for her to be rendered speechless, the situation had to be serious – very, very serious indeed. Firmly glued to the spot – motionless, like a statue – she stared at her phone for some time, at a complete loss as to how to respond, before deciding that discretion should be the order of the day and that it would therefore be better to ignore the message.

A few hours later...

The Jazz-Girl's telephone went "ding" and up popped François Pradel's name for the third time that day. Fearing the worst, she discovered a text message containing the following explanation:

"Nina,

What a truly terrible mistake to make. I actually meant to write: "he's just in FRONT OF me"... Oh my goodness! I'm thoroughly ashamed. On top of which, I added that we were having a really fantastic time together. Obviously I was referring to our work on the piano. I'm soooo embarrassed. You've no idea..."

No comment.

On the other hand...

It was an absolute gem of a mistake and the Jazz-Girl now had every intention of sharing it with as many friends as possible, *precisely* with a view to receiving their comments on the subject. Three of her female friends formed what she affectionately referred to as her reading club because they particularly liked to be kept informed of

François' latest adventures – linguistic and otherwise. And so it was that the Jazz-Girl wrote up the delicious anecdote and sent it to them by email, leaving the "Subject" box empty so as not to give them the slightest forewarning of its contents. Unsurprisingly, the replies came back, one after the other, at breakneck speed.

Number one:

"Thank you! Thank you!! THANK YOU!!! I'm at work and the day has been as dull as ditchwater thus far but, thanks to your email, it's turning out to be brilliant. You have to hand it to him. François Pradel makes some absolutely fabulous faux pas!!! You just couldn't script them any better!"

Number two:

"I'm currently alone in my kitchen and I'm laughing about it all to myself!"

And finally – the icing on the cake – number three:

"GI-FLIPPIN'-NORMOUS!!!"

Hmmm… The Jazz-Girl presumed that this last reply should be taken as a reference to the size of François' spectacularly huge linguistic error. Thus, tempted though she was to see it as a somewhat unsubtle invitation to continue writing on the theme of the moment, she ended up taking the very wise decision that it would probably be better to put the subject, once and for all, to bed… so to speak.

One month later…

The Jazz-Girl received a call from François Pradel who, yet again, required a favour.

'Hello, Nina, I'm calling because Martin Sixmann is coming back to Paris next Monday and he would like to meet up with me in the evening so that we can discuss the voicing which we're due to do on several new Steinways. These pianos are soon to be delivered to the big new concert hall prior to its opening in January. The problem is that the subject is really tricky and I just can't afford to get it wrong. However, I'm not sure my English is up to it, so I was wondering if you would be free to act as interpreter at the meeting.'

'Absolutely. I'd love to be there. And frankly, I don't think we have a choice, do you? I *have* to be there, given your propensity to make *the* most colossal linguistic errors whenever you go near Martin Sixmann,' she replied, lacing her words with a rather large dose of irony.

Feigning resignation, François conceded:

'Thank you, Nina, I guess you're right. Clearly, the aim is to come away from this meeting with a work contract and *not* a marriage certificate!'

The following Monday...

That evening, the Jazz-Girl and François made a punctual arrival at the elegant brasserie located near the Champs-Elysées where Martin Sixmann had arranged to meet them. However, to their surprise, the London tuner, in a bid to wind down from a rather trying day – a day which he had spent preparing a piano for a world-famous Russian pianist – had clearly been there for a while and now seemed to be particularly focussed on the serious business of consuming as much beer as he could possibly lay his hands on!

Having expected to set to work straight away, they were even more surprised when Martin Sixmann, who was evidently beginning to enjoy the feeling of relaxing slowly but surely, suggested that the three of them dine together before turning their attention to the professional matters at stake.

Now on a roll, Martin Sixmann insisted on washing the meal down with copious amounts of claret. Thinking it would be deemed impolite not to follow suit, the Jazz-Girl and François felt obliged to join in – with the result that when the time finally came to discuss the extremely complex technical issues regarding the pianos, they were no longer in any fit state to work.

That said, in spite of the challenge which this difficult interpreting assignment clearly posed, the Jazz-Girl found the job child's play compared to the real challenge of the evening: controlling her facial muscles! Maintaining a serious, dignified look, while stifling the desire to collapse into fits of giggles in the presence of Martin Sixmann, was no mean feat. François Pradel's fabulous faux pas kept on popping up in her mind and it required enormous powers of concentration on her part to keep them at bay. How she would have loved to be endowed with the Queen's superhuman levels of self-control at such times!

Fortunately, Apollo must have been on her side that night because, by dint of some miracle, the Jazz-Girl successfully managed to hold it together just long enough to wrap up the job in hand, without mishap.

Phew! What a relief. The Queen would have been extremely proud of her!

With the meeting over, the Jazz-Girl and François offered to accompany a by now extremely merry Martin Sixmann to his hotel. Which was just as well, really. As he happily zigzagged his way along the pavement for the entire length of the Avenue George V, they were on hand to steer and guide him safely to his end destination!

The Jazz-Girl then took it upon herself to congratulate François on his unusually impressive verbal restraint during the meeting with his London colleague while, at the same time, secretly congratulating herself for having managed to prevent anything untoward happening between the pair of them that night!

In turn, François congratulated the Jazz-Girl on her incredible professionalism in what had been a rather delicate situation and offered to take her to a Champagne bar to thank her – an offer which she was delighted to accept.

And so it was that they raised their glasses to their great working relationship that evening, in happy celebration of the fact that on this occasion, just for once, there would, thank goodness, be no legendary linguistic errors to report.

Good old François! The Jazz-girl had always really enjoyed translating and interpreting but, due to his absolutely fabulous faux pas, François Pradel had succeeded in taking that enjoyment to a completely different level, thereby affording her some of *the* most truly memorable, utterly hilarious moments of her entire translation career!

The Shoemaker's Children Always Go Barefoot

The Serial Fixer had just signed the lease on a new flat and having spent many a long telephone conversation asking the Jazz-Girl for advice on the matter, now wished to invite his "Scary Bat" – as he had taken to calling her – to celebrate this great news with him.

As luck would have it, that night the Scary Bat was actually booked to play her fortnightly slot in a local brasserie but upon hearing the news that her Serial Fixer had finally managed to secure this particular flat – a property he had long been coveting – she was so utterly delighted that, once she had finished playing, she leapt into a taxi, grabbing a bottle of Champagne on the way, to join him in his new abode.

They began by "inspecting" the premises. Situated on the eleventh floor of a 1970s building, the flat was spacious and extremely well laid out – two significant points in its favour. However, these were nothing compared to a third feature, the major attraction, *the* characteristic which spectacularly eclipsed all the others to transform what was already a good-sized, extremely functional flat into a truly exceptional dwelling.

François had already talked to her about it, but nothing, neither a detailed description, nor indeed any photograph, could possibly have prepared her for what followed next. Stepping out of the sitting room and onto the terrace, she found herself literally gasping for breath as she endeavoured to take in the stunning view across the entire, magnificent city of Paris. And it has to be said that Paris was looking particularly lovely on that March evening, shimmering in magical, iridescent light beneath a remarkably clear, star-studded sky.

The day had been mild and sunny but it was late now and

consequently rather cold outside. Be that as it may, the spectacular vista was not to be ignored. On the contrary, it appeared to be beckoning its public to stay outside and admire it. Consequently, the Serial Fixer and the Scary Bat wrapped up warmly in their jackets and woollen scarves so they could drink the Champagne on the terrace, where they proceeded to raise toasts to absolutely everything and anything they wished to celebrate – François Pradel's future, the city of Paris, blues…

Ah, yes. Blues, indeed!

Some weeks previously, François, who enjoyed playing guitar blues in his spare time, had asked the Jazz-Girl if they could arrange a jam session together. To their mutual regret, however, they had still not managed to find a suitable date. And now it seemed that music would no longer be a priority since François was about to embark on the daunting task of redecorating the entire flat prior to moving in.

The Jazz-Girl nevertheless decided to broach the subject in preparation of the day when he would finally be free. With an increasingly large and varied repertoire – a mix of traditional blues and boogie-woogie, together with several jazz arrangements of well-known classical pieces – she could provide plenty of material to work on and was eager to share it.

'So,' she asked him, 'if we're going to jam together one day, what would you like to play? Do you have any favourite pieces?'

True to form, François managed to throw her completely off-balance with a totally unexpected answer.

'Dead easy. Absolutely no contest. What I like is Bach!'

Pretending to take him seriously, she replied:

'Fair enough, but this poses two slight problems for me. First of all, Bach is not my favourite composer. In my view, he's way too mathematical. And secondly, I don't know if you're aware, after all it's just a tiny little detail, but Johann Sebastian Bach does not, at least not to my knowledge, have *that* great a reputation as a blues musician!'

Now adopting the pose of a stubborn two-year-old, his arms firmly crossed as he stamped his right foot, François persisted:

'I don't care. What I like is Bach!'

'Okay, I get the point,' she said as she burst out laughing. 'Thank goodness what I *like* is a challenge. I'll see what I can do. And even if Bach is not my favourite composer, there is one piece that I do like very much: "Jesu Joy of Man's Desiring". My husband and I chose it for our wedding. We have a friend who's an opera singer and she performed it at the religious ceremony. Just talking about it reminds me how much I really do love this piece. So, a jam session on Bach it is then. I'm in!'

♪

A few days later, recalling this conversation, the Jazz-Girl managed to dig out a copy of the sheet music to "Jesu Joy of Man's Desiring" and set about studying the piece.

This exercise turned out to be surprisingly rewarding and musically enriching beyond anything she could possibly have imagined. In order to write a jazz arrangement of any given piece of music, the first step is to analyse the harmony. This enables the musician to establish a series of chords that form the grid. In the case in point, this initial phase also enabled the Jazz-Girl to begin to comprehend the true depth and density of Bach's compositions. As eight bars of sheet music transformed into a sixteen-bar blues grid, the harmony of the piece revealed itself in all its complexity.

The next step was to try to find a way of applying a jazz rhythm to the melody. It was at this point that the task proved to be much more difficult than she had bargained for. Indeed, it looked like it was going to be just *too* difficult for her. Admittedly, she had already written jazz arrangements of some pieces by Mozart, as well as of a few well-known arias from Verdi's operas, but Bach posed a real problem. The regular structure of this composition, a shining example of mathematical perfection, simply did not seem to lend itself to a swing rhythm. Consequently, as it became increasingly clear that her endeavours to "jazzify" a work by the great musical genius were highly unlikely to jeopardise or indeed make the slightest dent in Jacques Loussier's reputation,[20] having relentlessly pursued the matter for two hours, the Jazz-Girl finally conceded defeat and, in a brutal descent from the sublime to the downright banal, abandoned Bach in favour of the weekly supermarket shop!

It turned out that Bach, or at any rate his music, was not quite ready to abandon the Jazz-Girl... Barely had she stepped outside

---

20 Jacques Loussier is a French pianist and composer known for his jazz interpretations of many of Bach's works.

her flat when suddenly "Jesu Joy of Man's Desiring" began singing inside her head in a true jazz style – proof, if proof were required, that music could never fail to surprise her, particularly at times when she was least expecting it. Accordingly, she found herself literally racing around the supermarket, desperate to return to her instrument as soon as possible.

This time, as she sat down at the piano, the Jazz-Girl started to play a really bluesy arrangement of the piece, her left hand adding a traditional New Orleans bass line with the greatest of ease. And to her utter astonishment, it turned out that Bach's work was actually rather compatible with blues. Could it be that this genius of classical music had been a closet jazzman, after all? Any possible answer to that question would have to wait for she was currently riding the crest of a wave with her music, which she proceeded to record and then send to her tuner – who responded by giving it a serious thumbs-up.

Now all they had to do was free up a date for a jam session...

The Easter vacation was soon upon them and, together with her family, the Jazz-Girl left Paris to spend two weeks in Normandy. During this time, she was kept informed, via numerous epistolary exchanges, of the trials and tribulations of François' decorating activities and subsequent move into his new home – or "palace" as he liked to call it.

Then, miraculously, upon the Jazz-Girl's return to Paris, François *finally* managed to find a date for a jam session. In his busy schedule, there was one day when he was booked to prepare a piano for an evening concert and would therefore not be required until five o'clock.

The Jazz-Girl arrived mid-morning and began by admiring the results of François' hard toil. Pristine layers of white paint had replaced the old floral wallpaper to make the flat look light and airy and even more spacious than before. Admittedly, a few vestiges of the recent decorating activities remained – a pot of paint here, two or three paintbrushes there – but the Jazz-Girl was also utterly delighted to observe that there was more than enough equipment laid out for the ensuing jam session: three guitars, two amplifiers and, naturally, a piano – an upright Schimmel. Better still, since the piano was placed facing the window, when the Jazz-Girl sat down to play, she noticed that – in spite of the grey mist which was descending on the city from the rainy April sky that day – the view from the flat was just as magical by day as by night. All of a sudden, it felt as if she were in a dream;

here she was, about to start playing blues – one of her favourite things – with a very dear friend while, to top it all, the entire beautiful city of Paris appeared to be at her feet. And to think that it was only Monday morning. What a truly wonderful way to start the week!

Once she had finished testing the piano, the Jazz-Girl and her tuner took the time to exchange various bits of news – anecdotes about her recent holiday in Normandy, talk of his imminent trip to his favourite country getaway in Burgundy – and then decided that finally, at long last, they were ready to play blues together. On the musical menu that day: the jazz arrangement of "Jesu Joy of Man's Desiring" followed by a slow and bluesy version of "When the Saints Go Marching In"[21].

The tuner grabbed one of the guitars – his favourite – and began to, well… tune it, of course!

Turning towards the Jazz-Girl, he said:

'Okay, Scary Bat, give me an E, will you?'

In response, she played the E of the middle octave.

'No. I need a lower E than that.'

She thus moved down an octave and once again played an E.

As for the tuner, he turned the pegs of his guitar, strummed a few chords, then stopped, looking really frustrated, slightly horrified even, as he exclaimed:

'Did you hear that? It's so out of tune. It's at four hundred and thirty-eight!'

The Jazz-Girl endeavoured to put on her best "seriously horrified" look but unfortunately laughter got the better of her, which in turn incited her to explain to him, as gently as she could, that this type of exclamation could not possibly come from anyone other than a true professional. Pianos are usually tuned to a general standard of four hundred and forty hertz – a value that remained a source of sheer mystery to the Jazz-Girl. And it was her sincere belief that only a trained tuner would be able to assess the state of his instrument, completely unaided by any machine, with such precision as to be able to proclaim it to be at a mere – shock, horror! – four hundred and thirty-eight. This comment from François served, above all, to reinforce the Jazz-Girl's view that piano tuners, as highly gifted members of an exclusive club entirely dedicated to all aspects of sound, form a breed apart.

---

21 These arrangements can be heard on my YouTube channel: Nicky Gentil.

Accepting these compliments with good grace, François finally managed to tune his guitar and together they embarked on a joyful jam session, which turned out to be somewhat surprising…

In the normal course of things, it would take the Jazz-Girl a while to feel at ease in the presence of another musician, with the result that her playing initially suffered, becoming rushed and irregular in tempo. This, however, was not the case when she played with her tuner and very dear friend. On the contrary, the relaxed atmosphere brought about by their friendship had a truly positive influence on their performance. Consequently, the Jazz-Girl was pleased to discover that the tempo of her playing was perfectly regular from the outset.

Their friendship also influenced their recordings. Usually, once the "record" button is pressed, a musician, inhibited by the machine, tends to start off with a performance that is unworthy of his or her ability. The Jazz-Girl had already experienced this on many other occasions during which several attempts had been necessary before she and her fellow musicians had relaxed sufficiently to record a version that could be deemed worthy of their true level of playing.

That day, the opposite was the case. Once they had finished rehearsing, the Jazz-Girl and her tuner recorded their pieces in one take – for the simple reason that this take was by far their best performance; better than the rehearsal by a very long chalk. With the machine rolling, it appeared that these two musical spirits just wanted to give their very best for each other.

Time was passing and, eventually, they stopped playing in order to enjoy a late lunch. What followed appealed to the Jazz-Girl even more than their jam session, which is really saying something! Flying in the face of tradition, with radical role reversal, François proceeded to prepare the lunch while the Jazz-Girl dealt with the recording.

François declared himself to be an expert at making omelettes and the Jazz-Girl confirmed that his self-congratulations were indeed justified. The omelette, served with a fresh green salad, was absolutely perfect – just as delicious as the beautiful sound he would give to her Steinway each time he tuned it. And so it was that together they tucked into the food, while at the same time listening to the results of their session.

Personal recordings raise further challenges for musicians, who tend to be incredibly self-critical – hearing only those elements they consider to be the weak points of their performance. It turned out that François was no exception to this rule, exclaiming, as the blues version of "When the Saints Go Marching In" started to play:

'Oh no, that F chord is way too low!'

That day, the Jazz-Girl, on the other hand, was *not*, for once, listening so much to her music as to the sound of the piano. Complacent in the knowledge that she would have plenty of time to analyse her performance later at home, for the time being her immediate concern lay with the state of the instrument and, more precisely, with whether or not it was in tune. Admittedly, during the entire jam session she had not been able to detect the slightest imperfection in the tuning. However, were there to be any flaws at all, it was now or never that she would detect them because a recording is always ferociously unforgiving.

Concentrating to the very best of her ability, the Jazz-Girl was surprised to observe that, out of the entire keyboard, only one note – the G of the middle octave – was beginning to go out of tune. And it has to be said that the difference was so very slight as to be perfectly tolerable – even for her highly demanding Scary Bat ear.

So what, you might be tempted to say. This piano did, after all, belong to a tuner. But here's the thing: that morning, upon the Jazz-Girl's arrival, François had proudly announced that he had not tuned his piano for a good ten years – on top of which, during that time he had actually moved house at least twice[22]!

Ten years of neglect and still sounding good? How could this be? How was the mysterious phenomenon of this apparently extraordinary instrument to be explained? After thinking long and hard about the matter, the Jazz-Girl came to a rather astonishing, extremely unscientific conclusion: a tuner's piano stays in tune, come what may, quite simply out of deep respect for the master in whose home it has the good fortune to live.

As for the fact that François, just like the vast majority of professional tuners, never bothered to take care of his own piano... well, let's face it, there was nothing very mysterious about that, was there? After all, as the saying goes, the shoemaker's children always go barefoot!

---

22 A household piano should generally be tuned at least once a year and *always* after a removal.

Epilogue

That day, as I made my way home from my piano tuner's, I suddenly realised that, as ever after a really good jam session, I was in a state of near euphoria. The sky was grey, the Metro jam-packed with stressed-out Parisians racing to reach their various destinations, but I was untouchable, floating around for the entire journey in a bubble of happiness, deliciously high from the intoxicating effects of playing music, temporarily propelled from the mundane surroundings of underground transport to a completely different planet – Planet Jazz.

$$\oint$$

It is my sincere hope, dear readers, that through my stories I have managed to convey to you some of the immense joy that my passion for jazz improvisation never ceases to bring to me.

If, while reading this book, you began to think: "I should never have given up the piano, the guitar, the violin (or whatever instrument you used to play) but it is too late now", my answer to you would be to say that it is never too late to return to music. I am living proof of that. Furthermore, music has taught me, and regularly reminds me, that, in life, an awful lot more is possible than we actually realise. And just occasionally, music even goes so far as to give me the impression that everything and anything is possible.

Obviously, in order to take up playing an instrument, two key elements – motivation and having the time to practise – are essential. Be that as it may, music is paradoxically the perfect activity when time is in short supply because regular practice on an instrument, even if each session only lasts as little as fifteen to twenty minutes, actually produces much better results than the odd sporadic long session[23].

And if it *is* possible to find just a few minutes to practise every day, the benefits can be huge. Playing a musical instrument is actually an amazing form of relaxation – similar, in many respects, to meditation. By this, I mean that a good performance depends on the musician's ability to become completely absorbed in his or her own universe, withdrawing into a kind of melodious secret garden to focus on the music to the exclusion of everything else, in just the same way that meditation requires its subject to empty the mind of all thoughts but, in this case, to concentrate solely on his or her breathing.

In addition to being an amazing form of relaxation, improvising on the piano provides me with a wonderful way to enjoy the present moment. And if I refer to everything I have read on this subject, from ancient spiritual texts to the most recent studies carried out by neurologists, enjoying the present moment is actually considered to be *the* best way to live.

It is also wonderful to be able to sit back, from time to time, and allow the creative process to take over. The pace of life in today's world is increasingly frenetic, partly because the speed at which information is distributed on the Internet incites us all to expect things to happen or be obtained immediately. With the creative process, however, this is out of the question. The process is in charge. It is the process that decides. And the pace, as I know from personal experience, is highly unpredictable. Sometimes I can work really hard on a piece, an improvisation or a composition and become extremely frustrated because, in spite of all my efforts, results do not appear

---

23 In his compelling book, *Play It Again*, Alan Rusbridger documents his achievement of what at first appears to be an almost unattainable goal: to learn, in the space of just one year, to play Chopin's Ballade N°1 – a piece generally acknowledged to be one of *the* most difficult in the classical repertoire. Admittedly, it takes him slightly over a year, but the point is that he goes on to achieve his aim despite the fact that, as the then editor of *The Guardian,* his working day would last at least sixteen hours – often more – since this particular year was highly eventful for anyone in his profession but especially for Alan Rusbridger given that it included – in addition to the Arab Spring, the Japanese tsunami and the English riots – *The Guardian's* breaking of both Wikileaks and the *News of the World* hacking scandal. So, just how did this excessively busy editor of a national newspaper actually manage to achieve his seemingly impossible pianistic goal? By resolving to practise, whenever and wherever possible – a decision which even sees him playing on one memorable occasion in a hotel in Libya – for just twenty minutes a day!

to be forthcoming. At other times, I sit down at the piano and have an immediate revelation; unexpected results, better than anything I previously thought I was capable of producing, seem to pop up from nowhere, without any particular effort on my part. I never cease to be amazed by this magical aspect of the creative process, which appears to be particularly present in musical activity in its various forms.

𝄞

In conclusion, I would like to extend my most heartfelt thanks to my husband, my children and three of my friends – Carine, Lama and Virginie – for proofreading the original book and making some valuable corrections and suggestions, for encouraging me through my moments of doubt to continue writing and, more generally, for being on board to accompany me on this literary adventure.

I would like to thank my piano tuner not only for everything he has taught me about pianos and the nature of sound but also for the crucial role he played in helping me to obtain the best possible treatment for my injured hand.

I will never forget my jazz teacher and that momentous day when he gave me such a precious key – a key which enabled me to open a very large door and step into the magical world of improvisation – so I thank him too.

And last but not least, for that most valuable gift which is my passion for music, I would just like to take this opportunity to thank Apollo from the bottom of my heart.

My very best musical wishes to you all!

Related works

Film

For anyone wishing to become visually acquainted with the piano tuning profession, I highly recommend *Pianomania* – a documentary which shadows Stefan Knüfner (a truly talented Steinway concert technician) on his quest to obtain the perfect sound.

Books

The following is, in no particular order, a list of books, all to do with music and pianos, which I very much enjoyed reading and therefore also highly recommend.

The Piano Shop on the Left Bank – Thad Carhart
Play It Again – Alan Rusbridger
Piano Girl – Robin Meloy Goldsby
Piano Notes – Charles Rosen
A Natural History of the Piano – Stuart Isacoff
The Pianist – Wladyslaw Szpilman
Wild Harmonies – Hélène Grimaud
Broken Music – Sting
An Orchestra Beyond Borders – Elena Cheah
This is Your Brain on Music – Daniel Levitin
The World in Six Songs – Daniel Levitin
Musicophilia – Oliver Sacks